GW00455527

Język angielski

365 zadań i ćwiczeń

z rozwiązaniami

Klaudyna Hildebrandt, Magdalena Grala

Langenscheidt

Warszawa

Opracowanie: zespół *Quendi Language Services,* www.quendi.pl, w składzie:
Autorki: **Klaudyna Hildebrandt, Magdalena Grala**
Konsultacja metodyczna: *Maria Birkenmajer-Hodgart*
Korekta: *Jadwiga Kosmulska, Inga Stępkowska*
Koordynacja prac merytorycznych: *Anna Wojciechowska*

Koordynacja projektu: *Małgorzata Kapuścińska*

Skład i łamanie: *GABO s.c.,* Milanówek
Druk i oprawa: *Zakład Poligraficzno-Wydawniczy POZKAL*

© 2006 Langenscheidt Polska Sp. z o.o., Warszawa

02-548 Warszawa
ul. Grażyny 13

ISBN-10 83-7476-103-2
ISBN-13 978-83-7476-103-1

Cena: 24,50 zł

WSTĘP

365 ZADAŃ I ĆWICZEŃ to książka, która stanowi owoc naszych doświadczeń w nauczaniu języka angielskiego i pracy z uczniami w różnym wieku i o zróżnicowanych potrzebach.

Zauważyłyśmy, że niejednokrotnie podręczniki i zbiory ćwiczeń napisane przez autorów zagranicznych, nawet tych bardzo wybitnych, nie uwypuklają problemów gramatycznych i językowych, z którymi Polacy mogą mieć szczególne problemy; nic dziwnego, skoro powstają z myślą o uczniu „nieangielskojęzycznym", nie zaś po prostu polskim. Postanowiłyśmy więc opracować nowy zestaw zadań i ćwiczeń, ze szczególnym uwzględnieniem potrzeb Polaków.

Obejmuje on zakres gramatyki kursów języka angielskiego od poziomu *beginner* (podstawowego) do *upper intermediate* (wyższego średnio zaawansowanego), opracowany na podstawie najpopularniejszych programów obowiązujących na polskim rynku, a także nieco ćwiczeń dotyczących słownictwa; główny nacisk spoczywa jednak na gramatyce. Aby wyjść naprzeciw potrzebom Polaków uczących się języka angielskiego, zaprojektowałyśmy klucze do naszych ćwiczeń w sposób nieco nietypowy: zawierają one nie tylko prawidłowe odpowiedzi i rozwiązania zadań, lecz także wyjaśnienia „dlaczego tak, a nie inaczej" oraz uwagi dotyczące typowych błędów i struktur gramatycznych, które Polakom najczęściej sprawiają trudności. Oczywiście wyjaśnień takich nie zamieszczałyśmy przy każdym punkcie, lecz tylko tych najtrudniejszych – w przeciwnym razie klucz rozrósłby się do zbyt dużej objętości, a wiele uwag niepotrzebnie by się powtarzało.

Zbiór podzielony jest na rozdziały. Wewnątrz poszczególnych rozdziałów ćwiczenia różnią się trudnością, co jest wyróżnione graficznie: ćwiczenia oznaczone ☺ są łatwe (*beginner*), ćwiczenia z ☺☺ (*lower intermediate*) wymagają nieco więcej wysiłku, zaś ☺☺☺ mają ćwiczenia na poziomie wyższym średnio zaawansowanym (*upper intermediate*). W niektórych unitach, w zależności od potrzeb, mogą występować np. jedno ćwiczenie łatwe i dwa trudniejsze albo trzy ćwiczenia, po jednym na poziom średnio zaawansowany, niższy i wyższy. Ćwiczenia dotyczące zagadnień gramatycznych, które uczeń poznaje dopiero po kilku latach systematycznej nauki, są oczywiście wszystkie oznaczone ☺☺ lub ☺☺☺.

Układ zagadnień i wyjaśnienia podane w kluczu pozwalają samodzielnie powtórzyć materiał lub przygotować się do testu; zakładamy więc, że osoby korzystające z naszego zbioru nie będą wykonywać wszystkich ćwiczeń „jak leci", lecz po prostu wybiorą te zagadnienia, które potrzebują utrwalić lub co do których czują, że przyda im się dodatkowa praktyka. Mamy też nadzieję, że ten zbiór pomoże nauczycielom i korepetytorom, jako źródło pomysłów na prace domowe, a także osobom, które uczyły się kiedyś angielskiego, teraz nieco go zapomniały i chciałyby ten język szybko odświeżyć. Książka powstała raczej z myślą o starszej młodzieży i dorosłych niż o dzieciach; zdania są więc napisane tak, by bawić i interesować osoby z tych grup wiekowych. Starałyśmy się unikać monotonii ćwiczeń; stąd w naszym zbiorze znajdują się nie tylko zadania typu „transformacja" lub wymagające podania właściwej formy gramatycznej, lecz także ćwiczenia wielokrotnego wyboru lub wymagające połączenia dwóch lub trzech części zdania, usunięcia zbędnych słów, uzupełnienia dialogu itd., a także ćwiczenia otwarte. Starałyśmy się, by większość zdań, jakie piszemy, należała do wypowiedzi, które można spotkać w rzeczywistości; nie mogłyśmy się jednak oprzeć pokusie napisania kilku ćwiczeń, w których zdania lub historyjki należą do świata humoru absurdalnego; jeśli choć jedno z nich rozbawi naszych Czytelników, będzie nam bardzo miło.

Autorki
Langenscheidt Polska 2006

SPIS TREŚCI

NOUNS AND NOUN PHRASES

ARTICLES

1. ☺ Trzy spośród poniższych zdań są bezbłędne. Znajdź te zdania, a w pozostałych popraw błędy w użyciu przedimków (*a/an*, *the* oraz „zero" article).

1. John is one of youngest teachers in our school but he's also one of the best.
2. A politician is not the same as statesman.
3. She has job in a leading software company.
4. Practice makes perfect.
5. The fear is not a good motivator for better work.
6. Is teaching just a job or a vocation?
7. Sir Winston Churchill was Prime Minister in Britain during Second World War.
8. Internet is a mine of useful information.
9. It's the experience that counts!
10. The Internet resources are not always used correctly.

2. ☺ Wstaw *a/an*, *the*, *some* lub Ø („zero" article).

People in (1)_____ Europe eat very different breakfasts. For instance, (2)_____ usual English breakfast consists of (3)_____ bacon and (4)_____ eggs, (5)_____ baked beans and (6)_____ black pudding, which is (7)_____ kind of sausage. In Scotland, you may get (8)_____ porridge and (9)_____ kippers, that is smoked herrings, first thing in (10)_____ morning. (11)_____ Italian will have (12)_____ cappuccino and (13)_____ few biscuits or (14)_____ sweet roll, while in Greece (15) _____ breakfast may consist of just (16)_____ bread and (17)_____ olives, (18)_____ lump of goat cheese and (19)_____ slice or two of (20)_____ melon.

3. ☺ Zakreśl właściwy przedimek: *a/an*, *the* lub Ø.

Sending (1) *a/an/the/Ø* postcard of (2) *a/an/the/Ø* place you're visiting is (3) *a/an/the/Ø* good way to keep in touch with friends and family. So, if you happen to be visiting (4) *a/an/the/Ø* Euroland, buy (5) *a/an/the/Ø* postcard, write (6) *a/an/the/Ø* message and their name and address and pop it into (7) *a/an/the/Ø* post box. But watch out! Sometimes there is (8) *a/an/the/Ø* international post box. By the way, (9) *a/an/the/Ø* standard letter is (10) *a/an/the/Ø* same price as your card.

4. ☺☺ Uzupełnij zdania odpowiednim wyrażeniem.

1. To care for _____ has always been the aim of our institution.
   - a) old and infirm
   - b) the olds and infirms
   - c) the old and infirm
2. We watched _____ rise slowly above the calm surface of the sea.
   - a) moon
   - b) a moon
   - c) the moon
3. My grandmother went to _____ every Sunday.
   - a) a church
   - b) the church
   - c) church

4. We went to _____ to see the famous altarpiece.
   a) a church   b) the church   c) church
5. The fridge was completely empty. It turned out that while I was taking a shower, my boyfriend ate everything I bought _____. He left only the ice cubes.
   a) for dinner   b) for the dinner   c) for a dinner
6. The painting shows a sea battle between _____.
   a) the Greek and the Turk   b) the Greeks and the Turks   c) Greeks and Turks
7. She is _____ completely honest person I know. It always lands her in trouble.
   a) an only   b) the only   c) only
8. _____ are not the same.
   a) bravery and courage   b) the bravery and the courage   c) a bravery and courage
9. 'Can you play _____ ?'
   a) piano   b) on the piano   c) the piano
   'No, but I can play _____.'
   d) golf   e) in golf   f) in the golf

5. ☺☺ Niektóre nazwy geograficzne występują z przedimkiem określonym *the*. Wpisz go tam, gdzie jest potrzebny.

1. _____ Hague is not the capital of _____ Netherlands, but it is their centre of government.
2. My husband was born in _____USA, and I come from _____ north of Italy, but we have been living in _____ Poland since 1992.
3. _____United Kingdom comprises the whole of the island called _____ Great Britain, and that is why the name 'Britain' is sometimes used to refer to the country as a whole.
4. Sir Ernest Shackleton, the British explorer who attempted to reach _____ South Pole, described his experiences in the book *The Heart of* _____ *Antarctic*.
5. In the 18th century, it was very fashionable to go on a trip to _____ Italy, cross _____ Alps, see famous cities, admire works of art and climb _____ Vesuvius.
6. In 1488, the Portuguese navigator Bartolomeu Diaz saw a rocky promontory at the southern tip of _____ Africa. One account says that he called it _____ Cape of Storms, but that it was later renamed _____ Cape of Good Hope because its discovery indicated that it was possible to reach India by sea.
7. Nina Nikolayevna Berberova left _____ Soviet Union in 1922 and lived in _____ Germany, _____ Czechoslovakia, and _____ Italy. She settled in _____ Paris in 1925 and became a writer, biographer, editor, and translator, often writing about the lives and problems of exiles.

6. ☺☺ Niektóre nazwy własne występują z przedimkiem określonym *the*. Wpisz go tam, gdzie jest potrzebny.

1. During the ball given last month by Her Majesty _____ Queen, _____ Duchess of C. danced with _____ Captain A. all the time. Since that memorable night the two are rumoured to have been inseparable.
2. During our day-trip to London we visited _____ National Gallery and _____ Tower of London, we saw _____ London Bridge, went to _____ Chinatown and walked along _____ Strand.
3. My friend was sailing across the Atlantic and he swears he saw _____ *Flying Dutchman*, or perhaps the ghost of _____ Columbus's ship _____ *Santa Maria*, emerge from the mist just before his yacht and dissolve again without a sound.
4. Our neighbours _____ Grants went for holidays to the Bahamas, whereas _____ Joneses next door could only afford Majorca.

5. On the train I was sitting next to a serious-looking old gentleman who was at first reading _____ *Financial Times*, but later took out _____ *Fight Club* by Palahniuk and began to listen to _____ Beatles, _____ Boney M and _____ ABBA on his portable stereo.
6. 'She says she danced with _____ Orlando Bloom.' – 'You're kidding, _____ Orlando Bloom? I don't believe it!'

7. ☺☺☺ Zakreśl właściwy przedimek: *a/an, the* lub *Ø*.

1. In *a/an/the/Ø* Middle Ages it was believed that only *a/an/the/Ø* virgin is able to tame *a/an/the/Ø* unicorn.
2. Even if very powerful *a/an/the/Ø* computers are invented, *a/an/the/Ø* weather will forever remain unpredictable in *a/an/the/Ø* long run.
3. *A/An/The/Ø* steel ball has more *a/an/the/Ø* potential energy raised above the ground than it has after falling to *a/an/the/Ø* Earth.
4. Could you remove your briefcase from the corridor? It is getting in *a/an/the/Ø* way.
5. John grabbed his coat and left in *a/an/the/Ø* hurry.
6. What, Mary has left you? I was under *a/an/the/Ø* impression you were getting married!
7. Both my grandfathers were sailors, and both were lost at *a/an/the/Ø* sea.

8. ☺☺☺ Uzupełnij tekst odpowiednimi przedimkami tam, gdzie są one potrzebne.

It is said that J. K. Rowling's first Harry Potter novel was turned down again and again by (1)_____ major publishing houses. Now (2)_____ new Harry Potter book, *Harry Potter and the Half-Blood Prince*, has broken (3)_____ records, selling over two million copies in (4)_____ first 24 hours of its release in (5)_____ UK and 6.9 million in (6)_____ US. The release of (7)_____ sixth Harry Potter novel is (8)_____ good news for (9)_____ English learning across (10)_____ globe since many kids everywhere want to read about (11)_____ Harry Potter's adventures in English. However, translating J. K. Rowling's novels is also (12)_____ big business. (13)_____ Harry Potter books have been translated into 62 languages and sold 270 million copies in 200 different countries, making J. K. Rowling (14)_____ richest woman in Britain, with (15)_____ *Forbes* magazine estimating her fortune at US $ 1 billion (£575,000,000).

(adapted from *ELT Gazette*, September 2005)

COUNTABLE AND UNCOUNTABLE NOUNS

9. ☺ Zakreśl rzeczowniki niepoliczalne.

duck	coffee	bag	church	thunder	sadness	sea
luggage	mountain	watch	gold	dish	darkness	yacht
water	rose	finger	knowledge	poetry	chimney	joy

10. ☺ Są cztery rodzaje rzeczowników. Dodaj po pięć rzeczowników każdego rodzaju:

Common nouns:	*island, lamp, diamond ...*
Abstract nouns:	*courage, cruelty, death ...*
Collective nouns:	*team, jury, club ...*
Proper nouns:	*Africa, Robinson Crusoe, Hollywood ...*

11. ☺☺ Niektóre rzeczowniki są policzalne lub niepoliczalne i w zależności od tego zmieniają znaczenie. Wybierz właściwą formę.

1. All the guests stood up and the bride's father began *toast/a toast* to the newlyweds.
2. Don't move! I will run to the village and get *help/a help*.
3. If you want to get slimmer, eat *chicken/a chicken* instead of beef.
4. My sister-in-law is *gossip/a gossip* and a prude.
5. Is Forth Bridge made of *iron/an iron*?
6. I bought complete *work/works* of Shakespeare for £5.
7. I am writing *paper/a paper* on Romantic poetry.
8. On her nose the evil witch had a wart, from which three long *hair/hairs* grew.
9. Since the recession began, a lot of *business/businesses* have closed in our town.
10. All who saw Nancy Lehose admitted she was *beauty/a beauty*.
11. Put some more *woods/wood* in the fireplace, the fire is dying.

A teraz napisz 11 zdań, wykorzystując drugie znaczenie podanych powyżej rzeczowników.

12. ☺☺ Wybierz właściwą formę.

1. My daughter is afraid of *thunder and lightning/thunders and lightnings*.
2. Could you buy *a bread/a loaf of bread* and six eggs on your way home?
3. Clarice's boyfriend wrote her *a poetry/a poem* for a birthday present.
4. Who will help you move *furniture/furnitures*?
5. Before we make a decision, let's get more *informations/information* on our options.

13. ☺☺ Używając podanego rzeczownika, utwórz nowe zdanie o tym samym znaczeniu, co zdanie podane. Uwaga! W niektórych zdaniach trzeba także zmienić stronę czynną na stronę bierną.

1. Do you think we will find a cheap place to live in Crete?
   accommodation
   Do you think _____?
2. Could you please add some cumin to the soup?
   teaspoonful
   Could you _____?
3. They will bring some typewriters, monitors and a photocopier to the office today.
   equipment
   Some _____.
4. I am doing research on conditioned reflexes in dogs.
   experiments
   _____ making _____.
5. My mother allowed me to go to the party.
   permission
   My mother _____.

14. ☺☺☺ Wpisz właściwą formę czasownika.

1. The army (carry out) _____ relief operations in case of natural disasters.
2. The police (be) _____ looking for an escaped convict in our neighbourhood.
3. Everybody (want) _____ to be happy, but few achieve real happiness.
4. Judging by the long round of applause, the audience (have) _____ enjoyed the concert very much.
5. My family (be) _____ wonderful. I always get all the support I need, but nobody is nosy.

6. The coming Saturday our choir, which (have) _____ been very successful recently, will give a special concert to celebrate its centenary.
7. People (be) _____ so hard to understand sometimes!

PLURAL NOUNS

15. ☺ Dwa spośród poniższych zdań są bezbłędne. Znajdź te zdania, a w pozostałych popraw formy liczby mnogiej.

1. We saw some childrens crossing the busy street.
2. I like sweets, but I am not keen on chocolate.
3. Mother, there are three strange mans in our garden.
4. Can you bring me all the spoon from the sitting-room?
5. Please buy three mineral waters.
6. African women often carry baskets on their heads.
7. Remember to clean your teeths before you go to sleep.

16. ☺ Uzupełnij poniższe nieco absurdalne zdania właściwymi formami podanych rzeczowników.

1. (uncle, MP, letter, hug, kiss, X, box, chocolate)
   My three _____, who were _____, used to send me _____
   with _____ and _____ in the form of _____, and huge
   _____ of _____.
2. (kimono, kilo, potato)
   They put on colourful _____ and started peeling five _____ of
   _____.
3. (Bellamy, lady, baby, donkey)
   The _____ were sitting on the terrace having coffee when along the dusty road
   came two Greek _____ carrying their _____ and dragging heavily
   loaded pack _____ behind them.
4. (loaf, shelf, leaf)
   As I took the _____ from the _____, something rustled and
   _____ of old love letters fell to the floor.
5. (wharf, roof, scarf)
   When the women were walking along the _____, raindrops dripped on them
   from the warehouse _____ and a fierce wind tugged at their _____.

17. ☺ Wstaw podany rzeczownik we właściwej formie.

1. (university) There are two _____ in Glasgow.
2. (foot) You have to learn to stand on your own two _____ sometime!
3. (wife) When I was going to St. Ives I met a man with seven _____.
4. (deer) On the first day of the hunt the earl killed two great _____.
5. (scissors) I have two pairs of _____: the big kitchen ones and the small embroidery ones.
6. (tomato) These _____ have gone off, throw them away.
7. (mouse) I have a feeling we have some _____ in our house. There are

9

droppings all over, and the cheese just disappears!
8. (advice)   Let me offer you two pieces of _____, my boy. Think first, then speak. And always remember that silence is golden.
9. (wolf)   A pack of _____ ran silently through the wood.
10. (sheep)   A flock of _____ was grazing peacefully on the hillside.

18. ☺☺ Wybierz właściwą formę.

1. Both my *brothers-in-law/brother-in-laws* are stupid and have no sense of humour.
2. Several *crafts/craft*: yachts, fishing boats, rowing boats and even a small military vessel were rocking gently in the harbour.
3. All the evening the children were quietly playing *domino/dominoes*. I had a feeling they were up to something.
4. Look, your *pyjama/pyjamas* are dirty and really need washing!
5. He made a mistake, that's true, but he has later taken considerable *pain/pains* to make things right.
6. The single most important *criterion/criteria* of our choice is the qualifications of our future employee.
7. The government is just not prepared to cope with *crisises/crises* of this magnitude.
8. Let's have a pie and some *greenery/greens* for lunch.
9. Nowadays we rarely eat *game/games*, but in the past deer, partridge or pheasant would often appear on the table.
10. Glistening shapes of the *trout/trouts* shot above the surface of the stream.

MASCULINE AND FEMININE NOUNS

19. ☺ Połącz rzeczowniki w pary.

1. bachelor	a. tigress
2. father	b. aunt
3. stallion	c. lady
4. hero	d. widow
5. duke	e. mother
6. widower	f. heroine
7. lord	g. bitch
8. tiger	h. mare
9. dog	i. spinster
10. uncle	j. duchess

20. ☺☺ Uzupełnij zdania właściwymi słowami z ramki.

bride	ram	lioness	queen	gander	husband
vixen	ewe	actress	niece	cock	

1. The _____ (she-lion) stalked a young zebra through tall grass.
2. Often the _____ (married man) is more in love with his wife than the other way round.

3. Look at John talking to Mary and Jill! Doesn't he look like a _____ (a male chicken) showing off before his hens?
4. Jane is red-headed and quarrelsome – a real _____ (female fox).
5. The little boy, frightened by the angry hissing of a huge _____ (male goose), ran away crying.
6. When I was a little girl, I used to pretend I was a _____ (wife of a king) and my dolls were my ladies-in-waiting.
7. If you were a famous _____ (woman who appears on theatre stage), the paparazzi would follow you everywhere. Are you sure you would be happy then?
8. The cottager had a flock of several _____ (female sheep) and a large _____ (male sheep).
9. My _____ (sister's daughter) has passed her driving test the first time. I am very proud of her.
10. The _____ (woman who is getting married) walked down the aisle, leaning on her father's arm and smiling at the man who waited for her at the altar.

SAXON GENITIVE

21. ☺ Dopasuj połówki zdań.

1. I went to the butcher's
2. You can get the best scones and buns
3. I was so happy it was all over
4. I left my red shoes at the shoemaker's
5. Until the age of seventeen

a. that I left my coat at the dentist's.
b. Elizabeth lived at her grandmother's.
c. because they needed mending.
d. to get a kilo of chicken liver.
e. at the baker's at Nicolson Street.

22. ☺ Przekształć odpowiedzi według wzoru.

Wzór: Whose is the last house on the left-hand side of our street?
   It belongs to Mr Finch. It's Mr Finch's.

1. Whose briefcase is this?
   It belongs to the Prime Minister. It's _____.
2. Whom did this sword use to belong to?
   To William the Conqueror. It's _____ sword.
3. Who wrote *Great Expectations*?
   Charles Dickens. It's _____ novel.
4. What church did you get married in?
   In the church of St. Luke. We got married at _____.
5. Is this your bedroom?
   No, the children sleep here. It's _____ bedroom.
6. Who does this magnificent mare belong to?
   To the Sheikh of the Al Kathir. It's _____ best mare.

23. ☺☺ Wybierz właściwą formę dzierżawczą.

1. *Horace Walpole's house/The house of Horace Walpole* was called Strawberry Hill.
2. *The newspaper of today/Today's newspaper* is on your desk, sir, as usual.

3. *The arrival of the President/The President's arrival* was delayed by the demonstrators.

4. We listened to *Vivaldi's concerto/a concerto of Vivaldi.*

5. *A five minutes' conversation/A conversation of five minutes* was enough to break her heart.

6. *A total eclipse of the sun/Sun's total eclipse* will occur on Friday 17, at 9.05 am.

7. Please write your name and address at *the page's top/the top of the page.*

8. Old Mrs Hart sat down heavily and *the leg of the chair/the chair's leg* broke with a loud snap.

9. I put *the dog's bowl/the bowl of the dog* in the dishwasher.

KLUCZ

1. 1. *the* youngest **2.** *a* statesman **3.** *a* job **4.** correct **5.** ~~the~~ **6.** correct **7.** *the* Second World War **8.** *The* Internet **9.** correct **10.** ~~the~~

2. 1. Ø **2.** *a* (używamy *a/an*, kiedy nazwa posiłku jest poprzedzona przymiotnikiem) **3.** Ø **4.** Ø **5.** Ø **6.** Ø **7.** *a* **8.** *some* **9.** Ø **10.** *the* **11.** *An* **12.** *a* **13.** *a* **14.** *a* **15.** Ø **16.** Ø **17.** *some* **18.** *a* **19.** *a* **20.** Ø

3. 1. *a* **2.** *the* **3.** *a* **4.** Ø **5.** *the* **6.** *the* **7.** *a/the* **8.** *an/the* **9.** *a* **10.** *the*

4. 1. c) the old and infirm (bo jest to określona grupa osób)
2. c) the moon (bo jest jedyny, przynajmniej dla Ziemi)
3. c) church (bo dotyczy to funkcji kościoła, a nie danego budynku)
4. b) the church (aby zwiedzić jakiś szczególny budynek)
5. a) for dinner (nazwy posiłków zwykle bez przyimka [ale patrz ćw. 2.2])
6. b) the Greeks and the Turks (grupa osób danej narodowości)
7. b) the only (jedyny, a więc określony)
8. a) bravery and courage (rzeczowniki niepoliczalne)
9. c) the piano (*the* z nazwami instrumentów); d) golf (ale Ø z nazwami gier)

5. 1. *The Hague* (tłumaczenie holenderskiej nazwy Den Haag; uwaga – *The* wielką literą!); *the Netherlands* (nazwa kraju jest w liczbie mnogiej).
2. *the USA* (nazwa kraju zawiera rzeczownik); *the north of Italy* (*north* jest tu rzeczownikiem, więc wymaga *the*); Ø *Poland* (nazwa własna kraju).
3. *the United Kingdom* (nazwa kraju zawiera rzeczownik), Ø *Great Britain* (nazwa wyspy – nie używamy *the*).
4. *the South Pole* (zazwyczaj przy nazwach z *North, South* itd. nie ma *the*; the *North/South Pole* jednak go wymagają, bo dotyczą szczególnego miejsca na ziemi); *the Antarctic* (nazwa regionu).
5. Ø *Italy* (nazwa własna kraju); *the Alps* (nazwa łańcucha górskiego – używamy *the*) Ø *Vesuvius* (nazwa góry – nie używamy *the*).
6. Ø *Africa* (nazwa własna); *the Cape of Storms* (nazwa składa się z rzeczownika + *of* + rzeczownika); *the Cape of Good Hope* (nazwa składa się z rzeczownika + *of* + rzeczownika).
7. *the Soviet Union* (nazwa kraju zawiera rzeczownik); Ø *Germany*, Ø *Czechoslovakia*, Ø *Italy*, Ø *Paris* (nazwy własne).

6. 1. *Her Majesty the Queen* (bo jest tylko jedna monarchini); *the Duchess of C.* (tytuł zawierający *of* poprzedzamy *the*); Ø *Captain A.* (inne tytuły i rangi – bez *the*).
2. *the National Gallery* (nazwa własna składająca się z przymiotnika i rzeczownika); *the Tower of London* (nazwa własna składająca się z rzeczownika + *of* + rzeczownika); Ø *London Bridge* (nazwa własna składająca się z dwóch rzeczowników); Ø *Chinatown* (nazwa własna); *the Strand* (jedna z niewielu nazw ulic zawsze poprzedzana *the*).
3. *the Flying Dutchman, the Santa Maria* (nazwy statków poprzedzamy *the*); Ø *Columbus's ship* (nazwiska w l.p. poprzedzamy przedimkiem niezwykle rzadko [patrz 7.5]).
4. *the Grants, the Joneses* (nazwisko w liczbie mnogiej poprzedzone *the* oznacza „rodzina" – np. rodzina Grantów, rodzina Jonesów).
5. *the Financial Times*; Ø *Fight Club*; *the Beatles*; Ø *Boney M*; Ø *ABBA*. Ponieważ w przypadku tytułów czy nazw gazet i czasopism, nazw grup itp. wybór przedimka zależy od autora, wydawcy lub twórców,

w zasadzie trzeba w każdym wypadku sprawdzić, czy należy wstawić przedimek określony, nieokreślony czy „zero".

6. *Ø Orlando Bloom* (nazwiska bez przedimka...); *the Orlando Bloom* (...chyba że chcemy dać do zrozumienia, iż chodzi o danego znanego człowieka).

7. 1. *the Middle Ages*; *a virgin*; *a unicorn* (uwaga: *a/an* używamy zgodnie z wymową, a nie z pisownią – dlatego wyraz *unicorn*/jʊnɪkɔːn/poprzedzamy *a*).
2. *Ø computers* (rzeczownik policzalny w l.mn.); *Ø weather* (rzeczownik niepoliczalny); *in the long run* (wyrażenie).
3. *A steel ball* (przymiotnik + rzeczownik policzalny w l.p.); *Ø potential energy* (rzeczownik niepoliczalny); *the Earth* (Ziemia jest „jedyna w swoim rodzaju").
4. *in the way* (wyrażenie).
5. *in a hurry* (wyrażenie).
6. *under the impression* (wyrażenie).
7. *at Ø sea* (wyrażenie – tzn. w czasie podróży morskiej).

8. 1. *the* **2.** *the* **3.** *Ø* **4.** *the* **5.** *the* **6.** *the* **7.** *the* **8.** *Ø* **9.** *Ø* **10.** *the* **11.** *Ø* **12.** *Ø* **13.** *The* **14.** *the* **15.** *Ø*

9. coffee, thunder, sadness, luggage, gold, darkness, water, knowledge, poetry, joy

10. Na przykład:
Common nouns:	*car, fridge* ...
Abstract nouns:	*loneliness, sight* ...
Collective nouns:	*police, government* ...
Proper nouns:	*Harry Potter, Glasgow Rangers* ...

11. 1. *a toast* – czyli uroczysta przemowa (*toast* to przypieczona kromka chleba)
2. *help* – pomoc (*a help* to pomocna osoba lub przydatna rzecz)
3. *chicken* – kurze mięso (*a chicken* to ptak domowy)
4. *a gossip* – plotkarka (*gossip* to plotki i pogaduszki)
5. *iron* – żelazo (*an iron* to żelazko do prasowania)
6. *works* – dzieła (*work* to praca lub robota)
7. *a paper* – wypracowanie, esej, artykuł (*paper* to materiał, na którym zazwyczaj piszemy)
8. *hairs* – pojedyncze włosy (*hair* to wszystkie włosy razem)
9. *businesses* – firmy (*business* to działalność gospodarcza, czyli biznes)
10. *a beauty* – piękność (*beauty* to piękno)
11. *wood* – drewno (*woods* to bory i lasy)

12. 1. *thunder and lightning* **2.** *a loaf of bread* **3.** *a poem* **4.** *furniture* **5.** *information*
Warto zapamiętać, że rzeczowniki niepoliczalne nie występują w liczbie mnogiej i nie poprzedzamy ich przedimkiem *a/an*.

13. 1. Do you think we will find cheap **accommodation** in Crete?
2. Could you please add **a teaspoonful of** cumin to the soup?
3. Some **equipment** will be brought to the office today.
4. I am making **experiments** on conditioned reflexes in dogs.
5. My mother **gave** me **permission** to go to the party.

14. Rzeczowniki, które odnoszą się do grup ludzi (*collective nouns*), łączą się z czasownikiem w liczbie pojedynczej, kiedy myślimy o grupie jako jednostce, ale z czasownikiem w liczbie mnogiej, gdy myślimy o grupie jako zbiorze poszczególnych osób.
1. the army carries out – bo wojsko działa jako jednostka.
2. the police are – *police* to rzeczownik zbiorowy, który **zawsze** łączy się z czasownikiem w liczbie mnogiej.
3. everybody wants – rzeczowniki typu *everybody*, *somebody*, *nobody* zawsze łączą się z czasownikiem w liczbie pojedynczej.
4. the audience have enjoyed – kiedy mówimy o uczuciach członków danej grupy, używamy czasownika w liczbie mnogiej.
5. my family are wonderful – kiedy mówimy o osobistych cechach członków danej grupy, używamy czasownika w liczbie mnogiej.

6. our choir, which has been – z zaimkiem względnym *which* używamy czasownika w liczbie pojedynczej, a z zaimkiem względnym *who* – w liczbie mnogiej.

7. people are – *people* to rzeczownik zbiorowy, który **zawsze** łączy się z czasownikiem w liczbie mnogiej.

15. **1.** children **2.** OK **3.** men **4.** spoons **5.** three bottles of mineral water **6.** OK **7.** teeth

16. Reguły tworzenia form regularnych liczby mnogiej w zależności od końcówki:

1. *uncles, MPs, letters, hugs, kisses, Xs/X's, boxes, chocolates* – do większości rzeczowników dodaje się końcówkę **-s**; jeśli rzeczownik kończy się na -ch, -sh, -ss lub -x, dodaje się -es. Liczbę mnogą nazw liter alfabetu można utworzyć z apostrofem lub bez, inicjałów – bez apostrofu.

2. *kimonos, kilos, potatoes* – kiedy rzeczownik ma końcówkę **-o**, liczbę mnogą tworzy się przez dodanie **-es**, z wyjątkiem rzeczowników mających skróconą formę i rzeczowników obcego pochodzenia.

3. *Bellamys, ladies, babies, donkeys* – kiedy rzeczownik ma końcówkę: spółgłoska + **-y**, liczbę mnogą tworzy się przez usunięcie **-y** i dodanie **-ies**, oprócz nazw własnych (np. nazwisk); ale kiedy rzeczownik ma końcówkę: samogłoska + **-y**, liczbę mnogą tworzy się przez dodanie **-s**.

4. *loaves, shelves, leaves* – liczbę mnogą kilkunastu rzeczowników kończących się na **-f/-fe** tworzy się przez usunięcie **-f/-fe** i dodanie końcówki **-ves**.

5. *wharfs/wharves, roofs, scarfs/scarves* – oprócz l.m. z końcówką **-ves**, rzeczowniki *wharf, scarf* i *hoof* mogą także tworzyć zwyczajną liczbę mnogą z **-s** na końcu, a wszystkie inne rzeczowniki kończące się na **-f/-fe** tworzą ją zawsze z **-s** na końcu.

17. **1.** universities **2.** feet **3.** wives **4.** deer **5.** scissors **6.** tomatoes **7.** mice **8.** advice **9.** wolves **10.** sheep

18. **1.** *brothers-in-law* **2.** *craft* **3.** *dominoes* **4.** *pyjamas* **5.** *pains* **6.** *criterion* **7.** *crises* **8.** *greens* **9.** *game* **10.** *trout*

19. **1.** i **2.** e **3.** h **4.** f **5.** j **6.** d **7.** c **8.** a **9.** g **10.** b

20. **1.** lioness **2.** husband **3.** cock **4.** vixen **5.** gander **6.** queen **7.** actress **8.** ewes, ram **9.** niece **10.** bride

21. **1.** d **2.** e **3.** a **4.** c **5.** b.
Przy nazwach firm, sklepów i czyichś mieszkań używamy formy z Saxon Genitive i opuszczamy następujący po nim rzeczownik (np. *shop* czy *place*).

22. **1.** It's the Prime Minister's.
2. It's William the Conqueror's sword.
3. It's Charles Dickens's/Charles Dickens' novel.
Jeśli rzeczownik w l.p. kończy się na -s, Saxon Genitive można zapisać na dwa sposoby.
4. We got married at St. Luke's.
Kościołów też dotyczą reguły zapisywania Saxon Genitive, jakie ilustruje ćwiczenie 21.
5. It's the children's bedroom.
6. It's the Sheikh of the Al Kathir's best mare.

23. **1.** *Horace Walpole's house* **2.** *Today's newspaper* **3.** *The arrival of the President/The President's arrival* (obie wersje dopuszczalne) **4.** *Vivaldi's concerto* **5.** *A five minutes' conversation* **6.** *A total eclipse of the sun* **7.** *the top of the page* **8.** *the leg of the chair* **9.** *the dog's bowl*

PRONOUNS AND DETERMINERS

DEMONSTRATIVE PRONOUNS

24. ☺ Uzupełnij poniższe zdania zaimkami *this/that* lub *these/those*.

1. _____ car here belongs to my daughter; _____ one in the garage belongs to my son.
2. 'How do you like _____ shoes?'
   'They're nice, but I preferred _____ blue ones you were wearing yesterday'.
3. _____ top is just too bright, I'll take _____ one.
4. Hello, _____ is Lucinda Smith speaking, could I talk to Albert, please?
5. We've got an important meeting scheduled for _____ Friday.
6. _____ of you who have finished the exam may leave earlier.
7. Mr. President, _____ two boys here would like to ask you a question!
8. Look at _____ two girls sitting at the table in the corner! What on earth are they wearing?!

25. ☺☺ Uzupełnij poniższe luki zaimkami *this/that* lub *these/those*.

1. Albert, is _____ you singing in the bathroom?
2. My boss avoided talking about _____ situation yesterday. _____ is a clear sign of his weakness.
3. To be or not to be, _____ is the question!
4. Listen to _____! There has been another robbery in our street!
5. All right, _____'s all for today, see you next week!
6. Now, there was once _____ old shoemaker in London…
7. As long as you live in _____ house you are not going to smoke in your room!
8. Can you remember _____ long, summer evenings we used to spend playing bridge in the garden?

THERE, IT

26. ☺ Utwórz z podanych wyrazów zdania, używając wyrażeń *there is/are*. Niektóre zdania są pytaniami lub przeczeniami.

Wzór: Only one, good café, my town *There is only one good café in my town.*

1. Warsaw, interesting art galleries, a lot of

2. some birthday cake, fridge, still

_____

3. Poland, many foreigners?

_____

4. two men, my door, stand

_____

5. questions, any more, this topic?

_____

6. I, you, anything else, can get?

_____

7. we, not much, help him, can do

_____

8. any, you, English grammar books, could recommend?

_____

9. not enough, this project, volunteers

_____

10. so many, world, why, wars?

_____

27. ☺☺ Połącz zdania z górnej kolumny z odpowiednimi komentarzami z dolnej kolumny, uzupełniając je *it* lub *there*, według wzoru:

1. The sun is shining bright today.
2. You have argued with all your friends and now you need help.
3. Lucinda left Albert, because he told her the truth about his past.
4. In Poland, temperatures in winter may fall below -5°C!
5. We will cross the border unnoticed.
6. You have to be able to buy the tickets via the Internet!
7. We're still stuck in a traffic jam and the meeting starts at 5!
8. Peter is a very mysterious person and we know only a little about his life.
9. Albert has only just started working on the project.
10. Don't switch the telly off!

a) _____ must be freezing cold then!
b) _____'s hard to tell how he will cope with it.
c) _____ isn't anybody to help you now, I'm afraid.
d) _____ won't be any problems, I'm sure.
e) _____'s more news ahead, right after the break!
f) _____ was silly of him to do that.
g) _____ are many secrets in his life.
h) *It*'s beautiful weather today!
i) _____'s getting late!
j) _____ must be possible!

28. ☺☺ Przekształć poniższe zdania zgodnie z podanym początkiem. W każdym zdaniu masz jedną podpowiedź.

Wzór: We may not be able to talk to Mark today.
It *may not be possible to talk to Mark today.*

1. My daughter wants to marry him for several reasons.
There _____why_____.
2. According to the weather forecast, this weekend will be very sunny.
It _____, according to_____.

16

3. We must find a way out of this embarrassing situation.
   There _____be_____.
4. There seem to be at least two solutions to your problem.
   It _____that_____.
5. Too many people in this town know about my past.
   There _____who_____.
6. There was so much noise in the office that nobody heard the phone call.
   It _____noisy_____.
7. We may not have any more chances to escape.
   There _____be_____.
8. This year the English exam might be particularly difficult to pass.
   It _____this year.

PERSONAL AND POSSESSIVE PRONOUNS

29. ☺ Uzupełnij poniższe zdania odpowiednimi formami zaimków osobowych
i dzierżawczych.

1. You can hand in (you) _____ essays now or leave (they) _____ in (I) _____
   box downstairs. The choice is (you) _____.
2. 'Look at that couple over there! Do you think it is (he) _____ mother shouting at
   (they) _____ or is it (she) _____?'
   'I'm not sure. I can't see (she) _____ too well, so it's hard to tell.
3. Make sure that the car you get into after the party is (we) _____. Albert has told (I)
   _____ that last time you tried to get into (they) _____!
4. When (she) _____ husband arrived, she bombarded (he) _____ with stories about
   everything that had happened in (they) _____ family.
5. (We) _____ son sometimes surprises (we) _____ with (he) _____
   inventiveness. We can't believe that some of the amazing ideas we hear about are really
   (he) _____.
6. Some people get on really well with (they) _____ brothers or sisters, but I can't get
   on with (I) _____.
7. This is a problem that concerns the whole company, and that means all of (we) _____:
   not only other managers or (me) _____, but each and every one of (you) _____.

30. ☺ Uzupełnij zdania, wybierając odpowiedź A lub B.

1. You shouldn't be jealous of Mark, he is nobody, just _____!
   A. my friend   B. a friend of mine
2. It is _____ responsibility to clean up after the party.
   A. your responsibility   B. a responsibility of yours
3. Their baby is so sweet and calm that I can hardly believe it is _____.
   A. their   B. theirs
4. We have recently met Barbara, who, it turns out, is _____.
   A. a cousin of my mothers   B. a cousin of my mother's
5. All right, so tell me about _____.
   A. this new crazy plan of yours B. this new crazy plan of you

6. When I finally get a job, I would like to buy _____.
   A. a flat of mine   B. a flat of my own
7. Did Lady Macbeth actually kill any of the characters with _____?
   A. her own hands   B. hands of her own
8. My parents are dreaming of starting _____.
   A. a business of theirs   B. their own business
9. I am going to do this project with Sarah, who is _____.
   A. a colleague of mine   B. a colleague of my own

31. ☺☺ Uzupełnij zdania, używając poniższych zaimków nieokreślonych.

Wzór: At my school *you* can photocopy books and materials for free.

~~you~~   you   your   one   they   their   their   he/she

1. I have heard that _____ are planning to renovate the National Museum.
2. Everybody would like to have a house of _____ own.
3. American supermarkets employ people who actually pack _____ shopping for _____.
4. It is better not to know and to know that _____ does not know.
5. At the end of the term each student should report to _____ mentor for an appraisal interview.
6. An employee must have a clear idea of what _____ is responsible for.

ONE

32. ☺ Uzupełnij poniższe wypowiedzi, używając zaimka *one* oraz wyrazów podanych w nawiasie.

Wzór: My sister was shopping for her wedding dress yesterday.
           (very long, veil) She chose *one with a very long veil.*

1. Albert often has lunch at a pub near his work. (the pub in Galford Street)
   He usually goes _____.
2. The sunglasses that you have ordered are already sold out. (different sunglasses)
   How about _____?
3. Why are so determined to buy this tiny car? (a bigger car)
   I think that you should buy _____.
4. These two TV sets are equipped with standard screens. (the TV sets in the shop window)
   _____ have flat screens.
5. My mom is thinking of buying a Yorkshire terrier. (a Yorkshire terrier with a very long fringe)
   She would particularly like _____.
6. Our family jewels are displayed in this case. (the large red jewel)
   _____ used to belong to the Duchess of York.
7. We have been invited to a company party. (a party with lots of food and drink)
   You know, it is probably going to be _____.
8. I usually get a bus to work. (the bus at 8 o'clock)
   I usually take _____.

33. ☺☺ Wykreśl zaimek *one* w tych zdaniach, w których został on błędnie użyty. Pozostaw go w tych zdaniach, w których został użyty poprawnie.

Wzór: I'll have three/~~three ones~~ of these apples, please.
My son is the tallest/the tallest one in his class. *Obie wersje poprawne.*

1. We've got two flavours of ice-cream today. Which/Which one are you having?
2. Among the girls in her class, Lucinda was always the smartest/the smartest one.
3. One necklace is really enough, are you sure you are buying both/both ones?
4. Having carefully looked at all the rabbits, she decided to take a black/a black one.
5. Albert didn't mind which of the two hotels he would stay at. He could stay at either/either one.
6. Stop asking about my work! You should worry about yours/yours one!
7. I love BMWs, especially the large/the large ones.
8. My wife couldn't decide which fur-coat to buy, so she bought all three/three ones.

34. ☺☺☺ W poniższych zdaniach zamień zaimki nieokreślone na odpowiednią formę zaimka *one*.

Wzór: You should always respect the opinion of your relatives.
One should always respect the opinion of one's relatives.

1. You must find time to eat and sleep properly.

_____

2. We tend to forget our weaknesses.

_____

3. You can never truly enjoy yourself in strange company.

_____

4. Maintaining good relations with your family may be a difficult task.

_____

5. At New Year's Eve we should ask ourselves an important question: how can we make our lives better this year?

_____

REFLEXIVE PRONOUNS

35. ☺ Zdecyduj, w których zdaniach należy użyć zaimków dzierżawczych, wykreślając błędną wersję.

Wzór: Expensive as it may sound, I like to dress –/~~myself~~ in silk.

1. Have you got any money on you/yourself?
2. My brother will start practising drums whenever I try to concentrate –/myself on studying.
3. She is going on a trip to Egypt and taking her 2-year-old daughter with her/herself.
4. The gladiator looked around –/himself and saw his opponent.
5. After a tiring day, the travelers allowed them/themselves a little break.
6. You needn't worry, this secret will stay between us/ourselves.
7. We washed –/ourselves and dried –/ourselves with cotton towels.

36. ☺☺ Połącz poniższe zdania, uzupełniając luki właściwymi zaimkami zwrotnymi.

1. Nobody can make this decision for you.
2. Thank you so much for the wonderful party!
3. If she keeps on riding without her helmet
4. The new haircut was very different from my old one
5. Have you two prepared _____
6. The Manager _____
7. One may be both scared of and attracted to
8. His parents are extremely selfish
9. All three of you are invited to the ceremony:
10. Now, after her partner has left for another company
11. Those who enjoy creating things with their own hands

a) congratulated me on that contract.
b) for the exam?
c) she may decide to run the business by _____.
d) and at first I couldn't recognize _____ in the mirror.
e) may want to buy one of our do-it-_____ kits.
f) and they only care about _____.
g) John, Mary and _____.
h) she may hurt _____ one day.
i) the idea of living by _____.
j) You must decide *yourself* what to do.
k) We have enjoyed _____ a lot!

37. ☺☺ Uzupełnij poniższe zdania, używając zaimka zwrotnego -*selves* lub *each other*.

Wzór:　　These kittens must have fleas, because they keep scratching *themselves*.
　　　　　My parents argued a week ago and are still not talking to *each other*.

1. At our company all computers are connected with _____.
2. What have you two been doing? Look at _____, you're all wet and dirty!
3. We looked at _____ and knew immediately what the other was thinking.
4. Increasingly, people in Poland see _____ as Europeans.
5. We should first know _____ before we try to understand other people.
6. Listen, class. You will do _____ no good if you try to crib during the test!
7. It really won't solve your problem, if you only keep on shouting at _____!

SOME, ANY, NO, NONE

38. ☺ Utwórz poprawne zdania, wybierając jeden z proponowanych zaimków.

Wzór:　　Can I get you ~~any~~/some more tea?

1. There's any/no need to hurry, we've got plenty of time.
2. My private life is no of/none of you business!
3. Robert says we might have any/some problems getting our Afghan visas.
4. Are there any/some questions? If there are no/none, let's continue.

5. Tony's parents didn't teach him <u>any/no</u> golden rules of behaviour.
6. <u>Any of/Some of</u> my friends can't stand my new boyfriend.
7. <u>Any/Some</u> student with a good knowledge of English may apply for the scholarship.
8. The President claims there is <u>no/any</u> risk of a natural disaster this summer.
9. Please, give us <u>any/some</u> tips on how to write a successful history essay.
10. Does <u>any/some</u> of your students speak Arabian by <u>any/some</u> chance?

39. ☺ Uzupełnij poniższe zdania zaimkami *some (-body/-one/-where/-how)* lub *any (-body/-one/-where/-thing)*.

Wzór: Are you going *anywhere* this summer?

1. _____ should take care of this old, deserted building in our street.
2. I rang the bell three times, but there wasn't _____ home.
3. Would you like _____ more brandy?
4. We are not going _____ until you tell us what's going on.
5. The police has still _____ crucial issues to explain in this case.
6. The prosecutor doesn't have _____ evidence that he is lying.
7. My family dreams of going _____ nice and warm for holiday.
8. Is there _____ else I could do to help you?
9. The salesman wasn't sure if there were _____ special offers on that car.
10. Jack managed to fix his motorbike _____ with just one nail and a wire.

40. ☺☺☺ Uzupełnij poniższy tekst właściwymi zaimkami *some (-body/-one/-where/-thing/ -how)*, *any (-body/-one/-where)* lub *no (-body/-one/-where/-thing)*.

My relationship with my husband had a rough beginning. We met in high-school. I agreed to go on a date with him, only because there wasn't (1) _____ else in our class whom I could possibly go out with. Mark invited me to a little restaurant (2) _____ in the centre of Cracow, which served (3) _____ resembling pizza. That date was a complete disaster, because my future husband said absolutely (4) _____ during the entire dinner. At first I was even trying to keep up the conversation, but simply gave up after a while and prayed that (5) _____ from my friends would see us together. And just as we had finished our pizzas and were about to leave, it turned out that Mark didn't have (6) _____ money on him! Now how could I possibly think of going on another date with (7) _____ that grumpy and irresponsible? Yet Mark managed to convince me (8) _____ to give him one more chance. Today, 15 years later, I can only laugh at those who dream about love at first sight. I can assure you: there is (9) _____ more beautiful than falling in love at second or even at third time…

EACH, EVERY

41. ☺ Uzupełnij poniższe zdania zaimkami *each* lub *every*.

Wzór: She had tattoos on both her hands.   *She had a tattoo on each hand.*

1. Both of the twins were given names after the mother's family.

_____

21

2. All candidates for school president had a short presentation for the teachers.

_____

3. Both competitors received gifts and certificates.

_____

4. We both carried our own luggage.

_____

5. All little boys dream of becoming firemen or soldiers.

_____

6. The doctor has advised me to use a special ointment for both feet.

_____

7. Both parties received a copy of the contract they signed.

_____

8. We are being pressed from all sides to make a decision.

_____

42. ☺☺ Uzupełnij zdania, używając zaimków *each* lub *every*.

1. _____ child in Poland knows the story of the dragon which lived under the Wawel Castle in Cracow.
2. During the recruitment of civil service workers, _____ candidate is carefully scanned for his/her employment history.
3. In your listening comprehension exam you will hear _____ text twice.
4. She bought _____ leather hat she could find in the shop.
5. _____ student should consider opening an online bank account.
6. The ghost of the girl held a candle in _____ hand.
7. _____ of our sales representatives has received a company car.
8. My sister is a true animal lover and would gladly adopt _____ homeless dog she happens to see in the street.
9. My boyfriend has got three earrings in _____ ear.
10. _____ competitor will get one chance to withdraw from the contest.

43. ☺☺☺ Przekształć poniższe zdania, używając zaimków *each* lub *every*.

Wzór: I was in a bad mood and argued with almost every/~~each~~ person I met that day.

1. Every/Each cloud has a silver lining.
2. You're coming late every/each single day!
3. My father has got five brothers, of whom every/each has at least three children.
4. Before buying anything, the lady tried on each/each of the one hundred-and-fifty hats in the shop.
5. My mom gave us three pieces of cake every/each.
6. Each/Each of our cats has got its own little bed. But they all sleep with me anyway.
7. Global warming is something that every/each one and every/each of us should take seriously.
8. Can you imagine: only every/each fourth student in Poland gets a scholarship!
9. My wife has seen nearly every/each film made by that director.
10. Every/Each single book that this author has written became a bestseller.

EVERY, ALL, WHOLE

44. ☺ Uzupełnij poniższe zdania, wybierając jedną z podanych odpowiedzi: A, B lub C.

1. Many young people dream of travelling and seeing _____ world.
   A. all   B. whole   C. the whole

2. _____ Mark tells you must be taken with a grain of salt.
   A. All   B. Every   C. Everything

3. Thank you very much for your letters from Egypt; I enjoyed _____ of them.
   A. everyone   B. every one   C. the all

4. My sister is a very sociable person who knows _____ in the neighborhood.
   A. every one   B. everyone   C. all

5. _____ banks should have 24/7 cash dispensers.
   A. All   B. All the   C. Every

6. It's not easy for lower-level employees to see the company as _____.
   A. whole   B. a whole   C. the whole

7. Jane has invited her _____ class to the wedding.
   A. whole   B. the whole   C. all

8. I don't feel like going out, I've been working _____ day.
   A. all   B. whole   C. a whole

9. Hurry up, will you? We don't have _____ time in the world!
   A. all   B. all the   C. every

10. Just a bit more patience: that's _____ I ask of you.
    A. everything   B. all the   C. all

11. Do you swear to tell us _____ truth?
    A. all   B. the whole   C. whole

12. The holiday was a disaster, it rained _____ time.
    A. all   B. whole   C. the whole

13. The actress gave almost _____ money she had to charity.
    A. all   B. every   C. all the

14. _____ families came to see the famous show.
    A. the whole   B. whole   C. every

45. ☺☺ Przekształć poniższe zdania, zamieniając wyrażenia z zaimkiem *all* na *every* (*-one/-body*).

Wzór: All children need to express their emotions.
          Every child needs to express his/her emotions.

1. All students should be allowed to listen to their music during exams.

   _____

2. All girls in our family have been trained in knitting and calligraphy.

   _____

3. In the past, nearly all marriages were arranged by the parents.

   _____

4. Hopefully all people affected by the earthquake have received food and shelter.

   _____

5. All schools in our district are to be provided with their own Internet access.

_____

6. All suspicious travellers had their luggage checked by airport police.

_____

46. ☺☺ Popraw błędy w poniższych zdaniach.

Wzór: All birds cannot fly.   *Not all birds can fly.*

1. All children don't enjoy English lessons.

_____

2. Every school doesn't have a football field.

_____

3. Every car doesn't have an automatic gear box.

_____

4. All persons in my class are not nice to hang around with.

_____

5. All of your ideas are not useful for our company.

_____

6. Every one of us did not contribute to the project.

_____

7. Everything we did in this course was not interesting.

_____

MANY, MUCH, LITTLE, FEW

47. ☺ Uzupełnij poniższe zdania zaimkami *many* lub *much*.

1. How _____ people work in your department?
2. We ought to hurry, we haven't got _____ time left.
3. There are _____ advantages of living on your own.
4. _____ politicians believe that politics is about being powerful.
5. How _____ money have you got on you?
6. Are _____ of your friends chess players like yourself?
7. Claire has _____ annoying habits; for example, she talks too _____.
8. There was not _____ the police could do about the robbery, because the gangster had too _____ connections in town.

48. ☺☺ Uzupełnij zdania, wykreślając błędną wersję.

1. She said she needed little/a little more time to finish the project.
2. Paul seems a loner, with only few/a few friends, but I've heard he's got few/a few relatives in Warsaw, whom he visits from time to time.
3. We know little/a little about prehistoric life. The few/A few things we know are mainly about hunting.
4. Few/A few of my friends proved to be very selfish, because they offered me little/a little support during my problems.
5. 'Could you give me few/a few tips on how to keep a healthy diet?'

6. 'Well, remember that eating healthy is not about eating <u>little/a little</u>, but choosing food that contains <u>few/a few</u> calories'.

49. ☺☺ Uzupełnij poniższe wypowiedzi podanymi wyrazami.

1. much, much, many, a little, ~~a few~~, few
Let us get <u>*a few*</u> things straight: I don't care _____ about your family life or other personal problems, of which you seem to have so _____ nowadays. All I want is _____ of your time and concentration here at work. Is that too _____ to ask? I bet _____ people would say 'yes' to this question.

2. a few, few, few, a little, many, a lot, plenty
I've had _____ of job offers recently! _____ of them are not really worth considering, but quite _____ are potentially interesting. I am only _____ disappointed that so _____ have come from Robsters, whom I've been contacting _____ in the past _____ months.

3. a lot, many, most, much, a few, little
Although _____ Polish people claim they know _____ about Polish history, just _____ questions are enough to prove them wrong. In reality, _____ of them know very _____ about post-war Poland, because so _____ time at schools is devoted to earlier periods.

4. much, many, fewer, few, least, a little
Mary, it's not really about your talking too _____. Just try to have _____ arguments with the people around you and be _____ more friendly to them. _____ of the things you say are simply mean and _____ of your friends will tolerate that in the long-run. So not being nasty to others is the _____ you can do.

BOTH, NEITHER, EITHER

50. ☺☺ Przekształć poniższe zdania, używając wskazanych zaimków *both, neither* oraz *either*.

Wzór: My older sister is an architect and so is the younger one.
         (both) *Both my sisters are architects.*

1. The first squad didn't know about the ambush and the second squad didn't know about the ambush either.
(neither) _____.

2. The first examiner did not notice the mistake and the second examiner did not notice it either.
(neither) _____.

3. Why don't you try on this dress and that one as well?
(both)   _____.

4. The students may use this exit or that exit.
(either) _____.

5. The first film starred Al Pacino and the second one starred Al Pacino as well.
(both)   _____.

6. My boss didn't like the first and he didn't like the second project either.
(neither) _____.

7. You can take the first or the second bus.

(either) _____.

51. ☺☺ Uzupełnij zdania zaimkami *both, neither* oraz *either*, w razie potrzeby dodając **of**.

Wzór: I don't mind which translator will accompany me. I'm sure *either of* them will do fine.

1. I begged _____ my ex-boyfriends to help me, but _____ them did.
2. There are two alarm bells in each office. In case of emergency, _____ may be used to call for help.
3. Since _____ us understands this theory, we should _____ consult a third person.
4. The police cross-examined _____ the two perpetrators, but _____ admitted the guilt.
5. It doesn't matter whether Martin chooses the job at the bank or at the post office; _____ way he will have to go through some training.
6. Although _____ your daughters are lovely, I cannot marry _____ of them.

52. ☺☺ Przeczytaj poniższe zdania i wybierz odpowiedź pasującą do danej sytuacji.

1. You are trying on two T-shirts and you like the first and the second one equally well. You say to the saleswoman:
   A. I'll take both of these T-shirts.
   B. I'll take either T-shirt.
2. You have borrowed a book from a friend and the book isn't exciting or even amusing. You say to your friend:
   A. The book is either exciting or amusing.
   B. The book is neither exciting nor amusing.
3. Your mother is taking a new medicine, which makes her feel dizzy. You say to her:
   A. You should either stop taking this medicine or see a different doctor.
   B. You should either stop taking this medicine and see a different doctor.
4. You have played the guitar and sung in a choir for many years. You say to your friend:
   A. I can both play the guitar and sing well.
   B. I can play both the guitar and sing well.
5. Your friend asks you whether you would like to meet up on Saturday or Sunday and you don't mind. You say to him:
   A. It's up to you, I can come both days.
   B. It's up to you, I can come either day.
6. Your boss asks your opinion on a new project. You think the project isn't brilliant, but it's not completely pointless either. You say to him:
   A. I must say the project is neither brilliant or completely pointless.
   B. I must say the project is neither brilliant nor completely pointless.

ALL, SEVERAL, SOME, MOST, NONE

53. ☺ Zdecyduj, czy w poniższych zdaniach właściwe jest użycie zaimka z **of** i zakreśl poprawną wersję.

1. I've tried <u>several/several of</u> her recipes and they are amazing!
2. <u>Some/Some of</u> the tips you gave me proved very helpful.
3. <u>All/All of</u> people are equal, but <u>some/some of</u> people are more equal than others.
4. <u>Most/Most of</u> things we do in life are either difficult or useless.
5. The king could make <u>either/either of</u> his two sons his heir, but decided to honour his nephew.
6. Although <u>all/all of</u> the students in my class claimed they had read the book, <u>none/none of</u> them was able to tell me how it begun.

54. ☺☺ Uzupełnij poniższe zdania zaimkami *some, none, all, most*. Znajdź zdania, w których poprawne są także formy z **of**.

1. _____ the lawyers I know are actually quite cooperative.
2. _____ students take up a job in the last year of their studies, it's a common practice.
3. _____ people should be entitled to free education.
4. Before we let him go, let's ask him _____ questions about last night.
5. I asked all passengers on the bus for directions, but _____ them knew where the cinema was.
6. I'm not saying she should have known the answers to _____ the questions in the exam… but at least to _____ them!

55. ☺☺ Uzupełnij poniższy tekst na temat wyścigów konnych, używając podanych zaimków i dodając **of**, gdzie to konieczne.

several   none x2   some x2   all x3

Horse racing in the UK became a professional sport under the reign of Queen Anne (1702-1714), who founded (1) _____ the most famous racecourses in England, including Ascot. At first, only two horses would compete in one race, but gradually the system changed to (2) _____ horses participating in one event. The most popular horse racing event became the thoroughbred race; the best-known event also today. From 1750 onward, (3) _____ horse races in England were overseen by the Jockey Club, which also took steps to regulate the breeding of racehorses, since (4) _____ the early breeders were in any way monitored. As a result, (5) _____ modern thoroughbred horses descend from just three stallions. Actually, (6) _____ them came from England, but (7) _____ them were imported from the Middle East. Just as prestigious the breed is, can be seen by the prices of the horses: (8) _____ the most successful thoroughbred racehorses have been sold for hundreds of thousands of dollars.

KLUCZ

24. **1.** this, that **2.** these, those **3.** this, that **4.** this **5.** this **6.** those **7.** these **8.** those

25. **1.** that **2.** that, this **3.** that **4.** that **5.** that **6.** this **7.** this **8.** those

26. **1.** There are a lot of interesting art galleries in Warsaw. **2.** There is still some birthday cake in the fridge. **3.** Are there many foreigners in Poland? **4.** There are two men standing at my door. **5.** Are there any more questions on this topic? **6.** Is there anything else I can get you? **7.** There is not much we can do to help him. **8.** Are there any English grammar books you could recommend? **9.** There are not enough volunteers for this project. **10.** Why are there so many wars in the world?

27. **2.** c there **3.** f it **4.** a it **5.** d there **6.** j it **7.** i it **8.** g there **9.** b it **10.** e there

28. **1.** There are several reasons why my daughter wants to marry him. **2.** It will be very sunny at the weekend, according to the weather forecast. **3.** There must be a way out of this embarrassing situation! **4.** It seems that there are at least two solutions to your problem. **5.** There are too many people in this town who know about my past. **6.** It was so noisy in the office that nobody heard the phone call. **7.** There may be no more chances to escape. **8.** It might be particularly difficult to pass the English exam this year.

29. **1.** your, them, my, yours **2.** his, them, hers, her **3.** ours, me, theirs **4.** her, him, their **5.** Our, us, his, his **6.** their, mine **7.** us, me, you

30. 1 B   2 A   3 B   4 B   5 A   6 B   7 A   8 B   9 A

31. **1.** they **2.** their **3.** your, you **4.** one **5.** their **6.** he/she

32. **1.** to the one in Galford Street **2.** different ones **3.** a bigger one **4.** The ones in the shop window **5.** one with a very long fringe **6.** The large red one **7.** one with lots of food and drink **8.** the 8 o'clock one

33. **1.** which/which one **2.** the smartest/the smartest one **3.** both **4.** a black one **5.** either/either one **6.** yours; po zaimkach dzierżawczych nie używamy 'one'. **7.** the large ones **8.** all three; po liczebnikach nie używamy 'one'.

34. **1.** One must find time to eat and sleep properly. **2.** One tends to forget one's weaknesses. **3.** One can never truly enjoy oneself in strange company. **4.** Maintaining good relations with one's family may be a difficult task. **5.** At New Year's Eve one should ask oneself an important question: how can one make one's life better this year?

35. **1.** you **2.** – **3.** her **4.** – **5.** themselves **6.** us **7.** – , ourselves

36. **2.** k ourselves **3.** h herself **4.** d myself **5.** b yourselves **6.** a himself **7.** i oneself **8.** f themselves **9.** g yourself **10.** c herself **11.** e yourself

37. **1.** each other **2.** yourselves **3.** each other **4.** themselves **5.** ourselves **6.** yourselves **7.** each other

38. **1.** no **2.** none **3.** some **4.** any, none **5.** any **6.** some of **7.** any **8.** no **9.** some **10.** any, any

39. **1.** somebody **2.** anyone **3.** some **4.** anywhere **5.** some **6.** any **7.** somewhere **8.** anything **9.** any **10.** somehow

40. **1.** anybody **2.** somewhere **3.** something **4.** nothing **5.** nobody **6.** any **7.** somebody **8.** somehow **9.** nothing

41. **1.** Each of the twins was given a name after the mother's family. – Przed rzeczownikiem z rodzajnikiem dodajemy 'of'. **2.** Each candidate for school president had a short presentation for the teachers. **3.** Each competitor received a gift and a certificate. **4.** Each of us carried our own luggage. – Przed zaimkiem osobowym dodajemy 'of'. **5.** Every little boy dreams of becoming a fireman or a soldier. **6.** The doctor has advised me to use a special ointment for each foot. **7.** Each party received a copy of the contract it signed. **8.** We are being pressed from every side to make a decision.

42. **1.** every **2.** each **3.** each **4.** every **5.** every **6.** each **7.** each **8.** every **9.** each **10.** each

43. **1.** every; gramatycznie możliwe byłoby także 'each', ale w przysłowiu jest 'every'. **2.** every **3.** each; 'every' nie może wystąpić jako samodzielny zaimek. **4.** each of; przed rzeczownikiem z rodzajnikiem dodajemy 'of'. **5.** each; oznacza „każdemu z nas". **6.** each of; przed rzeczownikiem z zaimkiem dzierżawczym dodajemy 'of'. **7.** each, every; jest to wyrażenie. **8.** every; oznacza „co czwarty". **9.** every; używamy przy wyrażeniach 'nearly', 'almost', 'single' itp. **10.** every

44. **1** C **2** C **3** B **4** B **5** A **6** B **7** A **8** A **9** B **10** C **11** B **12** C **13** C **14** B

45. **1.** Every student should be allowed to listen to his/her music during exams. **2.** Every girl in our family has been trained in knitting and calligraphy. **3.** In the past, nearly every marriage was arranged by the parents. **4.** Hopefully every person/everyone affected by the earthquake has received food and shelter. **5.** Every school in our district is to be provided with its own Internet access. **6.** Every suspicious traveller had his/her luggage checked by airport police.

46. **1.** Not every child enjoys English lessons. **2.** Not every school has a football field. **3.** Not every car has an automatic gear box. **4.** Not everyone in my class is nice to hang around with. **5.** Not all of your ideas are useful for our company. **6.** Not every one of us contributed to the project. **7.** Not everything we did in this course was interesting.

47. **1.** many **2.** much **3.** many **4.** many **5.** much **6.** many **7.** many, much **8.** much, many

48. **1.** a little; 'a little' oznacza „trochę", podczas gdy 'little' oznacza „mało", „niewiele". **2.** few, a few; 'few' oznacza „mało", „niewiele", podczas gdy 'a few' oznacza „kilka". **3.** little, the few; 'the few' oznacza tu „tych kilka konkretnych rzeczy, które znamy". **4.** a few, little **5.** a few **6.** little, few

49. **1.** much, many, a little, much, few **2.** plenty, many, a few, a little, few, a lot, few **3.** many, a lot, a few, most, little, much **4.** much, fewer, a little, many, few, least

50. **1.** Neither squad knew about the ambush. **2.** Neither examiner noticed the mistake. **3.** Why don't you try on both dresses? **4.** The students may use either exit. **5.** Both films starred Al Pacino. **6.** My boss liked neither project. **7.** You can take either bus.

51. **1.** both (of), neither of; 'of' jest konieczne przed zaimkami osobowymi. **2.** either **3.** neither of, both **4.** both of, neither; 'of' jest konieczne przed rzeczownikami z rodzajnikami. **5.** either **6.** both, either

52. **1** A **2** B **3** A **4** A **5** B **6** B

53. **1.** several of; 'of' jest konieczne przed rzeczownikami z zaimkami dzierżawczymi. **2.** some of; 'of' jest konieczne przed rzeczownikami z rodzajnikami. **3.** all, some **4.** most **5.** either of **6.** all/all of, none of; 'of' jest konieczne przed zaimkami osobowymi.

54. **1.** all (of) **2.** most **3.** all **4.** some **5.** none of **6.** all (of), some of

55. **1.** some of **2.** several **3.** all **4.** none of **5.** all **6.** none of **7.** all of **8.** some of

ADJECTIVES AND ADVERBS

COMPARATIVE AND SUPERLATIVE ADJECTIVES

56. ☺☺ Wstaw podany przymiotnik we właściwym stopniu: wyższym lub najwyższym. Pamiętaj, że przymiotnik w stopniu najwyższym poprzedzamy przedimkiem *the*.

1. (beautiful) _____ things in life come free.
2. The moment he slid his hand (far) _____ down her back she slapped him hard.
3. Nethybridge is (quiet) _____ little village you can imagine.
4. Ned's ideas get (crazy 2x) _____ and _____. Soon he will go mad altogether.
5. He had (blue) _____ eyes I have ever seen in my life.
6. Which painter was (well-known) _____ in his lifetime: Rubens or Van Dyck?
7. In the past, Chinese women had their feet broken and bound to make them appear (tiny) _____.
8. Which car is (fast) _____: a Mercedes or a Porsche?
9. I have just bought (new) _____ book by Guy Gavriel Kay. It was published just three days ago.
10. Your last homework is (good) _____ than the previous one, but you still have to work hard on the irregular verbs.

57. ☺☺ Wstaw podany przymiotnik we właściwym stopniu.

Old Sir Ronald Merridew's daughter was 1. (**sweet**) _____ girl you could imagine, and a lot 2. (**clever**) _____ than her father. Sir Ronald, after sixty years of life, was 3. (**wise**) _____ than clever. So when on the morning after the ball his darling girl came down to breakfast (and a very 4. (**late**) _____ breakfast it was) and announced: 'Count Belmonte is by far 5. (**good-looking**) _____ man I've ever danced with, Papa!', Sir Ronald answered seriously: 'It was indeed 6. (**kind**) _____ of the Count to invite us to his ball. I have never seen 7. (**spectacular**) _____ fireworks. But what a pity he was so 8. (**attentive**) _____ to Lady Julia DeForest that he danced with you only once. I was quite offended for you, my dear.'
The girl frowned and seemed slightly 9. (**little**) _____ certain of Count Belmonte's charm. Sir Ronald thought the moment of danger was over. He couldn't have been 10. (**wrong**) _____ ...

MAKING COMPARISONS

58. ☺ Uzupełnij zdania. W każdą lukę możesz wpisać tylko jedno słowo.

1. My father is better at maths _____ yours!
2. This class is as boring _____ the previous one.
3. I have never seen you look _____ lovely than you're looking today.
4. Are you feeling all right? You are getting paler and _____.
5. Diamonds are far _____ expensive than zirconias.
6. I should have added a _____ less salt to the soup. It's too salty now.
7. Ingrid enjoyed the party much _____ than her husband did.
8. I have never eaten such delicious doughnuts _____ these!
9. Our present flat is _____ so sunny as the previous one.
10. I don't enjoy watching football as _____ as you do. I'd rather read a book.

59. ☺☺ Dodaj do podanych dalsze dwa przykłady potraw, które są według ciebie:

exotic	Singapore noodles, _____
tasty	roast beef, _____
fattening	moussaka, _____
expensive	lobster, _____
easy to cook	pasta bolognese, _____
spicy	tandoori curry _____
sweet	sweetcorn and pineapple salad, _____
bland	boiled cauliflower, _____
filling	casserole, _____
vegetarian	vegetable stew, _____

Jak stopniują się te przymiotniki?

A teraz porównaj potrawy, używając podanych struktur:

Wzór: Curry vindaloo is more exotic *than* ossobuco: the first is Indian, the other Italian.

1. _____ than _____.
2. _____ less _____ than _____.
3. _____ as _____ as _____.
4. _____ not so _____ as _____.
5. _____ and _____than _____.
6. _____ like _____: they are both _____.
7. _____ the most _____ of all.
8. _____ more _____than _____.
9. _____, _____ and _____ are all _____.

60. ☺☺ Wstaw podaną frazę z przymiotnikiem we właściwym stopniu: wyższym lub najwyższym.

1. **an absent-minded person**
   Robert is _____ I know.

2. **a home-loving woman**
   My mother-in-law thinks her son ought to have married _____
   than me.
3. **a joyless meal**
   The family dinner we had after my grandmother's funeral was _____
   I remember.
4. **a heated discussion**
   After Professor Bolingbroke's ill-timed remark, _____ became even
   _____ than before.
5. **a horrifying experience**
   Meeting the madman in the woods was _____ of
   my life.
6. **a lifeless smile**
   I could see how depressed she was when she gave me the saddest, _____
   _____ that I ever saw on her face.
7. **harmful chemicals**
   The factory in our town has stopped polluting the river with its
   _____, but it is still pumping water from the
   cooling system into it.
8. **a hen-pecked husband**
   You couldn't find _____ than Gerald if you tried!
9. **a heartless remark**
   Shame on you! This was _____ you could have
   made in the circumstances!
10. **a helpful reference book**
    I found _____ that Jessie had lent me _____ than
    Morag's manual.

61. ☺☺ Poniżej podano dwadzieścia idiomów, których możesz używać przy porównaniach.
Uzupełnij je wyrazami z ramki.

a fox	a picture	a fiddle	a grave
life	a bat	a rake	chalk from cheese
a horse	a church mouse	a hatter	a cucmber
a lamb	a judge	lead	two peas in a pod
a daisy	a bee	a lord	gold

1. as blind as _____
2. as busy as _____
3. as cool as _____
4. as cunning as _____
5. as different as _____
6. as drunk as _____
7. as fit as _____
8. as fresh as _____
9. as good as _____
10. as heavy as _____
11. as large as _____
12. as like as _____
13. as mad as _____
14. as meek as _____

15. as poor as   _____
16. as pretty as   _____
17. as silent as   _____
18. as sober as   _____
19. as strong as   _____
20. as thin as   _____

Zastanów się, jakie są polskie odpowiedniki tych wyrażeń.

ORDER OF ADJECTIVES

62. ☺☺ Uzupełnij zdania, wpisując podane przymiotniki we właściwej kolejności.

1. **thin knitting steel long**
   My grandmother used to have _____ needles.
2. **diamond-shaped glittering blue purple**
   The dragon had _____ scales all over its body.
3. **lovely buckled silver tiny**
   On her feet, Cinderella was wearing _____
   shoes.
4. **lace finest white/Meissen best porcelain**
   On special occasions Mrs Weatherwane put a _____
   tablecloth on her table and took out her _____
   tea service.
5. **raisin delicious fresh honey**
   Aunt Theresa made some _____ cakes for us.
6. **terrifying black huge poisonous hairy**
   Seeing a _____ spider crawling into her tent,
   Alice screamed at the top of her voice.
7. **elegant leather silk black**
   Ella brought from Florence a/an _____
   handbag.
8. **nineteenth-century portrait renowned Venetian**
   This portrait of Countess Pemberley was painted by a _____
   _____ painter.
9. **modest Renaissance symmetrical/Baroque richly-decorated splendid**
   The _____ façade of the church oddly clashed
   with the _____ interior.

63. ☺☺☺ Wpisz podane przymiotniki do właściwej kolumny.

colossal aluminium grey-green cast-iron oval helpful pearly silk Roman ocean-
-going bluish Australian frozen octagonal medieval gold catastrophic eighteenth-
-century triangular huge Buddhist ancient outdoor lovely rosewood sour boring
leather bitter amoral linen star-shaped prehistoric cool Castilian military scarlet
lethal famous pea-sized Amazonian arched brand-new petite Navajo yellow

1. Opinion   _____

2. Size   _____

3. Shape   _____

4. Age   _____

5. Colour   _____

6. Origin   _____

7. Material   _____

8. Type/Purpose _____

ADVERBS

64. ☺ Przyporządkuj przysłówki podane w ramce do odpowiednich grup.

however	usually	hence	stupidly
maybe	fortunately	definitely	sometimes
perhaps	seldom	quietly	anyway
reasonably	sort of	downstairs	soon
here	today	fast	beforehand
in Scotland	almost	partly	hungrily

adverbs of certainty   _____

adverbs of comment   _____

adverbs of completeness   _____

adverbs of indefinite frequency   _____

adverbs of manner   _____

adverbs of place   _____

adverbs of time   _____

connecting adverbs   _____

65. ☺☺☺ Uzupełnij poniższe zdania odpowiednią formą czasowników podanych w nawiasach, a następnie dobierz z poprzedniego ćwiczenia i wpisz w odpowiednie miejsce w zdaniu przysłówek, który najlepiej wzmocni sens całej wypowiedzi.

Wzór:

Go to bed, but (clean) _____ your teeth _____.

Go to bed, but <u>clean</u> your teeth <u>beforehand</u>.

1. Helen is addicted to coffee. She (drink) _____ seven or eight coffees a day.
2. Don't worry, Sigurd is very hard-working. He (finish) _____ _____ the project on time.
3. The plane nearly crashed. _____, in the end the pilot (manage) _____ to make it land safely.
4. The alley cat (eat) _____ the mouse it caught.
5. My daughter is a well mannered girl. She (behave) _____ ____ rudely. But when she does, she can be horrid!
6. We don't have enough money to finish our summer house. Before winter, it will be only (finish) _____.

7. Your glasses are not upstairs. I last saw them in the kitchen, so (go) _____
_____ and you will find them there.
8. Mr Grant wanted to write a Ph.D. _____, Professor
Ralston (object) _____ to it.
9. Jack was late and Jill (suggest) _____ to wait
another five minutes and then phone him.

66. ☺☺☺ Oba zdania są prawidłowe. Wybierz to, które lepiej uzupełni wypowiedź.

1. A horrible gurgling sound intrrupted our talk. At a neighbouring table,
   a) a little boy noisily sucked at a straw.
   b) a little boy sucked at a straw noisily.
2. The team of marines was on its way home. Men were happy and relaxed.
   a) The mission has been completed successfully.
   b) The mission has been successfully completed.
3. Our language school is growing.
   a) Every summer more students come.
   b) More students come every summer.
4. Some national customs seem to us rather strange. For instance,
   a) men wear skirts in Scotland.
   b) in Scotland men wear skirts.
5. After she lost the letter, the Chairman gave his secretary a severe reprimand.
   a) Wisely, she remained silent.
   b) She wisely remained silent.

ADJECTIVES VS. ADVERBS

67. ☺ Uzupełnij poniższe zdania przymiotnikami lub przysłówkami podanymi w ramce.

obvious clear deeply quickly well smoothly clearly deep good obviously smooth quick

Wzór: The thieves were so *quick* that the police didn't manage to catch them.

1. The fog was getting thicker every minute and the climbers couldn't see the mountain top
   too _____.
2. Alice's boss told her to come to work on Sunday. So, she was furious,
   _____.
3. The fact that the company is withdrawing from the stock-exchange is a
   _____ sign of its financial difficulties.
4. They say this film is not really _____; it's just a light comedy.
5. The actors had practiced a lot, so the entire show ran very _____.
6. Everybody was waiting for me, so I _____ looked in the mirror and joined
   them.
7. What you have just said seems _____, but in fact not many people have
   heard about it.
8. Sandra was _____ moved by Albert Charlie's speech.

9. What I particularly like about these gloves is the _____ leather they are made of.
10. The musical that Greta stars in is not too _____. Half of the cast can't sing _____!

68. ☺☺ Uzupełnij poniższe zdania, zakreślając właściwy przysłówek.

1. Take it easy/easily, it's just a class test.
2. I have tried hard/hardly to gain her trust, but she still didn't speak free/freely.
3. Add a cucumber, washed and fine/finely chopped.
4. Already as little children, footballers must learn to play fair/fairly.
5. Our P.E. teacher made us jump very high/highly.
6. I found her remarks high/highly amusing.
7. Don't worry about your son, he's doing fine/finely!
8. Your leaving town tomorrow has sure/surely nothing to do with Lucinda's sudden business trip, has it?
9. Hold on tight/tightly, another wave is coming!
10. I've heard that when you work for that hotel you can eat free/freely in the canteen downstairs.

69. ☺☺ Uzupełnij zdania przysłówkiem lub wyrażeniem przysłówkowym.

Wzór: She laughed (quiet) *quietly.*
        She looked at me (friendly) *in a friendly way.*

1. He spoke (angry) _____ about his accident.
2. I can't believe Jane is acting (so silly) _____.
3. Dorris was singing a Christmas carol (lovely) _____.
4. If you study this book you will pass the exam (easy) _____.
5. In my class pupils are not allowed to write (ugly) _____.
6. Any ordinary object used (deadly) _____ can be considered a weapon by the court.
7. Joe's remark was (wrong) _____ interpreted as an accusation.
8. This book presents dry historic facts (lively) _____.
9. Eric got up very (early) _____ that day, to prepare a surprise for his wife.
10. The project was not Mary's responsibility, as she (right) _____ pointed out to her boss.

SO/SUCH... SO THAT

70. ☺ Połącz połówki zdań, uzupełniając je wyrażeniami z *so...* lub *such (a/an)...*

1. The Manager was *so* angry...
2. Our mother is _____ good cook...
3. My boss is _____ perfectionist...
4. Paul's wife is _____ obsessed with cleanliness...
5. Isabelle's parents are _____ old-fashioned...
6. My trip to Bangladesh was _____ important experience...

7. Some people are _____ jealous of other people's success...

8. Lucinda is _____ talkative...

   a) ...that she cleans the carpet three times a day.
   b) ...that he often leaves work past midnight.
   c) ...that they will do anything to end their good fortune.
   d) ...that hardly anyone wants to chat with her.
   e) ...that her recipes are often published in magazines.
   f) ...that he fired the entire department.
   g) ...that I've written a book about it.
   h) ...that they even travel by a horse-drawn carriage.

71. ☺☺ Przekształć wyrażenia z *so... that* na *such... that* i odwrotnie.

   Wzór: The view was so shocking that we had to turn our heads away.
              It was such a shocking view that we had to turn our heads away.

   1. The dress she was wearing was so beautiful that Arthur fell in love right away.
      _____

   2. My aunt gave me such a cheap fur-coat that it fell apart within a week.
      _____

   3. That idea was so brilliant that I could hardly believe it was yours.
      _____

   4. Juliet was wearing such dark sunglasses that I couldn't see the colour of her eyes.
      _____

   5. The winter was so cold that one morning my car's engine froze.
      _____

   6. It is such a warm evening that it would be a shame to spend it inside.
      _____

   7. It was so noisy in the pub that nobody could hear the singer.
      _____

   8. It has been such a busy day today that we didn't even manage to have lunch.
      _____

   9. That book was so gripping that I read it through the day I bought it.
      _____

   10. The dog had such sad eyes that several passers-by stopped by to pat it.
       _____

72. ☺☺☺ Uzupełnij poniższe wypowiedzi, używając wyrazów w nawiasach oraz konstrukcji *so... that* lub *such... that*.

   Wzór: Is Agnes very ambitious? (ambitious person, study, all day long)
              Yes. In fact, *she is such an ambitious person that she studies all day long.*

   1. Were you disappointed when you lost the race? (disappointed, nearly, cry)
      Yes. In fact, _____.
   2. Was it a good theatre play? (good play, receive, standing ovation)
      Yes. In fact, _____.
   3. Was your journey long? (long, read, all my books)
      Yes. In fact, _____.
   4. Is it true that the Manager gave a long speech? (long speech, back rows, fall asleep)
      Yes. In fact, _____.
   5. Has Judy really got such long hair? (long hair, people, trip over)
      Yes. In fact, _____.

6. Was your holiday really that boring? (boring, study maths, entertain oneself)
   Yes. In fact, _____.

7. Is the company powerful? (powerful, not fear, any competition)
   Yes. In fact, _____.

TOO... TO

73. ☺ Połącz poniższe zdania, używając wyrażeń z *too... to*.

Wzór: Lucinda is so rude that she doesn't have any friends.
    Lucinda is too rude to have any friends.

1. David loves Helen so much that he won't accept the truth about her.
   _____

2. This car is so large that it won't fit into our garage.
   _____

3. The film is so deeply-rooted in American culture that it will not appeal to other nations.
   _____

4. Our football team was so weak that they didn't defeat Manchester United.
   _____

5. It rained so much that day that it wasn't possible to continue climbing.
   _____

6. The boys looked so young that they couldn't buy beer at the bar.
   _____

7. The book was so dull that it didn't become a bestseller.
   _____

8. I have read so little of this author that I can't say if he's good.
   _____

74. ☺☺ Odpowiedz na poniższe pytania, używając wyrażeń z *too... to*.

Wzór: A friend asks you to help her with her luggage, which is very heavy. You can't carry it. What do you say?
    Sorry, but this luggage *is too heavy for me to carry.*

1. A shop assistant offers you a very skimpy dress. You don't want to buy it. What do you say?
   Sorry, but this dress _____.

2. You go to a disco, which is very crowded. You can't enjoy yourself. What do you say to your friends?
   Sorry, but this disco _____.

3. Your colleague asks you a question, which is very complex. You can't answer it right away. What do you say?
   Sorry, but this question _____.

4. Your new neighbour has told you little about his life. You can't trust him. What do you say to him?
   Sorry, but I _____.

5. Rebecca's dog is aggressive. You don't want your dog to play with it. What do you say to Rebecca?

Sorry, but your dog _____.

6. You are watching a film with a friend and find it very violent. You can't watch it. What do you say to your friend?

Sorry, but this film _____.

75. ☺☺☺ Uzupełnij poniższe zdania, wybierając poprawną spośród odpowiedzi A, B lub C.

1. She was _____ preoccupied with her own life _____ notice the problems of others.
   A. much ... to   B. too ... to   C. to... to

2. Your theory is too abstract for anybody _____.
   A. too understand   B. to understand   C. understand it

3. The truth about Lucinda is _____ to bear.
   A. too heavy burden   B. a too heavy burden   C. too heavy a burden

4. It is too soon _____ to decide what to do.
   A. that we   B. of us   C. for us

5. Isn't this book too boring to _____?
   A. talk about?   B. talk about it?   C. to talk?

6. The future of the world is _____ to predict.
   A. a too difficult   B. for anybody too difficult   C. too difficult for anybody

7. Ours is _____ company to tolerate mistakes like that.
   A. too professional   B. too professional a   C. too professional the

ENOUGH... TO

76. ☺☺ Przekształć poniższe zdania, używając podanych przymiotników oraz wyrażeń z *enough... to*.

Wzór: Larry is too rude to get the job. (POLITE)
           Larry isn't polite enough to get the job.

1. The salesman was too short to reach the upper shelf. (TALL)

   _____

2. The knight felt too weak to accept the challenge. (STRONG)

   _____

3. Some people are too bored with politics to vote in the elections. (INTERESTED)

   _____

4. The candidate has too little experience to work on this project. (EXPERIENCED)

   _____

5. Her paintings are too typical to receive more publicity. (ORIGINAL)

   _____

6. The highways are too narrow to ease traffic. (WIDE)

   _____

7. My computer is too slow to download this program. (FAST)

   _____

77. ☺☺ Uzupełnij poniższe zdania, używając wyrażenia *enough... to.*

Wzór: You know too little to argue with me on this topic.
You don't know enough to argue with me on this topic.

1. The policeman had slept too little to understand what the woman was saying.

_____

2. Albert loves Anna too little to forgive her the lie.

_____

3. We were offered too little to eat to enjoy the party.

_____

4. The couple had practised too little to perform the dance.

_____

5. Peter lived too far away to visit Peggy every day.

_____

6. The government is doing too little to prevent the conflict.

_____

7. The company is selling too little to make a profit this year.

_____

78. ☺☺ Uzupełnij poniższe zdania, używając podanych przymiotników oraz wyrażenia *enough... to.*

Wzór: Lucinda isn't polite. The company will not employ her.
Lucinda isn't polite enough for the company to employ.

1. The idea was not crazy. Olivier didn't accept it.

_____

2. The book isn't interesting. I won't recommend it to anybody.

_____

3. The cave wasn't safe. We didn't hide in it.

_____

4. Your arguments aren't convincing. Your boss will not accept them.

_____

5. The situation isn't clear. The army cannot intervene.

_____

6. The rollercoaster ride wasn't long. The children didn't enjoy it.

_____

7. The horse wasn't fast. We didn't bet on it.

_____

ADJECTIVES AND INFINITIVES

79. ☺☺ Przekształć poniższe zdania, używając konstrukcji z bezokolicznikiem.

Wzór: Albert was glad that he was home again.
Albert was glad to be home again.

1. I'm happy that I can help!

_____

2. Adrian was relieved that he was on the waiting list for the excursion to Egypt.

_____

3. It is certain that Caroline will win the beauty contest at her company.

_____

4. Was he angry when he discovered your little secret?

_____

5. It is likely that the population of the Earth will soon exceed 11 billion.

_____

6. I am very pleased that I can introduce to you our new colleague.

_____

7. The public was very disappointed when they heard that the band had a new lead singer.

_____

8. My brother got an A in his maths test, which was lucky.

_____

9. Is it certain that we will get the test results tomorrow?

_____

80. ☺☺ Skomentuj poniższe zdania, używając konstrukcji z bezokolicznikiem i podanych przymiotników.

Wzór:　　　Diana gave up her job because she felt exploited. (BRAVE)
It was brave of Diana to give up her job.

1. You helped your neighbour to clean the garage. (NICE)

_____

2. Stephen told Sarah about his previous girlfriend. (SILLY)

_____

3. My husband checked the bank carefully before opening his bank account. (SENSIBLE)

_____

4. I believed that the manager had good intentions. (NAÏVE)

_____

5. She told everybody in the class about that scandal. (NASTY)

_____

6. You have insulted your mother-in-law! (RUDE)

_____

7. Ian organized a charity action for the poorest families in our district. (THOUGHTFUL)

_____

8. Polish people complain a lot. (TYPICAL)

81. ☺☺ Przekształć poniższe zdania, używając konstrukcji z bezokolicznikiem i podanych przymiotników.

Wzór:　　　I can easily get some free tickets for you. (NOT DIFFICULT)
It won't be difficult (for me) to get some free tickets for you.

1. I enjoyed living near a big park. (NICE)

_____

2. Sean doesn't have to come with us to the meeting tomorrow. (NOT NECESSARY)

_____

3. Students usually start coming to lectures just before the exam session. (USUAL)

_____

4. We shouldn't eat too much of animal fats. (HEALTHY)

_____

5. You must listen carefully to what I say. (IMPORTANT)

_____

6. Jackie cannot win the beauty contest, she is too skinny! (IMPOSSIBLE)

_____

7. Milk shouldn't be kept in room temperature for more than one day. (GOOD)

_____

ADJECTIVES AND PREPOSITIONS

82. ☺ Uzupełnij poniższe zdania odpowiednim przyimkiem: A, B lub C.

1. My neighbours are very interested _____ our family life.
   A. for   B. at   C. in
2. Robbie is not very keen _____ exercising or sports.
   A. about   B. on   C. for
3. Just go up and talk to her! What are you afraid _____?
   A. of   B. about   C. against
4. I've studied all night but I still don't feel prepared _____ the exam.
   A. on   B. for   C. at
5. The President is worried _____ the political situation in our country.
   A. of   B. about   C. for
6. Children who solve a lot of puzzles are usually good _____ math.
   A. in   B. on   C. at
7. My friend's wife is very jealous _____ other people.
   A. about   B. for   C. of
8. I'm sorry _____ interrupting you, but you've got a phone call!
   A. for   B. about   C. at

83. ☺☺ Uzupełnij poniższy tekst odpowiednimi przyimkami.

My older sister, Agnes, has a truly colourful personality. She is interested (1) *in* martial arts and is genuinely fond (2) _____ all those Bruce Lee films, which normally only boys watch. She took up karate three years ago and has been quite successful (3) _____ all her competitions so far. Agnes is a tough person, very much obsessed (4) _____ good manners. I remember how disgusted she was (5) _____ our brother once, who had offended her friend at our house. She was so angry (6) _____ him that she made him apologize to the friend right away. I remember that I was very proud (7) _____ her. But Agnes is not made of steel. She has some little weaknesses which are typical (8) _____ women: she is scared (9) _____ spiders, for example, and ashamed (10) _____ talking to strangers. Whenever I see her like that, I am truly startled. However, it seems that Agnes herself is not aware (11) _____ this paradox.

84. ☺☺☺ Przekształć poniższe zdania, używając przymiotników podanych w nawiasach.

Wzór: My mother is not a good cook. (BAD)
          My mother is bad at cooking.

1. I really don't feel like forgiving you anymore! (TIRED)

_____

2. It's the manager's responsibility to organize the conference. (RESPONSIBLE)

_____

3. It's alright, I'm always the one getting all the blame, you know. (USED)

_____

4. I can't believe that you might want to buy this house. (INTERESTED)

_____

5. My son doesn't enjoy reading, I'm afraid. (KEEN)

_____

6. My parents were terrified whenever they had to get into the car I was driving. (HORRIFIED)

_____

7. Our students know how to avoid hard work. (VERY GOOD)

_____

8. Can't you concentrate for just 5 minutes? (CAPABLE)

_____

KLUCZ

56. **1.** The most beautiful **2.** farther/further (*far* stopniuje się nieregularnie) **3.** the quietest **4.** crazier and crazier (powtórzenie przymiotnika sugeruje ciągłość zmiany) **5.** the bluest **6.** better-known/more well-known (niektóre przymiotniki złożone można stopniować, zarówno dodając **-er/-est**, jak i opisowo) **7.** tinier **8.** faster **9.** the newest **10.** better

57. **1.** the sweetest **2.** cleverer **3.** more wise – zazwyczaj wise stopniuje się z **-er/-est**; kiedy jednak porównujemy dwa przymiotniki, mówiąc, że jeden jest bardziej odpowiedni niż drugi, używamy wyłącznie *more* **4.** late **5.** the most good-looking/the best-looking – niektóre przymiotniki złożone można stopniować, zarówno dodając **-er/-est**, jak i opisowo **6.** most kind – kiedy wyrażamy pochwałę lub naganę, zamiast *very* możemy użyć *most* (bez *the*) z przymiotnikiem; jest to charakterystyczne dla stylu oficjalnego **7.** more spectacular **8.** attentive **9.** less – little stopniuje się nieregularnie (*less – the least*) **10.** more wrong – *wrong* i *right* stopniuje się wyłącznie z *more*

58. **1.** than **2.** as **3.** more **4.** paler **5.** more **6.** little **7.** more **8.** as **9.** not **10.** much

59. Ćwiczenie otwarte; podane przymiotniki stopniują się następująco:
exotic, more exotic, the most exotic
tasty, tastier, the tastiest
fattening, more fattening, the most fattening
expensive, more expensive, the most expensive
easy, easier, the easiest (to cook)
spicy, spicier, the spiciest
sweet, sweeter, the sweetest
bland, blander, the blandest
filling, more filling, the most filling
vegetarian – nie stopniuje się! Potrawa albo jest wegetariańska, albo nie.

60. **1.** the most absent-minded person **2.** a more home-loving woman **3.** the most joyless meal **4.** the discussion (...) more heated **5.** the most horrifying experience **6.** the most lifeless smile **7.** most harmful chemicals **8.** a more hen-pecked husband **9.** the most heartless remark **10.** the reference book (...) more helpful
Przymiotniki kończące się na -ing, -ed, -ful i -less stopniuje się tylko i wyłącznie opisowo, niezależnie od ilości sylab.

61. **1.** a bat (ślepy jak kret) **2.** a bee (pracowity jak pszczółka) **3.** a cucumber (mniej więcej: wesoły jak szczygiełek) **4.** a fox (chytry jak lis) **5.** chalk from cheese (różniące się jak dzień i noc) **6.** a lord (pijany jak bela) **7.** a fiddle (zdrowy jak rydz) **8.** a daisy (świeży jak poranek) **9.** gold (szczery jak złoto) **10.** lead (ciężki jak ołów) **11.** life (wielki jak góra) **12.** two peas in a pod (podobne do siebie jak dwie krople wody) **13.** a hatter (stąd Szalony Kapelusznik z *Alicji w Krainie Czarów*!) (pokręcony jak kłębek włóczki) **14.** a lamb (łagodny jak baranek) **15.** a church mouse (biedny jak mysz kościelna) **16.** a picture (śliczny jak z obrazka) **17.** a grave (milczący jak kamień) **18.** a judge (trzeźwy jak świnia) **19.** a horse (silny jak koń) **20.** a rake (chudy jak patyk/jak chart)

62. 1. long and thin steel knitting needles – (shape, material, purpose). Dwa przymiotniki z tej samej kategorii (tu: shape) łączymy spójnikiem *and*.
2. glittering diamond-shaped blue and purple scales – (opinion, shape, colour). Dwa przymiotniki z tej samej kategorii (tu: colour) łączymy spójnikiem *and*.
3. lovely tiny silver buckled shoes – (opinion, size, colour, type).
4. a finest white lace tablecloth/best Meissen porcelain tea service – (opinion, colour, material/opinion, origin, material).
5. fresh and delicious raisin and honey cakes – (opinion, material). Mamy tu po dwa przymiotniki z tej samej kategorii, więc łączymy je spójnikiem *and*.
6. a terrifying, huge, black, hairy, poisonous spider – (opinion, size, colour, other qualities). Jeśli jednak chcemy użyć aż pięciu przymiotników, lepiej będzie utworzyć zdanie złożone:
Alice screamed at the top of her voice when she saw a terrifying, huge, black, hairy spider, which she knew was poisonous, crawling into her tent.
7. an elegant black leather and silk handbag – (opinion, colour, material). Dwa przymiotniki z tej samej kategorii (tu: material) łączymy spójnikiem *and*.
8. a renowned nineteenth-century Venetian portrait painter – (opinion, age, origin, type).
9. the modest and symmetrical Renaissance façade/the splendid richly-decorated Baroque interior – (opinion and opinion, age/opinion, decoration, age).

63. 1. Opinion   helpful, catastrophic, lovely, sour, boring, bitter, amoral, cool, famous
    2. Size   colossal, huge, pea-sized, petite
    3. Shape   oval, octagonal, triangular, star-shaped, arched
    4. Age   medieval, eighteenth-century, ancient, prehistoric, brand-new
    5. Colour   grey-green, pearly, bluish, scarlet, yellow
    6. Origin   Roman, Australian, Castilian, Amazonian, Navajo
    7. Material   aluminium, cast-iron, silk, gold, rosewood, leather, linen
    8. Type/purpose   ocean-going, frozen, Buddhist, outdoor, military, lethal

64. adverbs of certainty   maybe, definitely, perhaps
    adverbs of comment   fortunately, reasonably, stupidly
    adverbs of completeness   almost, partly, sort of
    adverbs of indefinite frequency   usually, sometimes, seldom
    adverbs of manner   quietly, fast, hungrily
    adverbs of place   downstairs, here, in Scotland
    adverbs of time   soon, today, beforehand
    connecting adverbs   however, hence, anyway

65. 1. usually drinks **2.** will definitely finish **3.** Fortunately/managed **4.** hungrily ate **5.** seldom behaves **6.** partly finished **7.** go downstairs **8.** However/objected **9.** reasonably suggested

66. 1. a). Przysłówek oznaczający sposób wykonywania czynności kończący się na **-ly** może występować w środku lub na końcu zdania, ale pozycja w środku zdania kładzie nań mniejszy nacisk. Tu ważne jest, *co* ssał chłopiec, a nie *jak*, bo już z poprzedniego zdania wiadomo, że wydawał bulgoczące dźwięki.
2. b). W przypadku zdań w stronie biernej przysłówek oznaczający sposób wykonywania czynności występuje najczęściej w środku zdania (po wszystkich czasownikach posiłkowych).
3. b). Przysłówek oznaczający czas/częstotliwość może występować na początku lub w środku zdania, ale pozycja na początku zdania kładzie nań mniejszy nacisk. W tym przykładzie (chodzi o szkołę letnią) ważne jest, że każdego lata przyjeżdża więcej słuchaczy; to, że przyjeżdżają, jest oczywiste.
4. b). Przysłówek oznaczający miejsce może występować na początku lub w środku zdania, ale pozycja na początku zdania kładzie nań mniejszy nacisk. W tym przykładzie ważniejsze jest, że mężczyźni noszą spódniczki.
5. Oba zdania są prawidłowe, chociaż a) jest bardziej typowe. Przysłówek wyrażający stosunek wypowiadającego zdanie występuje częściej na początku niż w środku zdania.

67. 1. clearly **2.** obviously **3.** clear **4.** deep **5.** smoothly **6.** quickly **7.** obvious **8.** deeply **9.** smooth **10**. good, well; przymiotnik 'good' stosujemy do opisania rzeczowników, a więc przedmiotów, osób itp. (*jaki* jest musical), natomiast przysłówek 'well' do opisania czasowników, a więc zdarzeń, czynności, umiejętności (*jak* ona śpiewa)

68. 1. easy **2.** hard, freely; 'try hard' oznacza tutaj bardzo mocno się starać, natomiast przysłówek 'hardly' ma inne znaczenie – ledwie, rzadko itp. 'Freely' oznacza swobodnie. **3.** finely; 'finely' oznacza bardzo drobno, cienko. **4.** fair; 'play fair' to grać uczciwie, natomiast 'fairly' ma inne znaczenie – całkiem, dosyć (np. dosyć ciekawy). **5.** high; oznacza wysoko (np. podskoczyć). **6.** highly; oznacza wysoce (np. zabawny, interesujący). **7.** fine; 'do fine' to dobrze sobie radzić. **8.** surely; oznacza z pewnością. **9.** tight; wyrażenie 'hold on tight' oznacza mocno się trzymać. **10.** free; tutaj oznacza za darmo.

69. 1. angrily **2.** in such a silly way **3.** in a lovely voice **4.** easily **5.** in an ugly manner/way **6.** in a deadly manner **7.** wrongly **8.** in a lively way/manner **9.** early **10.** rightly

70. 2. e such a **3. b** such a **4. a** so **5. h** so **6. g** such an **7. c** so **8. d** so

71. 1. She was wearing such a beautiful dress that Arthur fell in love right away. **2.** The fur-coat that my aunt gave me was so cheap that it fell apart within a week. **3.** It was such a brilliant idea that I could hardly believe it was yours. **4.** The sunglasses that Juliet was wearing were so dark that I couldn't see the colour of her eyes. **5.** It was such a cold winter that one morning my car's engine froze. **6.** The evening is so warm that it would be a shame to spend it inside. **7.** There was so much noise in the pub that nobody could hear the singer. **8.** It has been so busy today that we didn't even manage to have lunch. **9.** It was such a gripping book that I read it through the day I bought it. **10.** The dog's eyes were so sad that several passers-by stopped by to pat it.

72. 1. I was so disappointed that I nearly cried. **2.** it was such a good play that it received a standing ovation. **3.** the journey was so long that I read all my books. **4.** he gave such a long speech that the back rows fell asleep. **5.** she has got such long hair that people trip over it. **6.** my holiday was so boring that I studied maths to entertain myself. **7.** the company is so powerful that it doesn't fear any competition.

73. 1. David loves Helen too much to accept the truth about her. **2.** This car is too large to fit into our garage. **3.** The film is too deeply-rooted in American culture to appeal to other nations. **4.** Our football team was too weak to defeat Manchester United. **5.** It rained too much to continue climbing. **6.** The boys looked too young to buy beer at the bar. **7.** The book was too dull to become a bestseller. **8.** I have read too little of this author to say if he's good.

74. 1. Sorry, but this dress is too skimpy for me to buy. **2.** Sorry, but this disco is too crowded for me to enjoy myself. **3.** Sorry, but this question is too complex for me to answer it right away. **4.** Sorry, but I know too little about your life to trust you. **5.** Sorry, but your dog is too aggressive for my dog to play with. **6.** Sorry, but this film is too violent for me to watch..

75. 1 B   2 B   3 C   4 C   5 A   6 C   7 B

76. 1. The salesman wasn't tall enough to reach to the upper shelf. **2.** The knight didn't feel strong enough to accept the challenge. **3.** Some people are not interested enough in politics to vote in the elections. **4.** The candidate is not experienced enough to work on this project. **5.** Her paintings are not original enough to receive more publicity. **6.** The highways are not wide enough to ease traffic. **7.** My computer is not fast enough to download this program.

77. 1. The policemen didn't sleep enough to understand what the woman was saying. **2.** Albert doesn't love Anna enough to forgive her the lie. **3.** We weren't offered enough to eat to enjoy the party. **4.** The couple hadn't practised enough to perform the dance. **5.** Peter didn't live close enough to visit Peggy every day. **6.** The government is not doing enough to prevent the conflict. **7.** The company is not selling enough to make a profit this year.

78. 1. The idea was not crazy enough for Olivier to accept. **2.** The book is not interesting enough for me to recommend to anybody. **3.** The cave wasn't safe for us to hide in. **4.** Your arguments aren't convincing enough for your boss to accept. **5.** The situation isn't clear enough for the army to intervene. **6.** The rollercoaster ride wasn't long enough for the children to enjoy. **7.** The horse wasn't fast enough for us to bet on.

79. 1. I'm happy to help. **2.** Adrian was relieved to be on the waiting list for the excursion to Egypt. **3.** Caroline is certain to win the beauty contest at her company. **4.** Was he angry to discover your little secret? **5.** The population of the Earth is likely to exceed 11 billion. **6.** I am very pleased to introduce to you our new colleague. **7.** The public was very disappointed to hear that the band had a new lead singer. **8.** My brother was lucky to get an A in his maths test. **9.** Are we certain to get the test results tomorrow?

80. 1. It was nice of you to help your neighbour to clean the garage. **2.** It was silly of Stephen to tell Sarah about his previous girlfriend. **3.** It was sensible of my husband to check the bank carefully before opening his bank account. **4.** It was naïve of me to believe that the manager had good intentions. **5.** It was nasty of her to tell everybody in the class about that scandal. **6.** It was rude of you to insult your mother-in-law! **7.** It was thoughtful of Ian to organize a charity action for the poorest families in our district. **8.** It is typical of Polish people to complain a lot.

81. 1. It was nice to live near a big park. **2.** It is not necessary for Sean to come with us to the meeting tomorrow. **3.** It is usual for students to start coming to lectures just before the exam session. **4.** It's not healthy (for us) to eat too much of animal fats. **5.** It is important for you to listen carefully to what I say. **6.** It is impossible for Jackie to win the beauty contest, she is too skinny! **7.** It isn't good for milk to be kept in room temperature for more than one day.

82. 1 C **2** B **3** A **4** B **5** B **6** C **7** C **8** A

83. 2. of **3.** in **4.** with **5.** with/at **6.** with **7.** of **8.** of **9.** of **10.** of **11.** of

84. 1. I am really tired of forgiving you! **2.** The manager is responsible for organizing the conference. **3.** It's alright, I'm used to getting all the blame. **4.** I can't believe that you might be interested in buying this house. **5.** My son is not keen on reading, I'm afraid. **6.** My parents were horrified of getting into the car I was driving. **7.** Our students are very good at avoiding hard work. **8.** Aren't you capable of concentrating for just 5 minutes?

VERBS

IRREGULAR VERBS

85. ☺ Uzupełnij poniższe zdania odpowiednią formą czasowników w czasie Past Simple.

1. When my mother (be) _____ a little girl, the teachers (be) _____ stricter than nowadays.
2. The postman (come) _____ up to the postbox and (put) _____ a letter inside.
3. Last year we (go) _____ to Florida and (spend) _____ the whole summer on the beach.
4. Last night I (see) _____ a very interesting film, which (tell) _____ the story of American prisoners of war.
5. My boss (send) _____ us an e-mail yesterday, in which he (write) _____ about his splendid plans for the next month.
6. Some of the children (sit) _____ down on the floor and others (lie) _____ down on the carpet. The teacher (begin) _____ reading a story.
7. Mandy (feel) _____ very ill yesterday and (sleep) _____ all day.

86. ☺☺ W każdej z par czasowników jeden jest nieregularny. Znajdź wszystkie czasowniki nieregularne i użyj pięciu z nich, aby utworzyć zdania w czasie Past Simple i pięciu, aby utworzyć zdania w czasie Present Perfect.

1. snow – show	6. prove – move	11. find – found
2. kneel – peel	7. hold – fold	12. dine – shine
3. stay – lay	8. fly – flow	13. catch – match
4. say – pray	9. blink – think	14. rake – brake
5. raise – rise	10. kick – stick	15. trim – swim

Past Simple

1. _____
2. _____
3. _____
4. _____
5. _____

Present Perfect

1. _____
2. _____
3. _____
4. _____
5. _____

87. ☺☺☺ Przekształć poniższe zdania, zachowując ich znaczenie; użyj wyrazów podanych w nawiasach.

Wzór:

According to the Greek myth, Cronus was defeated by his own son, Zeus. (OVERTHROW)
According to the Greek myth, Cronus was overthrown by his own son, Zeus.

1. Angela has gone to court against her own company. (SUE)

   _____

2. The pilot hasn't managed to contact the airport so far. (BE ABLE)

   _____

3. This government has solved many basic problems of the healthcare system. (DEAL SUCCESSFULLY)

   _____

4. Many artists have hoped that they will find happiness in exotic countries. (SEEK)

   _____

5. I think you haven't quite understood what I mean. (MISUNDERSTAND)

   _____

6. Horses shouldn't be given too many apples to eat. (FEED)

   _____

7. You are not permitted to enter the professor's office with your hat on! (FORBID)

   _____

8. In the epic poem, Beowulf dies after his victorious fight with the dragon. (SLAY)

   _____

QUESTIONS

88. ☺ Utwórz pytania do poniższych odpowiedzi.

Wzór: Yes, my sister likes to tease others.
            Does your sister like to tease others?

1. _____
   'Yes, I can give you the details of the plan.'

2. _____
   'Yes, we have met Carl's new girlfriend.'

3. _____
   'That's right, Francis is not invited to my wedding.'

4. _____
   'No, I will not come in for a drink.'

5. _____
   'Yes, the patient was very tired after the operation.'

6. _____
   'Certainly, I would like to know your opinion.'

7. _____
   'You're right, a new chairman has not been appointed yet.'

8. _____

'Yes, definitely, the nights in Egypt were very cold.'

9. _____

'That's right we didn't tell our parents the truth.'

10. _____

'Yes, unfortunately, I broke up with my boyfriend two months ago'.

89. ☺ Używając *who, which, what, when, where, why* i *how*, utwórz pytania do podkreślonej części zdania.

Wzór:　　　My father gave me that dress.　　*Who gave you that dress?*

1. Belinda told me about your argument with the Manager.

_____

2. We appointed Ted for this job.

_____

3. I've been swimming and playing golf recently.

_____

4. The meeting is taking place on Friday.

_____

5. The award ceremony is being organized in Paris.

_____

6. Helen insulted Allan's parents during his birthday dinner.

_____

7. The first part of the film is about John's childhood.

_____

8. The second part is about John's journey to India.

_____

9. The Jacksons want to renovate the spare room in order to rent it to a foreign student.

_____

10. You can help me by leaving me alone right now.

_____

90. ☺☺ Utwórz pytania zależne, używając podanych wyrazów w odpowiedniej formie oraz *who, which, what, when, where, why* i *how*.

Wzór:　　(the nearest post office, be)

　　　　Do you know *where the nearest post office is?*

1. Can you tell me _____? 　　　　(the party, be like)

2. Do you know _____? 　　　　(Harry, leave earlier)

3. Did he say _____? 　　　　(he, go to)

4. Do you have any idea _____? 　　　　(he, get home)

5. Does anybody remember _____ that evening? 　(Nancy, talk to)

6. Could you explain _____? 　　　　(they, argue about)

7. Can you tell me _____? 　　　　(Nancy, go out with)

8. Do you have any idea _____? 　　　　(that guy, be from)

QUESTION TAGS

91. ☺ Uzupełnij poniższe zdania odpowiednimi pytaniami zwrotnymi.

1. She's not very excited about Jonathan's marriage, _____?
2. You have met my parents, _____?
3. We're not going to sit around and wait for something to happen, _____?
4. I don't know what Graham is going to do, I'm not a fortuneteller, _____?
5. Your mother can speak Chinese, _____?
6. There was a lot of confusion about the new law, _____?
7. Well, it's not Margaret who started the argument, _____?
8. The Management haven't got a clue what to do now, _____?
9. We shouldn't trust Lucinda's words, _____?
10. Leave me alone for a few minutes, _____?

92. ☺ Połącz poniższe zdania.

1. It's really hot in here.
2. I've been trying to get in touch wih Mary.
3. One of our colleagues has been surfing on the Internet all day.
4. I've heard this play is very good.
5. I don't think our conflict is very serious.
6. We are looking for somebody fluent in Spanish.
7. I don't feel like discussing this project here in the office.
8. I've told you a thousand times that I will not lend you my car, but you just keep asking me about it.

a) It's forbidden at our department, isn't it?
b) Open the window, will you?
c) You wouldn't know her telephone number, would you?
d) Jerry has lived in Madrid, hasn't he?
e) Let's see it at the weekend, shall we?
f) There's no need for us to call our lawyers yet, is there?
g) You never give up, do you?
h) Let's go to a café, shall we?

93. ☺☺ Uzupełnij poniższy dialog odpowiednimi pytaniami zwrotnymi.

'Hi, Albert! You haven't seen Lucinda by any chance, (1) _____?'
'No, sorry, I haven't. She isn't a person I often hang around with, (2) _____?'
'I guess she isn't. Just let me know if you do happen do see her, (3) _____?'
'Of course. But there isn't anything to worry about, (4) _____?'
'No, there isn't.
'Are you sure?'
'Yes! I would tell you if there was, (5) _____?'
'I hope so. I am still your best friend after all, (6) _____?'
'Of course you are!'
'So, let's go now, (7) _____?'

IMPERATIVE

94. ☺ Ułóż zdania rozkazujące, używając czasowników z ramki.

> write down   call   take away   be quiet   give back   not argue with   answer
> not go away   switch off   ~~listen to~~   not be angry with

Wzór: I know what's best for you.   *Listen to me!*

1. You've taken my wallet!   _____
2. I've asked you a question!   _____
3. I know I'm right about it.   _____
4. This was supposed to be just a joke!   _____
5. This is my e-mail address.   _____
6. I don't want to be alone now.   _____
7. I don't need that plate any longer, John.   _____
8. Anita wanted to speak to you.   _____
9. The radio is disturbing me.   _____
10. Children, stop shouting now!

95. ☺☺ Dokończ wypowiedzi, przekształcając zdania w nawiasach w zdania rozkazujące.

Wzór: If Amelia wants to emigrate to Africa, it's fine by me. (She should just go.)
              Let her go!

1. I don't know which bank loan will be best for our family. (I want my husband to decide.)
  _____

2. Ok, I see there are no more questions on this. (We're moving on to the next chapter.)
  _____

3. There's no use forcing students to study harder. (They should just fail the exam.)
  _____

4. This is not a major emergency. (We shouldn't panic).
  _____

5. You're not good at fixing cars. (Patrick should fix mine.)
  _____

6. I don't feel like staying home all weekend. (I feel like going dancing.)
  _____

7. Susan will not cope with this project. (Somebody else should handle it.)
  _____

8. It's not an easy decision to make. (We shouldn't rush with it.)
  _____

96. ☺☺ Połącz zdania w pary, uzupełniając je odpowiednią formą rozkazującą czasownika.

1. You shouldn't intervene in this situation.
2. Altogether your situation is not that bad.
3. Lucinda and Mark are getting married.
4. You and I are good at planning things.
5. I believe our discussion is over.

6. Your arguments are not very convincing.
7. There is a huge crowd in front of our office building.
8. Your father is working at the moment.

a) (not go) _____ outside for a while.
b) (not talk) _____ about it anymore!
c) (stay out) *Stay out* of it, that's my advice.
d) (face) _____ it, you'll never win this case!
e) (not exaggerate) _____!
f) (organize) _____ a surprise party for them!
g) (start) _____ our own business!
h) (not disturb) _____ him!

VERBS FOLLOWED BY GERUND, INFINITIVE, TO-INFINITIVE OR *THAT*-CLAUSE

97. ☺☺ Uzupełnij zdania właściwą formą bezokolicznika (**infinitive** lub *to*-**infinitive**).

1. I am ashamed that despite all my promises I have failed (write) _____ to my best friend.
2. I've finally arranged (meet) _____ Rick for a coffee and a chat.
3. Put your hand on my belly. Can you feel the baby (move) _____?
4. I regret (tell) _____ you that your dog's operation was not succesful.
5. We tried (turn) _____ the doorknob, but it wouldn't move, so we climbed in through the window.
6. In the middle of the night Luke heard the door (open) _____ quietly.
7. After her husband's death, Monica decided (leave) _____ the country forever.
8. Do you really expect me (make) _____ your bed? You must be joking!

98. ☺☺ Przekształć poniższe zdania, używając odpowiedniej formy bezokolicznika (**infinitive** lub *to*-**infinitive**).

Wzór: I forgot that I had an important letter to post.
       I forgot to post an important letter.

1. Jill and I agreed that we shall pay the debt fifty-fifty.
   Jill and I _____
2. The boys planned that they would go to the army together.
   The boys _____
3. I watched the rat until it disappeared in the dustbin.
   I _____
4. Please remember that the key has to be turned twice.
   Please _____
5. My mother expected that she shall be free by 7 pm at the latest.
   My mother _____

99. ☺☺ W podanych zdaniach wybierz właściwą formę.

1. You do realise that getting this train means <u>to stay/staying</u> up all night, don't you?
2. Grandmother always regretted <u>not to go/not going</u> to art school.
3. Leslie distinctly remembered <u>to put/putting</u> his book on the windowsill – yet it was not there now.
4. The dog stopped <u>to sniff/sniffing</u> the lamp-post.
5. I will never forget <u>to kiss/kissing</u> Belinda during the last dance of the prom.
6. This sauce is so bland! Why don't you try <u>to add/adding</u> some cinnamon to it?

100. ☺☺ Uzupełnij zdania za pomocą *how, what, when, where, whether, who* oraz odpowiedniej formy czasownika podanego w ramce.

become	blame	do	find	operate	keep

1. Michael has not decided yet _____ a sculptor or a painter.
2. Minnie never knew _____ her mouth shut.
3. I am wondering _____ a decent mechanic in this God-forsaken dump.
4. Can you tell me _____ the new photocopier?
5. Never forget _____ in case of fire.
6. I know _____ for opening the safe-box, but I am afraid to tell anyone.

101. ☺☺☺ Przekształć zdania, jak najmniej zmieniając ich znaczenie.

1. The secretaries still keep stealing office stationery. (STOPPED)
   The secretaries _____
2. Lucy noticed a strange boy waiting patiently at her gate. (THAT)
   Lucy _____
3. Randolph hoped to be promoted fast. (FOR)
   Randolph _____
4. Lillian said she won't come to Betsy's wedding ceremony. (REFUSED)
   Lillian _____
5. I hope you are not angry that I asked you to wash the dishes. (WASHING)
   You don't mind _____, do you?
6. If you can't sleep, I suggest you drink herb tea instead of coffee in the evening. (TRY)
   If you can't sleep, why _____?
7. I deeply regret that I decided to sell my grandfather's library. (DECISION)
   I _____
8. 'I want to see the Headmaster!', shouted the pupil's mother. (DEMANDED)
   The pupil's mother _____
9. My boss ordered me to write the report by 7 pm on Friday. (MADE)
   My boss _____
10. Jane is very sorry she doesn't have time to go to the dancing class anymore. (MISSES)
    Jane _____
11. I don't feel like watching a horror film tonight. (FANCY)
    I _____
12. I am sorry I did not buy that old grandfather clock. (BUYING)
    I regret _____

13. Cinderella's stepmother made her darn the stepsisters' socks. (WAS)
   Cinderella _____
14. 'Yes, I cheated in the exam', said Tim finally. (CHEATING)
   Tim finally _____

KLUCZ

85. 1. was, were **2.** came, put **3.** went, spent **4.** saw, told **5.** sent, wrote **6.** sat, lay, began **7.** felt, slept

86. Czasowniki nieregularne: **1.** show **2.** kneel **3.** lay **4.** say **5.** rise **6.** prove **7.** hold **8.** fly **9.** think **10.** stick **11.** find **12.** shine **13.** catch **14.** brake **15.** swim
Przykłady zdań: Past Simple **1.** John showed me around his house and garden. **2.** The people in the church knelt and prayed. **3.** My mother laid the presents under the Christmas tree. **4.** Mary said that she liked her job. **5.** The fog rose over the mountain range.
Present Perfect **1.** I have proven that my hypothesis is correct. **2.** This year we have held two conferences on this topic. **3.** The manager has flown over 5,000 miles this year. **4.** I have thought a lot about this problem lately. **5.** The teacher has stuck the children's drawings to the wall.

87. 1. Angela has sued her own company. **2.** The pilot hasn't been able to contact the airport so far. **3.** This government has dealt successfully with many basic problems of the healthcare system. **4.** Many artists have sought happiness in exotic countries. **5.** I think you have misunderstood me. **6.** Horses shouldn't be fed too many apples. **7.** You are forbidden to enter the professor's office with your hat on! **8.** In the epic poem, Beowulf dies after he has slain the dragon.

88. 1. Can you give me the details of the plan? **2.** Have you met Carl's new girlfriend? **3.** Isn't Francis invited to the wedding? **4.** Won't you come in for a drink? **5.** Was the patient very tired after the operation? **6.** Would you like to know my opinion? **7.** Hasn't a new chairman been appointed yet? **8.** Were the nights in Egypt very cold? **9.** Didn't you tell your parents the truth? **10.** Did you break up with your boyfriend two months ago?

89. 1. Who told you about my argument with the Manager? 'Who' w tym pytaniu odnosi się do wykonawcy czynności/podmiotu w zdaniu (*Belinda* told me), nie stosujemy więc operatora 'do'. **2.** Who did you appoint for the job? 'Who' w tym pytaniu odnosi się do odbiorcy czynności/dopełnienia (We appointed *Ted*), stosujemy więc operator 'do'. **3.** What have you been doing recently? **4.** When is the meeting taking place? **5.** Where is the award ceremony being organized? **6.** Who did Helen insult during Allan's birthday dinner? **7.** Which part of the film is about John's childhood? **8.** What is the second part about? Przyimki związane z czasownikiem stawiamy zwykle na końcu pytania. **9.** Why do the Jacksons want to renovate the spare room? *lub* What do the Jacksons want to renovate the spare room for? **10.** How can I help you?

90. 1. what the party was like – Jeżeli pytanie jest zdaniem podrzędnym, zostawiamy zwykły szyk zdania: podmiot-orzeczenie. **2.** why Harry left earlier **3.** where he went to **4.** how he got home **5.** who Nancy was talking to that evening **6.** what they argued about **7.** who Nancy went out with **8.** where that guy was from

91. 1. is she? **2.** haven't you? **3.** are we? **4.** am I? **5.** can't she? **6.** wasn't there? **7.** is it? **8.** have they? **9.** should we? **10.** will you?

92. 2 c 3 a 4 e 5 f 6 d 7 h 8 g

93. 1. have you? **2.** is she? **3.** will you? **4.** is there? **5.** wouldn't I? **6.** aren't I? **7.** shall we?

94. 1. Give it back. **2.** Answer it. **3.** Don't argue with me! **4.** Don't be angry with me. **5.** Write it down. **6.** Don't go away. **7.** Take it away. **8.** Call her. **9.** Switch it off. **10.** Be quiet!

95. 1. Let my husband decide. **2.** Let's move on to the next chapter. W trybie rozkazującym w 1 os. l. mn. forma 'let us' jest zwykle skracana do 'let's'. **3.** Let them fail the exam. **4.** Let's not/Don't let's panic. Przeczenia z 'let's' tworzymy w dwojaki sposób: za pomocą operatora 'do not/don't' lub za pomocą słówka 'not' wstawianego za konstrukcją, przed czasownikiem. **5.** Let Patrick fix mine. **6.** Let's go dancing. **7.** Let somebody else handle it. **8.** Let's not/Don't let's rush with it. Przeczenia z 'let's' tworzymy w dwojaki sposób: za pomocą operatora 'do not/don't' lub za pomocą słówka 'not' wstawianego za konstrukcją, przed czasownikiem.

96. **2 e** Don't exaggerate. **3 f** Let's organize a surprise party for them. **4 g** Let's start our own business. **5 b** Let's not talk/Don't let's talk about it anymore. **6 d** Face it/Let's face it, you'll never win this case. **7 a** Let's not go outside for a while. **8 h** Don't/Let's not/Don't let's disturb him.

97. **1.** to write **2.** to meet **3.** move **4.** to tell **5.** to turn **6.** open **7.** to leave **8.** to make
Warto zawsze sprawdzić w słowniku, czy dany czasownik łączy się z czasownikiem z **-ing**, czy też z bezokolicznikiem, a jeśli tak, to z którym rodzajem bezokolicznika.

98. **1.** Jill and I agreed to pay the debt fifty-fifty.
2. The boys planned to go to the army together.
3. I watched the rat disappear in the dustbin. (użycie **infinitive** podkreśla tu zakończenie czynności)
4. Please remember to turn the key twice.
5. My mother expected to be free by 7 pm at the latest.

99. Wiele czasowników łączy się zarówno z **-ing**, jak i z **to-infinitive**, lecz zmienia znaczenie w zależności od formy.
1. staying (*mean + to-infinitive* wyraża zamiar)
2. not going (*regret + to-infinitive* używamy w oficjalnych informacjach [patrz 97.4])
3. putting (*remember + to-infinitive* używamy, mówiąc o przyszłości)
4. to sniff (*stop + -ing* wyraża zaniechanie jakiejś czynności)
5. kissing (*forget + to-infinitive* używamy, mówiąc o tym, że zapomnieliśmy coś zrobić)
6. adding (*try + to-infinitive* używamy, mówiąc o próbach zakończonych niepowodzeniem [patrz 97.5])

100. **1.** Michael has not decided yet whether to become a sculptor or a painter.
2. Minnie never knew when to keep her mouth shut.
3. I am wondering where to find a decent mechanic in this God-forsaken dump.
4. Can you tell me how to operate the new photocopier?
5. Never forget what to do in case of fire.
6. I know who to blame for opening the safe-box, but I am afraid to tell anyone.

101. **1.** The secretaries have not stopped stealing office stationery.
2. Lucy noticed that a strange boy was waiting patiently at her gate.
3. Randolph hoped for a fast promotion.
4. Lillian refused to come to Betsy's wedding ceremony.
5. You don't mind washing the dishes, do you?
6. If you can't sleep, why don't you try drinking herb tea instead of coffee in the evening?
7. I deeply regret the/my decision to sell my grandfather's library.
8. The pupil's mother demanded to see the Headmaster.
9. My boss made me write the report by 7 pm on Friday.
10. Jane misses going to the dancing class.
11. I don't fancy watching a horror film tonight.
12. I regret not buying that old grandfather clock.
13. Cinderella was made by her stepmother to darn the stepsisters' socks.
14. Tim finally admitted to cheating in the exam.

PRESENT TENSES

PRESENT SIMPLE

102. ☺ Wybierz odpowiednią formę czasownika.

1. John _____ strawberries: he is allergic to them.
   a) don't eat   b) doesn't eat   c) eats

2. Susan never _____ horror films.
   a) watches   b) doesn't watch   c) watch

3. Not many students _____ their own car.
   a) don't have   b) have   c) has

4. A lot of teenagers _____ bikes.
   a) rides   b) to ride   c) ride

5. My two best friends _____ the violin.
   a) plays   b) play   c) not play

6. Björn _____ from Norway.
   a) come   b) coming   c) comes

103. ☺ Ułóż pytania do podanych odpowiedzi.

1. _____ like _____?
   No, I hate yoghurt. I am not very keen on dairy products in general.

2. _____ time _____?
   Jill starts her classes at 8.15 am. She is a primary school teacher.

3. Where _____?
   Your watch is on the kitchen table. You put it there yesterday.

4. _____ instrument _____?
   Rachel plays the violin. She wants to be a famous concert player.

5. _____ Rick and Mary _____?
   Rick takes sugar with his tea, but Mary doesn't. She is slimming.

6. _____ ever _____?
   No, my dog never barks. He was taught not to.

7. Excuse me, _____?
   The nearest post office is just round the corner, on the left. You can't miss it.

8. How _____?
   You press this button here and the box opens.

9. _____ you think of _____?
   I think the new University conference centre is extremely ugly.

10. _____ go round _____?
    No, it is the Earth that goes round the Sun, silly.

104. ☺☺ Przepisz podane zdania, zastępując podkreślony fragment odpowiednią formą czasownika z ramki i dokonując innych potrzebnych zmian.

agree	behave	consider	feel	love	~~suppose~~	think

Wzór: <u>My guess is that</u> John has done something wrong.
          I suppose John has done something wrong.

1. I <u>have the impression</u> that you are not telling me the truth.
2. My sister's daughter <u>is</u> often <u>naughty</u>.
3. <u>My opinion is</u> that the entire idea for this holiday was crazy.
4. Nellie considers her mother's novel badly written and her husband <u>thinks so too</u>.
5. Leslie <u>is very keen on</u> water sports.
6. We <u>think that</u> our rival company's proposal <u>is</u> strange.

PRESENT CONTINUOUS

105. ☺ Uzupełnij zdania właściwą formą czasownika.

Granny: Hello? Is that Lucy? Hi, sweetie! What (1. you/do) _____ now?
Lucy: Hello, Gran! (2. I/have) _____ breakfast.
Granny: And what (3. your mother/do) _____?
Lucy: (4. she/talk) _____ to Daddy. (5. he/go) _____ to work in a minute.
Granny: And your Kitty?
Lucy: (6. she/play) _____ with a piece of paper on the carpet. Granny, when (7. you/come) _____ to see us?
Granny: (8. I/come) _____ on Friday, sweetie, as planned.

106. ☺☺ Do podanych czasowników dopisz ich formy z -*ing*. Czy wiesz, według jakich reguł tworzy się te formy?

answer – _____   betray   – _____   catch   – _____
chat   – _____   collide – _____   complain   – _____
dare   – _____   destroy – _____   fly   – _____
love   – _____   quarrel – _____   sit   – _____
swim   – _____   travel   – _____

107. ☺☺ Zdecyduj, czy podkreślona forma czasownika odnosi się do teraźniejszości (**T**), czy do przyszłości (**P**).

1. I <u>am learning</u> Greek. (**T/P**)
2. You <u>are</u> definitely <u>not going</u> to this party! (**T/P**)
3. Delia <u>is considering</u> moving to Island. (**T/P**)
4. Our partners <u>are asking</u> for a meeting next Monday. (**T/P**)
5. They <u>are not showing</u> any good films all week. (**T/P**)
6. I am too fat. Next month, I <u>am not eating</u> chocolate at all. (**T/P**)
7. Lucy <u>is trying</u> to learn bellydancing. (**T/P**)

8. What <u>are you wearing</u> to the wedding reception? (**T/P**)

9. I <u>am getting</u> tired with your constant complaints. (**T/P**)

10. Bill <u>is not leaving</u> until the end of the month. (**T/P**)

108. ☺☺ Wybierz właściwą formę czasownika.

1. Mr and Mrs Langdon <u>think/are thinking</u> of moving to Singapore.

2. Why <u>do you smell/are you smelling</u> the milk? Has it gone off?

3. Jane <u>hears/is hearing</u> strange voices which order her to do things. Do you think she may have schizophrenia?

4. I <u>taste/am tasting</u> the stew to see if it is spicy enough. It could do with some pepper, actually.

5. I could swear I saw fairies dance in our garden at dawn. I must <u>see/be seeing</u> things.

109. ☺☺ Przepisz podane zdania, zastępując podkreślony fragment odpowiednią formą czasownika z ramki.

feel	have	hear	see	~~think~~

Wzór: I <u>may change</u> my job next year.
               I am thinking of changing my job next year.

1. What time <u>will you eat</u> supper tonight?

_____

2. I <u>have a meeting with</u> the new employees at 11 o'clock.

_____

3. The jury <u>will listen</u> to the witnesses tomorrow.

_____

4. You have gone pale. <u>Are you</u> OK?

_____

110. ☺☺ Wyraź niezadowolenie z poniższych sytuacji.

Wzór:

It drives you mad when your younger sister borrows your earrings without asking.
'*You're always borrowing my earrings!* You could at least ask!'

1. You hate it when the office door is left open, and your colleague never closes it.
'_____ Will you please start closing it?'

2. You have worked hard in your garden, and your neighbour's dog comes and digs holes there.
'_____ I have worked so hard to plant the flowers!'

3. It irritates you very much when your boyfriend leaves dirty dishes in the sitting-room.
'_____ Do you think I am your servant?'

4. Your brother keeps smoking in your room, although you many times told him not to.
'_____ How many times did I tell you not to?'

5. Your father often forgets his keys and phones you to let him in. You are telling your sister how much it irritates you.
'_____ I wish he would stop.'

PRESENT SIMPLE OR
PRESENT CONTINUOUS?

111. ☺ Zdecyduj, czy czasowniki w poniższych zdaniach powinny mieć formę Present Simple czy Present Continuous.

1. Don't disturb your brother. He (write) _____ a letter to his girlfriend.
   I (think) _____ he is going to ask her to marry him!
2. Fred (work) _____ in the International Department and often (write) _____ to other companies in English. He has bought an entire bookcase of dictionaries.
3. 'Would you like to have dinner with us?'
   'No, thanks. I (not want) _____ to eat anything until later tonight. My wife and I (go) _____ to this fancy restaurant, where you (pay) _____ $5 and get an "all-you-can-eat" menu'.
4. The Queen (live) _____ in the western wing of the Palace, but (think) _____ of moving to the southern one soon. She (believe) _____ that part has a better view and nicer furniture.
5. The Ambassador (not travel) _____ a lot, because it (put) _____ too much strain on his health, he (say) _____. However, he (not seem) _____ to be very stressed about his holiday trip to Egypt, where he (fly) _____ next week.
6. My girlfriend (eat) _____ tremendous amounts of carrots nowadays, because she (claim) _____ they are good for her complexion. Well, all I've noticed is that her skin (look) _____ orangey these days, which I would hardly consider healthy.
7. I should've known this present was just a joke! Albert always (make) _____ fun of me in front of other people!

112. ☺☺ Połącz poniższe zdania w pary, uzupełniając je odpowiednimi formami czasowników w czasie Present Simple lub Present Continuous.

1. Tony Parsons (write) _____ books about love, family and relationship.
2. I (do) _____ an interview with the Minister of Justice today, which I'm very angry about.
3. The club members (meet) _____ today to discuss the future of their organization.
4. The Duke and the Duchess are currently in Essex, where they usually (spend) _____ their holidays.
5. As an owner of a bodyguard organization, I often (work) _____ in stressful or dangerous conditions.
6. It (seem) _____ that we will have to wait for the President's signature under this Act.

a) They (fish) _____ and (hunt) _____ and generally (enjoy) _____ themselves.
b) Especially now, in summer, when we (cover) _____ many open-air mass events.
c) He currently (work) _____ on a novel about the problem of divorce.
d) Of course he (do) _____ all he can to speed up the decision process.

59

e) I (not enjoy) _____ talking to arrogant high-rank politicians.

f) The meeting is at the Green Palace, where they usually (hold) _____ their conferences.

113. ☺☺☺ Przeczytaj poniższą notatkę o zmianach w regulaminie Uniwersytetu w Chaste. Uzupełnij luki odpowiednimi formami podanych czasowników w czasie Present Simple lub Present Continuous.

Chaste University currently 1. (consider) _____ whether to change a decades-old policy that 2. (ban) _____ its employees from activities like drinking and smoking. In accordance with these regulations, lecturers and faculty 3. (abstain) _____ from drinking alcohol, smoking tobacco and gambling even in their private lives. However, increasingly, university staff 4. (feel) _____ that the policy may be slightly too restrictive. They 5. (criticize) _____ especially the ban on dancing and going to the cinema. They 6. (hope) _____ that these regulations will be changed. However, some authors of the policy 7. (not agree) _____ with any modifications. 'That's because I 8. (take) _____ it very seriously that I'm a role model for students here', says Sarah Still, Associate Professor at Chaste University, who 9. (try) _____ to gather a group of supporters. At present, a special committee 10. (study) _____ the policy. The committee members 11. (meet) _____ next month to give their verdict.

PRESENT PERFECT

114. ☺ Uzupełnij poniższe zdania w czasie Present Perfect najbardziej odpowiednim wyrażeniem A, B lub C.

1. My brother has been very nice to me _____, which I find rather suspicious.
   A. always   B. lately   C. already

2. The President is happy about the new law on forest protection, because he has _____ supported environment-friendly policies.
   A. always   B. never   C. before

3. Betty's sister is extremely busy and hasn't spoken with her own family _____ the past few weeks.
   A. for   B. since   C. from

4. Bob has been a very cautious ever _____ his accident last year.
   A. from   B. for   C. since

5. Have you _____ thought of publishing your diaries? I bet they would gain readership across the world.
   A. always   B. yet   C. ever

6. _____ the introduction of the new school regulations, we haven't had any problems with smoking in the toilets.
   A. since   B. from   C. ever

7. Have you managed to buy Christmas presents for all your children _____?
   A. already   B. just   C. yet

8. You don't need to ask the teacher's permission. Mary's _____ asked him.
   A. before   B. already   C. yet

9. 'Are you still putting your makeup on?' 'No, I've _____ finished. We can go now!'
   A. lately   B. just   C. yet
10. I think you should reconsider the bibliography for your end-of-term paper. Most of the authors on your list are people I've _____ heard of.
   A. just   B. before   C. never

115. ☺ Uzupełnij poniższe wypowiedzi, tworząc zdania w czasie Present Perfect z podanych wyrazów.

1. I can't find my wallet anywhere. (I, afraid, lose, it) _____.
2. (Maggie, play tennis, all life) _____ and she just can't imagine a weekend without a game or two.
3. (my parents, travel, a lot) _____ and they have many fascinating pictures from their excursions.
4. George's sister is 38, but (she, still, not finish, her studies) _____
   _____.
5. I know I'm late, but my bus broke down. (I, walk, work, all the way) _____
   _____.
6. I know most people living in this area by their first names, because (I, live, here, 5 years) _____.
7. Ed is still not sure whether he wants to join the yoga course. The idea is quite appealing to him, but (he, never, do yoga, before) _____.
8. (guests, arrive, already) _____ and I'm still in the middle of laying the table! Can somebody please offer them something to drink?

116. ☺ Uzupełnij poniższe pytania w czasie Present Perfect odpowiednim czasownikiem z ramki.

| decide | lose | meet | finish | forget | see | read | repair | be |

1. _____ the newest film with Brad Pitt?
   'No, but I'm going to do so this weekend.'
2. _____ your girlfriend's parents yet?
   'Yes, they invited me to dinner last week'.
3. _____ to any exotic countries?
   'Yes, we went to Taiwan 2 years ago'.
4. _____ what subjects you will take in your final exams?
   'No, I'm still considering the pros and cons'.
5. _____ writing your report yet?
   'Yes, I've even had time to put in some of the colourful diagrams our boss likes so much'.
6. _____ "Gone with the Wind" in the original?
   'Yes, but I also have the Polish version at home to compare some passages'.
7. What, you're quitting your job to take part in a reality show? _____ your mind?!
   'No, I just want to become famous'.
8. Philip, _____ the kitchen tap?
   'Of course, honey, I've even washed the dishes afterwards'.
9. Stop kidding around, _____ what we are here for? We need to get Bill to sign the contract.
   'I know, but being stressed and gloomy won't help us, will it?'

PRESENT PERFECT CONTINUOUS

117. ☺ Utwórz zdania w czasie Present Perfect Continuous, używając czasowników podanych w nawiasach.

1. I'm quite worried about Tony. I (try) _____ to call him all afternoon but his mobile seems to be out of range.
2. My brother (work) _____ for the fast-food chain for 2 years now. I'm surprised he is still as thin as he is.
3. Lucinda is very tired, because she (practise) _____ her piano lessons all day. She still finds them rather difficult.
4. My children (act) _____ very suspiciously lately. I'm sure they're up to something.
5. You (watch) _____ too much TV today. No wonder you've got a headache.
6. We (hear) _____ some rumours about John and Mary getting married. Do you know anything about it?
7. The Committee (investigate) _____ that bribery case for two years already and they don't seem to be anywhere near the end.

118. ☺☺ Połącz połówki zdań, uzupełniając je odpowiednimi czasownikami z ramki w czasie Present Perfect Continuous.

~~use~~ wait think try not be write get rain

1. No wonder we're lost!
2. I'm fed up with this essay.
3. Her husband looks annoyed.
4. My children are very excited about their Dad coming back.
5. What horrible weather!
6. What is your husband doing on the roof of your house?
7. I'm not going to Greg's party.
8. This job offer looks very promising.

a) We _____ on speaking terms since his last party.
b) It _____ for 3 hours now and the sky is still clouded!
c) They _____ for him since early morning.
d) I _____ it all day.
e) He _____ to fix the satellite dish, which broke down yesterday.
f) She _____ on his nerves all day.
g) I _____ of sending my application.
h) We *have been using* the wrong map!

119. ☺☺☺ Present Perfect czy Present Perfect Continuous? Wybierz właściwą wersję. W niektórych zdaniach obie wersje są możliwe.

1. Lucinda has been studying/has studied all day today and is still busy working. I think she has read/has been reading two books already!
2. I joined the Hamster Lovers' Club quite accidentally, but by now I have become/have been becoming deeply involved in its activity.

3. Most students <u>have found/have been finding</u> it difficult to adjust to the new curriculum.
4. That question was troubling me for years, but now at last I believe I <u>have found/have been finding</u> the answer.
5. What <u>have you done/have you been doing</u> lately? I <u>haven't seen/haven't been seeing</u> you for a while.
6. Now that all children <u>have sat down/have been sitting down</u> at last, I can break the news to them.
7. During her reign, the Queen <u>has received/has been receiving</u> hundreds of foreign delegations.
8. I'm not going to lend things to Lucy anymore. She <u>has broken/has been breaking</u> my mascara!

KLUCZ

102. 1. b **2.** a **3.** b **4.** c **5.** b **6.** c

103.
    1. Do you like yoghurt?
    2. What time does Jill start her classes?
    3. Where is my watch?
    4. What instrument does Rachel play?
    5. Do Rick and Mary take sugar with their tea?
    6. Does your dog ever bark?
    7. Excuse me, where is the nearest post office?
    8. How do I open this box?
    9. What do you think of the new University conference centre?
    10. Does the Sun go round the Earth?

104. 1. I feel that you are not telling me the truth.
    2. My sister's daughter often behaves naughtily.
    3. I think that the entire idea for this holiday was crazy.
    4. Nellie considers her mother's novel badly written and her husband agrees with her.
    5. Leslie loves water sports.
    6. We consider our rival company's proposal strange.

105. 1. are you doing **2.** I am having **3.** is your mother doing **4.** She is talking **5.** He is going **6.** She is playing **7.** are you coming **8.** I am coming

106. answering betraying catching chatting colliding complaining daring destroying flying loving quarrelling (BrE)/quarreling (AmE) sitting swimming travelling (BrE)/traveling (AmE)
Reguły, według których tworzy się formy *-ing* czasowników:
a) jeśli czasownik kończy się na spółgłoskę – dodajemy *-ing* (np. *answering*);
b) jeśli czasownik ma jedną sylabę i kończy się na samogłoskę + spółgłoskę – podwajamy spółgłoskę i dodajemy *-ing* (np. *chatting*);
c) jeśli czasownik kończy się na samogłoskę + spółgłoskę + 'e' – opuszczamy 'e' i dodajemy *-ing* (np. *colliding*);
d) jeśli czasownik kończy się na 'y' – dodajemy *-ing* (np. *betraying*);
e) w czasownikach kończących się na 'l' – wg brytyjskiej pisowni podwajamy 'l', wg amerykańskiej – nie (np. *quarrelling/quarreling*).

107. 1. T **2.** P **3.** T **4.** T **5.** P **6.** P **7.** T **8.** P **9.** T **10.** P

108. Wiele czasowników nie występuje w formie ciągłej (z *-ing*), ponieważ opisuje czynności, które z natury są długotrwałe. Takie czasowniki nazywamy *state verbs*. Część *state verbs* może jednak wystąpić w formie ciągłej, lecz zmienią wtedy swoje znaczenie. Wszystkie czasowniki w tym ćwiczeniu to *state verbs* zmieniające znaczenie w formie ciągłej.
1. are thinking
think = myśleć; ale *They are thinking of moving to Singapore* = Rozważają przeprowadzkę do Singapuru.
2. are you smelling
smell = pachnieć; ale *Why are you smelling the milk?* = Dlaczego obwąchujesz to mleko?

3. is hearing

hear = słyszeć; ale *Jane is hearing strange voices which order her to do things* = Jane słyszy dziwne „głosy", które nakazują jej robić pewne rzeczy (czyli ma omamy słuchowe).

4. am tasting

taste = smakować; ale *I am tasting the stew* = Próbuję smaku gulaszu (aby zdecydować, czy nie należy go doprawić).

5. be seeing

see = widzieć; ale *I must be seeing things* = Z pewnością mam halucynacje.

109. Wszystkie czasowniki w tym ćwiczeniu to *state verbs* zmieniające znaczenie w formie ciągłej.
  1. What time are you having supper tonight?
  2. I am seeing the new employees at 11 o'clock.
  3. The jury is hearing the witnesses tomorrow.
  4. Are you feeling OK?

110. Czasu **Present Continuous** używamy, narzekając na czyjeś denerwujące zwyczaje i przyzwyczajenia. W takich zdaniach koniecznie trzeba dodać przysłówek oznaczający częstotliwość (zwykle *always*).
  1. 'You're always leaving the office door open!'
  2. 'Your dog is always digging holes in my garden!'
  3. 'You are always leaving dirty dishes in the sitting-room!'
  4. 'You are always smoking in my room!'
  5. 'Dad is always forgetting his keys and then phoning me to let him in.'

111. 1. is writing, think; czasownik 'think' w znaczeniu „sądzić" stosowany jest w czasie Present Simple, podobnie jak czasowniki: believe, say, consider, claim itp. **2.** works, writes **3.** don't want, are going, pay **4.** lives, is thinking, believes; czasownik 'think' ma tu znaczenie „rozważać (obecnie)" i dlatego jest użyty w czasie Present Continuous. **5.** doesn't travel, puts, says, doesn't seem, is flying **6.** is eating, claims, is looking; czas Present Continuous czasownika 'eat' i 'look' podkreśla, że dana sytuacja jest nowa i nie-typowa (a w pierwszym przypadku sugeruje nawet, że zachowanie dziewczyny może być irytujące). **7.** is always making; czas Present Continuous używany jest w przesadnych sądach o sytuacjach i zachowa-niach, które irytują rozmówcę.

112. 1. c writes; is currently working **2. e** am doing; don't enjoy **3. f** are meeting; hold **4. a** spend; are fishing and hunting and generally enjoying **5. b** work; are covering **6. d** seems; is doing

113. 1. is currently considering **2.** bans **3.** abstain **4.** feel/are feeling **5.** criticise/are criticising **6.** hope/are hoping **7.** don't agree **8.** take **9.** is trying **10.** is studying **11.** are meeting

114. 1 B 2 A 3 A 4 C 5 C 6 A 7 C 8 B 9 B 10 C

115. 1. I'm afraid I have lost it **2.** Maggie has played tennis all her life **3.** My parents have travelled a lot **4.** she still hasn't finished her studies **5.** I have walked all the way to work **6.** I have lived here for 5 years **7.** he has never done yoga before **8.** The guests have already arrived

116. 1. Have you seen **2.** Have you met **3.** Have you been **4.** Have you decided **5.** Have you finished **6.** Have you read **7.** Have you lost **8.** have you repaired **9.** have you forgotten

117. 1. have been trying **2.** has been working **3.** has been practising **4.** have been acting **5.** have been watching **6.** have been hearing **7.** has been investigating

118. 2. d have been writing **3. f** has been getting **4. c** have been waiting **5. b** has been raining **6. e** has been trying **7. a** haven't been **8. g** have been thinking

119. 1. has been studying, has read; Present Perfect Continuous jest bardziej typowy przy wyrażeniach typu: 'all day', 'all week' itd. oraz jeżeli czynność wciąż trwa, podczas gdy Present Perfect stosowany jest dla czynności dokonanych. **2.** have become **3.** have found/have been finding; Present Perfect Continuous jeszcze mocniej podkreśla, że dany problem jest nowy i naglący. **4.** have found; Present Perfect stosowany jest dla czynności dokonanych. **5.** have you been doing, haven't seen; pytanie w Present Perfect Continuous jest ogólne, nie odnosi się do konkretnego osiągnięcia. Czasownik 'see' w znaczeniu „widzieć" nie tworzy czasów 'continuous', w przeciwieństwie do 'see somebody', czyli „spotykać się z kimś". **6.** have sat down; Present Perfect stosowany jest dla czynności dokonanych. **7.** has received; Present Perfect stosowany jest dla czynności dokonanych. **8.** has broken; Present Perfect stosowany jest dla czynności dokonanych.

PAST TENSES

PAST SIMPLE

120. ☺ Ułóż pytania w czasie Past Simple.

Wzór: _____ (*you/sleep*) well last night?
Did you sleep well last night?

1. _____ (*you/have*) anything for breakfast this morning?
2. _____ (*he/fail*) his driving test last month?
3. _____ (*you/feed*) the horses last night?
4. _____ (*she/play*) the piano when she was little?
5. _____ (*we/go*) to Spain three or four summers ago?
6. _____ (it/rain) a lot last March?

121. ☺ Z rozsypanych wyrazów ułóż pytania do podanych odpowiedzi. Użyj czasownika *be* w odpowiedniej formie.

Wzór: *at home/you/yesterday evening*
Were you at home yesterday evening?
No, I wasn't.

1. *long/the meeting*
_____?
No, it was quite short, actually.
2. *out/the cat/last night*
_____?
Yes, she was. I let her out.
3. *to leave/the hikers/at sunrise/ready*
_____?
Yes, they were. They left at four am.
4. *a quiet baby/Rilla*
_____?
No, she wasn't. She cried a lot.
5. *you/why/yesterday/so sad*
_____?
Because I broke up with my boyfriend.
6. *that snake/how long*
_____?
It was over two metres long.

122. ☺ Wstaw podany czasownik w czasie Past Simple.

Last summer we (1. go) _____ for a trip to Egypt. We (2. fly) _____ to Cairo and after a week (3. take) _____ a bus to Hurghada. In Cairo we (4. see) _____ the pyramids and the Sphinx. At the seaside, we (5. swim) _____ in the coral reef. The sea (6. be) _____ very warm and clean and there (7. be) _____ many big and colourful fish swimming all around us. We (8. meet) _____ some people we (9. know) _____ from our hometown and we also (10. make) _____ some new friends. We (11. drink) _____ a lot of very sweet and aromatic coffee, and mint tea. We (12. eat) _____ specialities of local cuisine. We (13. have) _____ a great time and (14. bring) _____ back wonderful memories.

123. ☺☺ Spośród podanych w ramce czasowników wybierz odpowiednie i uzupełnij zdania w czasie Past Simple. Pięć czasowników pozostanie niewykorzystanych.

bite cost cut dig flee hide lay light mistake ride seek shake wake wear

1. There is nothing that cannot be found, if _____.
2. On the anniversary of their old friend's death they _____ a candle in the window.
3. In the 1960s, the hippies _____ flowers in their hair.
4. Captain Silver _____ a deep hole beneath the oak tree and there he _____ the treasure he had found on a desert island.
5. She _____ some fresh flowers and then _____ the table with cakes and sweets.
6. When I was three, a huge black dog _____ me. Since then I've been afraid of dogs.
7. On the day after their arrival the travellers _____ late in the afternoon.

PAST CONTINUOUS

124. ☺☺ Wstaw podane czasowniki w czasie Past Continuous.

1. Last summer, it (rain) _____ all the time we were in the mountains.
2. While I (cook) _____ dinner, my husband (sleep) _____ on the couch in the sitting-room.
3. What (you/do) _____ yesterday evening? Your phone (ring) _____ all the time, but you never answered it.
4. Night after night, my new next-door neighbour (listen) _____ to classical music.
5. Jack (drive) _____ home when his car skidded and hit a tree.
6. We crawled out of our tent as the sun (rise) _____ over the treetops.

125. ☺☺ Zdecyduj, czy w poniższych zdaniach czas Past Continuous jest użyty prawidłowo.

1. <u>Were you eating</u> a lot of rice when you were in China? (YES/NO)
2. While June was eating, someone <u>was breaking</u> the kitchen window. (YES/NO)
3. My friends <u>were singing</u> sad songs, while I <u>was watching</u> the fire. (YES/NO)
4. When my sister was a baby, she <u>was</u> always <u>drawing</u> on my books. (YES/NO)

5. The market was very busy, hundreds of people <u>were talking</u> together, the sellers <u>were shouting</u>, the pigs <u>were squealing</u>, and the church bells <u>were ringing</u> deafeningly. (YES/NO)
6. It <u>was being</u> sunny all the time we were in Greece. (YES/NO)
7. Ben <u>was being</u> naughty all day, wasn't he? (YES/NO)
8. It <u>was growing</u> dark, so we decided to head home. (YES/NO)

PAST SIMPLE OR PAST CONTINUOUS?

126. ☺☺ Wybierz odpowiednią formę czasownika.

1. During my year abroad I <u>met/was meeting</u> many interesting people.
2. Why am I tired? Because when you <u>slept/were sleeping</u>, I <u>did/was doing</u> the cleaning!
3. When I <u>finished/was finishing</u> the report, there was a power cut and I <u>lost/was losing</u> half of my work.
4. I <u>arranged/was arranging</u> to see my dentist on Monday at 5 pm.
5. The weather <u>was/was being</u> warm and sunny all July.
6. I <u>cut/was cutting</u> my hand when I <u>cut/was cutting</u> sausage.
7. I can't transport these books myself, so I <u>wondered/was wondering</u> if you could organise the delivery for me.
8. My brother was really difficult to stand when he was a teenager. He <u>was always quarrelling/always quarrelled</u> with our Father.

127. ☺☺ Wybierz odpowiednią formę czasownika.

1. While Beauty was enjoying herself at her father's home, the Beast _____.
   a) die   c) died   c) was dying   d) were dying
2. Big Bad Wolf broke into Granny's house and _____ her.
   a) was eating   b) ate   c) eats   d) is eating
3. Cinderella _____ in the cellar, sorting out poppy seeds from ash.
   a) sit   b) sits   c) sat   d) was sitting
4. As the Prince _____ towards it, the dragon spat fire.
   a) rode   b) ride   c) rides   d) was riding
5. One day, while Sleeping Beauty was spinning, she _____ her finger.
   a) pricks   b) was pricking   c) pricked   d) prick
6. When Snow White walked into their house, the Seven Dwarves _____ at their supper.
   a) sat   b) was sitting   c) sits   d) were sitting

128. ☺☺ W poniższym tekście wpisz czasowniki w odpowiedniej formie (Past Simple lub Past Continuous).

A few weeks ago I (1. go) _____ for a business trip to China. The flight from Cracow to Beijing (2. take) _____ over twenty hours, but I was not bored because I (3. read) _____ James Clavell's novels about China. In Beijing, we (4. be) _____ quite busy: in the morning we (5. have) _____ business meetings, and in the afternoon we (6. go) _____ sightseeing. We (7. see) _____ the Old Beijing and the Forbidden City. And when I (8. walk) _____ along the Great Wall, I

(9. feel) _____ really moved. After all, it is one of the greatest structures ever built!
I had read a lot about China, but still it (10. not turn out) _____ exactly what I expected. I (11. find) _____ the Chinese very kind and helpful, but when they (12. speak) _____ English to me, I (13. not understand) _____ them very well. Anyway, they (14. be) _____ excellent hosts. They (15. take) _____ us to excellent restaurants.
I (16. not realise) _____ Chinese food could be so tasty. The conference (17. be) _____ well prepared, too. Every day I (18. meet) _____ interesting people. I (19. make) _____ some useful contacts.
I (20. not have) _____ much time for shopping, so I (21. buy) _____ very few souvenirs: a jade pendant for my mother, silk pyjamas for my husband, and a Chinese doll for my little daughter. I (22. not get) _____ anything for myself, but I (23. make) _____ photos all the time and these are going to be the best souvenirs for me.

PAST SIMPLE OR PRESENT PERFECT?

129. ☺☺ Wybierz odpowiednią formę czasownika.

1. Did you see/Have you seen my car keys anywhere?
2. All my friends went/have gone to work abroad.
3. Their best horse broke/has broken a leg during the last race.
4. Did you ever eat/Have you ever eaten octopus?
5. My grandfather studied/has studied in Cracow.
6. Did you see/Have you seen the horror on TV last night?
7. I managed/have managed to do only three exercises so far.
8. Mummy, I won/have won the race!
9. Look, John wrote/has written to me from New Zealand.

130. ☺☺ Napisz zdania o sobie.

Wzór: I have never been *to Singapore, but I have been to Turkey.*

1. I have never eaten _____ .
2. I have never seen _____ .
3. I have never read _____ .
4. I have never danced _____ .
5. I have never written _____ .

A teraz dodaj do każdego zdania więcej szczegółów.

Wzór: I have never been to Singapore, but I have been to Turkey. *I went to Ankara a year ago.*

1. _____
2. _____
3. _____
4. _____
5. _____

131. W poniższych zdaniach wpisz czasowniki w odpowiedniej formie (Past Simple lub Present Perfect).

1. Gillian (manage) _____ to trip her attacker. He (fall) _____ and she (run) _____ away.
2. 'Why is everybody standing in front of the lecture hall?'
   'The lecturer (ask) _____ us to leave the building. There (be) _____ a bomb scare!'
3. A week ago I (be) _____ accidentally entrusted with some very sensitive information and since then I (not be able) _____ to fall asleep even for a second.
4. You all realise that we (gamble) _____ heavily on this scheme. Now it appears that we (lose) _____.
5. Indians of the Great Plains (hunt) _____ and (live) _____ in tepees until white men (come) _____ and everything (change) _____.
6. So this is the Lyttons' house? It is smaller than I (expect) _____.
7. OK, we (study) _____ enough. Let's stop and get some sleep.

PAST PERFECT

132. ☺☺☺ Dopasuj połówki zdań.

1. Alice disregarded her father's warning...
2. Before his paintings became famous,...
3. The National Museum held an exhibition of ancient artifacts...
4. Half way there we realised...
5. By the time Anne returned my book...
6. I wasn't very keen on the present...
7. The couch was dirty...
8. The house was pulled down...

a) ...which had been excavated in Nubia.
b) ...I had already bought a new copy.
c) ...Lester had worked as a delivery man.
d) ...because he had told her just the same thing many times before.
e) ... because it had been damaged by the hurricane.
f) ... because their baby had spilt blackcurrant juice all over it.
g) ...we had left the presents at home.
h) ...my boyfriend had bought me for my last birthday.

133. ☺☺☺ Zdecyduj, czy w poniższych zdaniach niezbędne jest użycie czasu Past Perfect.

1. Only next morning did it dawn on me that I hadn't called my boss on arrival. (YES/NO)
2. By the time the speaker finished, the audience had lost interest. (YES/NO)
3. Before he began landing procedures, the pilot had checked wind force on the ground. (YES/NO)
4. Luke said he had known the secret, but denied that he had revealed it to our rivals. (YES/NO)

5. I was not worried about my wife's absence because she had been late from work many times before. (YES/NO)
6. Jill had taken off her coat and shoes, had switched the electric kettle on, and then she noticed the body on the floor. (YES/NO)
7. When Alice met Trevor, she had already been married to Mark for two years. (YES/NO)

PAST PERFECT CONTINUOUS

134. ☺☺☺ Dopasuj przyczynę do skutku.

1. The little boy was crying...
2. The old tree died...
3. The cashier was sacked...
4. The horses were tired...
5. The girl's shoes were wet...
6. The man's breath smelt horribly...

a) ...because she had been playing in the mud.
b) ...because the diggers had damaged its roots.
c) ...because they had been galloping all day.
d) ...because he had been eating garlic.
e) ...because he had been slapped by his mother.
f) ...because she had been stealing money from the till.

135. ☺☺☺ Wstaw podany czasownik w czasie Past Perfect Continuous.

1. When we were driving to my in-laws, the roads were slippery because it (rain) _____ all night.
2. After the party Nellie assured us that she (not eat) _____ anything she's allergic to.
3. I went to the doctor because I (have) _____ recurrent back ache.
4. The guests (dance) _____ since early afternoon and they were very tired.
5. My wrists ached because I (type) _____ for a long time.
6. Liz confessed that she (see) _____ her sister's boyfriend in secret.

PAST SIMPLE, PAST PERFECT OR PAST PERFECT CONTINUOUS?

136. ☺☺☺ Wybierz właściwą wersję zdania.

1. Delia knew/had known/had been knowing her boyfriend for only a month before he went to prison.

70

2. The boy finished/had finished/had been finishing his lunch and went to the garden.

3. We couldn't get in because our father accidentally locked/had locked/had been locking the door to which we did not have the key.

4. Before I started writing my own poems, I read/had read/had been reading a lot of poetry.

5. By the time the girls stopped talking, the thunderstorm passed/had passed/had been passing.

6. Arnold managed to convince Betsy that he meant/had meant/had been meaning to tell her of his infidelity.

137. ☺☺☺ Uzupełnij poniższy tekst odpowiednimi formami czasowników z ramki w czasach Past Simple, Past Perfect lub Past Perfect Continuous. Jedno zdanie wymaga użycia strony biernej (patrz ćw. 232–242).

agree cajole diagnose feel flop forget freeze have learn make ring rehearse seem sew snow think turn out work

Last Saturday was supposed to be our amateur theatre group's great day. Having chosen to stage Shakespeare's *Romeo and Juliet*, we 1._____ the text by heart, 2._____ the costumes ourselves, 3._____ the stage decorations and props. Success 4._____ sure. We 5._____ that we 6._____ the performance so many times that it was practically impossible for us to fail. But...
The first major disaster 7._____ to be the weather. It 8._____ all night before and on Saturday morning everything 9._____. People just 10._____ like going out on such a cold morning. So in the audience there were mostly members of our families. This was lucky, in a sense, considering what happened later.
Half an hour before the performance, Lillian's mother 11._____ to tell us that Lillian 12._____ with measles and would be unable to perform. We 13._____ no Juliet! Finally, when we 14._____ Rita, our lighting technician, to save the performance, she 15._____ to play the lead role. But of course she is not half as talented as Lillian, and she 16._____ her lines several times. The audience were very patient and understanding, but there were also a few laughs, often in the most dramatic moments.
Needless to say, the play we 17._____ so very hard to prepare 18._____ terribly. We are feeling very bitter about it and we are even considering disbanding the theatre group.

KLUCZ

120. Pamiętaj, że forma *did* czasownika posiłkowego *do*, której używamy w czasie Past Simple, jest taka sama dla wszystkich osób.
   1. Did you have anything for breakfast this morning?
   2. Did he fail his driving test last month?
   3. Did you feed the horses last night?
   4. Did she play the piano when she was little?
   5. Did we go to Spain three or four summers ago?
   6. Did it rain a lot last March?

121. 1. Was the meeting long?
   2. Was the cat out last night?
   3. Were the hikers ready to leave at sunrise?

4. Was Rilla a quiet baby?
5. Why were you so sad yesterday?
6. How long was that snake?

122. **1.** went **2.** flew **3.** took **4.** saw **5.** swam **6.** was **7.** were **8.** met **9.** knew **10.** made **11.** drank **12.** ate **13.** had **14.** brought

123. **1.** sought **2.** lit **3.** wore **4.** dug, hid **5.** cut, laid **6.** bit **7.** woke

124. **1.** was raining **2.** was cooking, was sleeping **3.** were you doing, was ringing **4.** was listening **5.** was driving **6.** was rising

125. **1.** NO Takie pytania zadajemy w czasie Past Simple.
2. NO Czas Past Continuous podkreśla trwanie czynności, a w tym zdaniu czynność trwająca (*June was eating*) została przerwana nagłym wydarzeniem (*someone broke the window*); por. pkt. 3.
3. YES Zdanie opisuje dwie czynności ciągłe trwające jednocześnie.
4. YES Narzekając na czyjeś denerwujące zwyczaje i przyzwyczajenia w przeszłości, używamy czasu Past Continuous. W takich zdaniach koniecznie trzeba dodać przysłówek oznaczający częstotliwość (zwykle *always*).
5. YES Czasu Past Continuous używamy w opowiadaniach przy opisach tła głównej akcji, a więc wszystkie czasowniki w tym czasie są tu użyte prawidłowo.
6. NO W tym zdaniu wystarczy Past Simple.
7. YES *Was being* ma często zabarwienie negatywne.
8. YES *Was growing* (lub *was getting*) używamy, mówiąc o zmianach następujących w przeszłości.

126. **1.** met
2. were sleeping, was doing
3. was finishing, lost
4. arranged
5. was
6. cut, was cutting
7. was wondering – czasownik *wonder* w czasie Past Continuous to forma grzecznościowa
8. was always quarrelling – Past Continuous nadaje wypowiedzi zabarwienie krytyczne

127. **1.** c **2.** b **3.** c **4.** d **5.** c **6.** d

128. **1.** went **2.** took **3.** was reading **4.** were **5.** were having/had **6.** went **7.** saw **8.** was walking **9.** felt **10.** did not turn out **11.** found **12.** were speaking **13.** did not understand **14.** were **15.** were taking **16.** did not realise **17.** was **18.** was meeting **19.** made **20.** did not have **21.** bought **22.** did not get **23.** was making

129. Past Simple używamy z tymi określeniami czasu, które dotyczą zamkniętego już okresu w przeszłości; Present Perfect z tymi, które znaczą „kiedykolwiek aż do chwili obecnej". W wielu wypowiedziach (patrz np. pkt. 2 lub 5) określenie czasu pozostaje w domyśle.
1. Have you seen
2. have gone
3. broke
4. Have you ever eaten
5. studied
6. Did you see
7. have managed
8. have won
9. has written

130. Ćwiczenie otwarte; przykładowe odpowiedzi:
1. I have never eaten snails, but I have eaten squid. I ordered it in a restaurant in Greece. It was horrible.
2. I have never seen the original of *Mona Lisa*, but I have seen the *Lady with an Ermine*. I liked that portrait very much.
3. I have never read *War and Peace* by Leo Tolstoy, but I have read his *Anna Karenina*. At the end, when Anna commits suicide, I cried.

4. I have never danced a tango, but I have danced the waltz. I danced it with my cousin at my sister's wedding.

5. I have never written a short story, but I have written a poem. I wrote it for my mother when I was seven.

131. 1. managed, fell, ran

2. has asked, has been – mówiąc o wydarzeniach ostatniej chwili, używamy czasu Present Perfect

3. was, haven't been able

4. gambled/have gambled, have lost

5. hunted, lived, came, changed

6. expected – mówiąc o przekonaniach, które okazały się fałszywe, używamy Past Simple

7. have studied

132. 1. d **2.** c **3.** a **4.** g **5.** b **6.** h **7.** f **8.** e

133. Czas Past Perfect określa, co wydarzyło się wcześniej niż inne wydarzenie w przeszłości. Jeśli jednak sekwencję wydarzeń wystarczająco wyjaśnia jakieś określenie czasu, nie trzeba używać dodatkowo czasu Past Perfect.

1. YES Zdanie jest skomplikowane, więc czas Past Perfect wyjaśnia sekwencję wydarzeń.

2. YES W zdaniu wydarzenie późniejsze jest wymienione jako pierwsze.

3. NO Przysłówek *before* wystarczająco określa, co wydarzyło się najpierw.

4. YES Relacjonując, co ktoś powiedział w przeszłości (Reported Speech, patrz ćw. nr 267-281), używamy czasu Past Perfect.

5. YES Wprawdzie przysłówek *before* określa, co wydarzyło się najpierw, ale w zdaniu wydarzenie chronologicznie późniejsze jest wymienione jako pierwsze; lepiej więc jest użyć czasu Past Perfect.

6. NO Wydarzenia następują bezpośrednio po sobie. W takich sytuacjach używamy Past Simple.

7. YES W zdaniach mówiących o czynnościach, które rozpoczęły się w dalszej przeszłości, czas Past Perfect jest odpowiednikiem czasu Present Perfect.

134. Czasu Past Perfect Continuous używamy, mówiąc m.in. o przyczynach wydarzeń w przeszłości.

1. e **2.** b **3.** f **4.** c **5.** a **6.** d

135. 1. had been raining – czasu Past Perfect Continuous używamy, mówiąc o czynnościach, które trwały przez jakiś czas aż do określonego momentu w przeszłości

2. had not been eating – czasu Past Perfect Continuous bardzo często używamy w mowie zależnej (Reported Speech, patrz ćw. nr 267-281), gdzie zastępuje on czas Present Perfect Continuous

3. had been having – czasu Past Perfect Continuous używamy, mówiąc o wcześniejszych przyczynach określonego wydarzenia w przeszłości

4. had been dancing – czasu Past Perfect Continuous używamy, mówiąc, jak długo (do określonego momentu w przeszłości) trwała jakaś czynność

5. had been typing – czasu Past Perfect Continuous używamy, kiedy chcemy podkreślić, że jakaś czynność w przeszłości trwała przez jakiś czas (ale nie została zakończona)

6. had been seeing – Past Perfect Continuous jest tu uwarunkowany użyciem mowy zależnej (Reported Speech, patrz ćw. nr 267-281); czasownik *to see* jest użyty w formie ciągłej, gdyż ma znaczenie „spotykać się", a nie „widzieć" (patrz ćw. 134.1)

136. 1. had known – niektórych czasowników (tzw. *state verbs*) nie używamy w czasach ciągłych, nawet jeśli z kontekstu wynika, że byłoby to uzasadnione

2. finished – dwie czynności następujące bezpośrednio jedna po drugiej opisujemy w czasie Past Simple

3. had locked – czas Past Perfect określa sekwencję wydarzeń

4. had been reading – czas Past Perfect Continuous podkreśla długotrwałość czynności

5. had passed – czas Past Perfect określa sekwencję wydarzeń

6. had been meaning – *mean* należy do *state verbs*, których w podstawowym znaczeniu nie używa się w czasach ciągłych (patrz ćw. nr 108, 109). Mówiąc jednak o czyichś intencjach, można użyć odpowiednio form Present lub Past Perfect Continuous tego czasownika.

137. 1. learnt **2.** sewed **3.** made **4.** seemed **5.** thought **6.** had rehearsed **7.** turned out **8.** had been snowing **9.** had frozen **10.** didn't feel **11.** rang **12.** had been diagnosed **13.** had **14.** had cajoled **15.** agreed **16.** forgot **17.** had worked **18.** flopped

FUTURE TENSES

FUTURE SIMPLE

138. ☺ Używając podanych wyrazów, utwórz zdania w czasie Future Simple.

1. Our baby daughter is very pretty. (grow, beautiful, woman, future)
   We hope that _____.
2. Chris's party was extremely boring. (party, next week, boring, his, too)
   I bet that _____.
3. Emma keeps a little frog in a jar near her bedside. (bring, luck)
   She believes that _____.
4. My brother and I are not looking forward to our sister's wedding. (our parents, tell, wear, suits)
   We are afraid that _____.
5. I am not going to tell any of my friends about my moving to Togo. (not understand, decision, they)
   I'm sure that _____.
6. The lawyer has advised us not to take our case to court. (not win, canny, against, businessman)
   He says it's obvious that _____.
7. The government has promised to finish the construction of these new highways by 2008. (not have, resources, enough, do it)
   However, most analysts are convinced that _____.

139. ☺☺ Uzupełnij poniższe wypowiedzi odpowiednią formą jednego z podanych czasowników w czasie Future Simple.

give	shut	submit	ask	not argue	talk	clean up

1. My daughter has spilled the soup. I _____ it _____!
2. I'm sorry, but we have forgotten to bring our history assignments with us. We _____ them tomorrow.
3. It's time somebody told Lucy that her dress is inappropriate for the office. I _____ to her!
4. You shouldn't carry those heavy suitcases by yourself. My husband _____ you a hand.
5. People next door are very loud. If you don't mind, I _____ the door.
6. Greg wants to wear a pink shirt on his wedding and I can't do anything about it.
   I _____ with him anymore.
7. I'm not sure why the President has told all of us to dress up nicely tomorrow.
   I _____ him at lunch and tell you right away.

140. ☺☺ Przyjrzyj się poniższym zdaniom w czasie Future Simple, a następnie przypisz do każdego z nich jedno ze znaczeń podanych poniżej.

1. Rupert <u>will be</u> 37 next year.
2. I'<u>ll help </u>you with this essay, if you want.
3. We think our son <u>will</u> never <u>grow up</u>.
4. This dress is too big for me, I'<u>ll take </u>that one!
5. We're sorry about that mistake, it <u>won't happen</u> again.
6. If your company doesn't cooperate, we'<u>ll call </u>the police!
7. I believe the zloty <u>will drop</u> after the elections.
8. You <u>will prepare</u> the report by Friday.

a) promise
b) belief
c) command
d) prediction
e) future fact
f) offer
g) sudden decision
h) threat

FUTURE CONTINUOUS

141. ☺ Uzupełnij poniższe wypowiedzi odpowiednią formą podanych czasowników w czasie Future Continuous.

1. The company is sending me on a business trip to Australia, so this time tomorrow I (sit) _____ on the hotel terrace watching kangaroos.
2. Winter holidays are starting this Friday! For the next two weeks hundreds of children (run) _____ around the park playing snowballs all day long.
3. 'Could I come round at 8 am on Sunday to pick up the books?' 'That's impossible, my whole family (sleep) _____'.
4. Those two years of high school have passed very quickly. I can't believe that this time next year we (take) _____ our final exams.
5. Peter isn't coming to our yoga training tonight. He (work) _____ on his new novel.
6. 'Can I come and see you at 12 tomorrow?' 'I'm sorry, but I (have) _____ lunch with the district judge then'.
7. The Board haven't had time yet to decide on Mary's promotion, but since they have a meeting on Wednesday, they (probably discuss) _____ also this issue then.

142. ☺ Używając podanych czasowników, uzupełnij poniższe wypowiedzi zdaniami w czasie Future Continuous.

1. My father always leaves the house at 10 am and drives to work, where he arrives at 10:45.
   So tomorrow at 10:15 _____. (DRIVE)
2. Susie is going to France on a student exchange program which starts on 6th June.
   So on 5th June _____. (FLY)

3. George has bought tickets for the 'Cats' musical, which is on at 9 pm tonight.
   So tonight at 9:30 _____. (WATCH)
4. My chemistry presentation is scheduled for next Wednesday morning.
   So next Wednesday morning _____. (DO)
5. The next rehearsal of our show is planned for Sunday.
   So on Saturday _____. (REHEARSE)
6. My rental agreement expires on 26th July and the landowner hasn't agreed to extend it.
   So on 26th July _____. (MOVE OUT)
7. The Jones's got married exactly 4 years ago and are celebrating their 4th anniversary.
   So this time next year _____. (CELEBRATE)

143. ☺☺ What will you be doing then? Uzupełnij poniższe wypowiedzi dowolnymi zdaniami w czasie Future Continuous.

What will you be doing…
1. … at 8 pm tomorrow?

   _____

2. …on Wednesday evening?

   _____

3. …next June?

   _____

4. …this time on Friday?

   _____

5. …at 10 pm next Sunday?

   _____

6. …in two years' time?

   _____

7. …the coming summer?

   _____

FUTURE PERFECT

144. ☺ Future Perfect to czas przyszły stosowany do opisania czynności, której zakończenie przewidujemy w danym momencie w przyszłości. Uzupełnij poniższe wypowiedzi, używając podanych czasowników w czasie Future Perfect.

exceed	resit	be eaten	win	sell	complete	fall asleep

1. By the time the students get to their final year, most of them _____ at least one exam.
2. I'm worried that by the time I arrive at the conference gala dinner most of the food _____.
3. There's no use going to the auction at noon because they _____ everything potentially worth buying.
4. According to some analysts, by 2009 the population of the Earth _____ 3 billion people.

5. This lecture is extremely tedious! I think that by the time the professor finishes talking, most of the students _____.
6. We estimate that by June next year, our company _____ 300 new contracts.
7. The City Council promises that they _____ the construction of the third underground line by 2050.

145. ☺☺ Uzupełnij poniższe zdania odpowiednimi formami czasowników w czasach Present Simple lub Present Perfect oraz Future Perfect.

1. By the time the author (finish) _____ the third chapter of his book, the proofreaders (correct) _____ the first two.
2. I'm afraid that by the time Robert (discover) _____ that he loves Ann, she (marry) _____ somebody else.
3. It's sad that by the time people (realize) _____ the importance of environmental protection, many of our forests and rivers (be polluted) _____.
4. The scientists hope that by the time the avian flu (become) _____ a real danger, they (find) _____ a successful cure.
5. By the time the support squad (arrive) _____, many of our soldiers (surrender) _____.
6. The university board is afraid that by the time Mark (write) _____ his dissertation, his mentor (retire) _____.
7. Let's hurry up! By the time we (struggle) _____ through the traffic, our boss (arrive) _____ at the office.

146. ☺☺☺ Ułóż 10 zdań w czasie Future Perfect, wykorzystując w nich poniższe wyrazy:

computers/Mars/scientists/space travel/Internet/mobile phones/English language /discover/invent/end

What will have changed in the world by 2150?
I think that by 2150 …

_____
_____
_____
_____
_____
_____
_____
_____
_____
_____

GOING TO

147. ☺ Uzupełnij poniższe zdania wyrażeniem *going to* oraz podanymi czasownikami.

1. Kevin has already decided on the topic of his Matura essay. He (write) _____ about Elvis Presley.

2. My boyfriend and I study international communication and both of us would like to spend at least a year abroad. After college we (apply) _____ for a scholarship in Brussels.
3. Look, the swimmer is standing at the edge of the trampoline! He (jump) _____!
4. I've decided to talk to Cathy about her behavior. I (tolerate) _____ her bad moods any longer.
5. Your son is clearly experiencing some teenage problems. (you talk) _____ to him?
6. The air feels very frosty today. I think it (snow) _____.
7. It seems that the students' protests have not been in vain. The school (extend) _____ the holidays by 10 days!
8. The Manager is furious about Caroline's comments during the last meeting of the Board. I wonder if he (invite) _____ her to the next one?

148. ☺☺ Połącz poniższe zdania w pary, uzupełniając jedne z nich wyrażeniem *going to* oraz podanymi czasownikami.

1. We believe our customers like our special offer and will accept it.
2. I promise I won't bother you with any more questions, Sir.
3. The President has not taken a decision yet.
4. Lucinda doesn't like her new job, which she began last week.
5. I really enjoyed the book you gave me to read.
6. Albert isn't sure when he will arrive.
7. We have planned the party very carefully.
8. I'm afraid I'll have to change schools after the next parent-teacher day.

a) They (inform) _____ us about their decision next week.
b) I (read) _____ the second part as well.
c) She says she (change) _____ it after her first pay-check.
d) My parents (take part) *are going to take part* in a parents' football game.
e) But he (call) _____ us beforehand so that we can pick him up.
f) We (start) _____ at 8 pm, with a glass of champagne.
g) As a matter of fact, I (take out) _____ a few books on this topic and read more about it myself.
h) But he (review) _____ your case tomorrow, as he has promised.

149. ☺☺ Ułóż pytania z wyrażeniem *going to* z podanych wyrazów.

1. Brad Pitt, weekend, see, new film, you

   _____

2. take, the organization, when, decision

   _____

3. this grant, apply, our company

   _____

4. its, continue, government, employment policy, coming years

   _____

5. do, you, what, your grandfather's stamp collection

   _____

6. dogs, from, be banned, public parks

   _____

7. after, your sister, college, move out

   _____

8. during, where, Queen, stay, Poland, visit

_____

PRESENT FOR THE FUTURE

150. ☺ Dla wyrażenia czynności zaplanowanych na przyszłość można użyć czasu Present Continuous. Uzupełnij poniższe zdania jednym z podanych czasowników w czasie Present Continuous.

have	leave	fly	come back	give	start	take

1. My father can't come to my wedding, because he _____ to Japan to the annual meeting of his company's shareholders.
2. Would you like to join our discussion panels? We _____ next Thursday.
3. Mark _____ our company. We haven't managed to convince him to stay.
4. The Jones's are on the long-planned holiday to New Zealand. They _____ in 5 weeks.
5. Albert and Lucinda _____ a date tonight. All their friends are very excited.
6. Patricia has invited me to her party, which she _____ to celebrate her promotion.
7. I'm sorry, but I have to cancel our appointment tomorrow. I'm feeling very weak and I _____ a few days off.

151. ☺☺ Dla wyrażenia przyszłych czynności zgodnych z harmonogramem, planem, kontraktem itp. można użyć czasu Present Simple. Uzupełnij poniższe zdania jednym z podanych czasowników w czasie Present Simple.

end	leave	start	be	see	take place	meet	join

1. Don't be late! The conference _____ at 9 am sharp.
2. The last train to Dorchester _____ at 4 pm from the Central Station.
3. According to our timetable, Sir, you _____ with the Ministers first and then _____ the rest of your delegation for lunch.
4. The trade fair _____ on Friday, so there _____ a short briefing for the staff on Thursday evening.
5. The application process _____ on 20th October, so the candidates are advised to send their documents by 19th October at the latest.
6. I'm sorry, but I cannot make an appointment for you for Thursday, because the doctor already _____ ten patients that day!

152. ☺ Present Continuous, Present Simple czy Future Simple? Uzupełnij poniższe zdania właściwą formą czasownika: A, B lub C.

1. The opening lecture of the conference is by Albert Jones. I believe we _____ some interesting conclusions from his recent research.

    A. hear   B. are hearing   C. will hear

2. The plane _____ at 8 am, so please make sure you are at the airport at least an hour earlier.
   A. takes off   B. will take off   C. is going to take off

3. I _____ Anthony and Alice today, because they want to discuss some details of their weddding.
   A. am meeting   B. will meet   C. meet

4. Do you think that you _____ the translation by tomorrow?
   A. are going to finish   B. are finishing   C. will finish

5. I want to watch the football game tonight. The Chicago Bulls _____ against the Los Angeles Clippers, so it should be interesting.
   A. will play   B. are playing   C. will be played

6. The new Parliament session _____ for January.
   A. will be scheduled   B. is scheduled   C. schedules

7. I _____ to give you the details as soon as I can. I _____ with my staff today and I should have some information tonight already.
   A. will try, will meet   B. am trying, am meeting   C. will try, am meeting

WHEN I DO... AS SOON AS I HAVE DONE...

153. ☺☺ Uzupełnij poniższe zdania odpowiednią formą podanych czasowników w czasie przyszłym.

1. When I (come back) _____ from my holidays, we (talk) _____ about it again.
2. Before you (go off) _____ , we (take) _____ a look at the last exercise.
3. The committee (select) _____ three candidates after they (review) _____ all applications.
4. Try to contact me as soon as you (find out) _____ what the situation is like.
5. When you (enter) _____ the room, you (see) _____ a large, colourful picture on the wall. I'd like you to take a good look at it.
6. My sister (probably go) _____ to work as a volunteer in a Third World country after she (complete) _____ an introductury course.
7. I guarantee that after you (read) _____ this book, your idea of phantasy literature (change) _____ completely.

154. ☺☺☺ Połącz poniższe zdania, uzupełniając je odpowiednimi formami czasowników podanych w nawiasach.

1. We (take) _____ the patient to the X-ray division
2. After the Manager (hear) _____ your story
3. (you let) _____ me know
4. Once the students (solve) _____ the task individually
5. Our proof-reader (go over) _____ your text

6. When you (see) _____ Hilary

7. Your mother (be) _____ quite pleased

8. Until Paul (change) *has changed* his mind about my family

a) the class (discuss) _____ it together.

b) as soon as the nurse (take) _____ his blood pressure.

c) when she (find out) _____ that you did so well in your math test.

d) before we (send) _____ it off.

e) I (can) *won't be able* to be friends with him again.

f) when you (decide) _____ if you're going to the party?

g) (you ask) _____ her to call me right away?

h) I'm sure he (excuse) _____ your absence from the meeting.

155. ☺☺☺ Przekształć poniższe zdania, używając podanych wyrazów.

1. First we will learn something about the history of ballet. Then we will start practical classes.
   After _____.

2. First you need to calm down. Then we will discuss the situation.
   _____ once _____.

3. The students are taking their exams in May. They will have a mock exam session.
   Before _____.

4. We will get to the top of the mountain. We will have to set up the tents immediately.
   As soon as _____.

5. The delegation will arrive. It will be greeted by the Ambassador.
   When _____.

6. You will hear the results of the competition. Will you call me afterwards?
   _____ after _____.

7. First the plane will land. Then the band will start playing the welcome song.
   When _____.

8. I will meet the professor tomorrow. I will quickly ask him to sign my student's book.
   As soon as _____.

WILL, SHALL

156. ☺ Uzupełnij poniższe wypowiedzi, używajac *shall* i podanych czasowników.

not tolerate	return	see	collect	not disappoint	explain	be

1. 'We are leaving at 5 o'clock tomorrow'.
   'Great, I _____ at your house ay 4:30 then'.

2. 'I've put much trust in you, Tony'
   'I know Sir, and I _____ you'.

3. 'Are we going to see the National Musuem when we're in London?'
   'It depends on how much we have left, we _____'.

4. 'Our project consists of three stages. I _____ each of them to you in turn'.

5. 'I recommend that your company reconsiders its position. We _____ such arrogance anymore'.

6. 'Could you please make sure that the postman arrives on time? This package *is* urgent'. 'Don't worry, madam. We _____ the letter at 4 o'clock, as promised'.

7. 'There's no need arguing about such details in front of our guests. We _____ to it later'.

157. ☺ *Shall* używane jest często dla wyrażania uprzejmych propozycji. Przeczytaj poniższe sytuacje i ułóż odpowiednie propozycje, używając *shall* i podanych czasowników.

Wzór: It's late at night and your friend is afraid to walk home alone.
          Shall I walk you home? (WALK)

1. It's very stuffy in the room, because all the windows are shut.
_____ (OPEN)

2. A friend is visiting you and says that he is thirsty.
_____ (GET)

3. You see an old lady carrying heavy bags with shopping.
_____ (HELP)

4. You are planning to go to a cinema with your friends and the ticket office is near your house.
_____ (BUY)

5. Your brother is complaining that his wife doesn't want to cook for him.
_____ (TALK)

6. Your boss has an important meeting tomorrow and needs some data on the company's performance.
_____ (PREPARE)

7. You are a teacher and notice that some of your students seem not to have understood a certain topic.
_____ (DISCUSS)

158. ☺☺ W niektórych z poniższych zdań użycie *shall* i *will* jest niepoprawne. Przeczytaj ćwiczenie uważnie i popraw błędne zdania.

1. My wife and I <u>will go</u> to a Chinese restaurant tonight; we've been invited by my boss.
_____

2. The next incentive trip at our company <u>will</u> probably <u>be</u> to Japan.
_____

3. There's no use inviting John to our party. I'm sure he <u>won't come</u>.
_____

4. What video <u>will</u> you girls <u>watch</u> tonight at Cindy's sleep-over party?
_____

5. Don't worry; Mark is a very trustworthy person. He <u>shall finish</u> the project on time.
_____

6. We <u>shall be</u> at your house at 6 o'clock to help you with the cleaning-up.
_____

7. This picture is hanging by just one nail! It <u>will fall</u> down.
_____

8. <u>Will</u> I <u>offer</u> you something to drink?
_____

FURTHER TENSE PRACTICE

159. ☺☺ Uzupełnij poniższe zdania właściwymi formami czasowników: A, B lub C.

1. When the teacher _____ the room, he _____ that the whole class _____.
    A. has entered, saw, laughed
    B. entered, saw, laughed
    C. entered, saw, was laughing
   The teacher also _____ that somebody _____ into the class book, because it _____ open.
    A. had noticed, looked, lay
    B. had noticed, looked, laid
    C. noticed, had looked, lay

2. One of the questions I _____ on asking myself these days is: what _____ we all _____ this time next year?
    A. keep, will… be doing
    B. am keeping, will... be doing
    C. keep, will.. do
   And, strangely enough, what _____ me most is whether my boyfriend and I _____ to stay together.
    A. troubles, will manage
    B. will trouble, will have managed
    C. have troubled, will manage

3. _____ you _____ that nitrogen _____ at −219°C?
    A. Have… known, freezes
    B. Do… know, will freeze
    C. Did… know, freezes
   That's something I _____ only today. Actually, I _____ about it in the paper this morning.
    A. found out, read
    B. have found out, read
    C. have found out, have read

4. My mom _____ a very good swimmer, even though she never actually _____ swimming as a little girl. I, on the contrary, _____ afraid of water since early childhood.
    A. is, has enjoyed, was
    B. is, enjoys, is
    C. is, enjoyed, have been
   However, this year I _____ to the seaside on holiday, and it _____ the first time I _____ the sea.
    A. go, will be, see
    B. will go, will be, see
    C. am going, will be, have seen

5. Ever since Tom _____ the company, Jean _____ to take his place.
    A. has left, tried
    B. left, has been trying
    C. left, is trying

Currently, she _____ on the cases that Albert _____ before he _____ .

    A. is working, had been handling, left

    B. works, handled, had left

    C. is working, handled, had left

160. ☺☺☺ Uzupełnij poniższe zdania właściwymi formami czasowników: A, B lub C.

1. Can you imagine I _____ 'food' with a 'u' in my last English essay? Why _____ I always _____ silly mistakes like that?!

    A. have written, do… make

    B. wrote, have… made

    C. wrote, am… making

2. Our CEO _____ in June, so we presume the Board _____ a farewell party in May.

    A. retires, will be organizing

    B. retires, will have organized

    C. is retiring, is organizing

3. Ever since Fay _____ with Richard, he _____ a much more cheerful person.

    A. broke up, is

    B. has broken up, is

    C. broke up, has been

4. When exactly _____ you _____ me that you were engaged to a prince from Burma?!

    A. did… tell

    B. were… going to tell

    C. were… telling me

5. That was the first time the children _____ by plane, so they _____ obviously excited.

    A. have flown, are

    B. flew, had been

    C. had flown, were

6. The author is looking forward to the press conference today. It _____ the first time he _____ to so many journalists at once.

    A. will be, has spoken

    B. is, speaks

    C. will be, speaks

7. Your eyes are all red and swollen! _____ you _____ ? What _____ ?

    A. Did… cry, 's happened

    B. Have… been crying, 's happened

    C. Were… crying, happened

8. When Lucinda first _____ to New York looking for work, she _____ 15.

    A. came, only just turned

    B. come, have only just turned

    C. came, had only just turned

9. I'm sorry I was so sulky when you _____ to visit, but I _____ all day and felt rather stressed.

    A. had come, worked

    B. came, worked

    C. came, had been working

10. It _____ years since I last _____ waltz with somebody as graceful as yourself, madam.
   A. 's, danced
   B. 's been, danced
   C. 's been, have danced

161. ☺☺☺ Uzupełnij poniższy tekst odpowiednimi formami czasowników podanych w nawiasach.

One of China's most remote ethnic groups, the Dulong, (1. move up) recently _____ to the top of the list of world's most popular tourist destinations. Numbering about 6,000, the Dulong (2. be) _____ once known for tattooing the faces of their women. That tradition (3. develop) _____ in early times to discourage neighbouring Tibetans from kidnapping the women. This practice gradually (4. vanish) _____ over the years and (5. now cease) _____ completely, so that only a handful of women actually (6. wear) _____ tatooes today. However, other aspects of the Dulong way of life still (7. survive) _____ in the Dunlong Valley in northwestern Yunnan province. The recent outburst of interest in the Dulong tribe (8. be) _____ facilitated by the construction of a new dirt road connecting the valley to the nearest town, Gongshan, which (9. reduce) _____ the journey to about 10 hours. The local travel agencies (10. predict) _____ that more and more tourists (11. come) _____ to the valley in the nearest months. The committed travelers, after they (12. reach) _____ the valley, (13. be) _____ welcomed by one of the remaining tattooed women with a steaming cup of tea. An experience you (14. never forget) _____ !

Adapted from 'Time', August 22, 2005/Vol. 166, No. 8

KLUCz

138. 1. she will grow into a beautiful woman in the future **2.** his party next week will be boring too **3.** it will bring her luck **4.** our parents will tell us to wear suits **5.** they won't understand my decision **6.** we won't win against that canny businessman **7.** they won't have enough resources to do it

139. 1. 'll clean it up **2.** will submit **3.** 'll talk **4.** will give **5.** 'll shut **6.** won't argue **7.** 'll ask

140. 1. e **2.** f **3.** b **4.** g **5.** a **6.** h **7.** d **8.** c

141. Future Continuous to czas przyszły stosowany m.in. do opisania czynności, która będzie trwała w danym momencie w przyszłości.
1. will be sitting **2.** will be running **3.** will be sleeping **4.** will be taking **5.** will be working **6.** will be having **7.** will probably be discussing

142. 1. he will be driving to work. **2.** she will be flying to France. **3.** he will be watching the musical. **4.** I will be doing my chemistry presentation. **5.** we will be rehearsing our show. **6.** I will be moving out. **7.** they will be celebrating their 5th aniversary.

143. Propozycje zdań:
1. I will be driving to work. **2.** I will be playing tennis. **3.** I will be spending holiday in Egypt. **4.** I will be sitting in my biology class. **5.** I will be having family breakfast with my parents. **6.** I will be taking my final exams. **7.** I will be looking for a summer job.

144. 1. will have resat **2.** will have been eaten **3.** will have sold **4.** will have exceeded **5.** will have fallen asleep **6.** will have won **7.** will have completed

145. 1. finishes, will have corrected – Present Perfect podkreśla zakończenie dłuższego procesu/dłuższej czynności. **2.** discovers, will have married **3.** realize, will have been polluted **4.** becomes, will have found **5.** arrives, will have surrendered **6.** has written, will have retired **7.** struggle, will have arrived

146. Ćwiczenie otwarte; przykłady zdań:

1. I think that by 2150 pocket computers will have been invented. **2.** I think that by 2150 Mars will have become a human colony. **3.** I think that by 2150 scientists will have found a cure for AIDS. **4.** I think that by 2150 space travel will have become a common practice. **5.** I think that by 2150 the Internet will have reached all corners of the world. **6.** I think that by 2150 mobile phones will have fully replaced fixed-line phones. **7.** I think that by 2150 the English language will have become a global language. **8.** I think that by 2150 several new planets will have been discovered. **9.** I think that by 2150 new technological equipment will have been invented. **10.** I think that by 2150 many wars will have ended.

147. **1.** is going to write **2.** are going to apply **3.** is going to jump **4.** am not going to tolerate **5.** Are you going to talk **6.** is going to snow **7.** is going to extend **8.** is going to invite

148. **1** a) are going to inform **2** g) am going to take out **3** h) is going to review **4** c) is going to change **5** b) am going to read **6** e) is going to call **7** f) are going to start

149. **1.** Are you going to see the new film with Brad Pitt this weekend? **2.** When is the organization going to take the decision? **3.** Is our company going to apply for this grant? **4.** Is the government going to continue its employment policy in the coming years? **5.** What are you going to do with your grandfather's stamp collection? **6.** Are dogs going to be banned from public parks? **7.** Is your sister going to move out after college? **8.** Where is the Queen going to stay during her visit to Poland?

150. **1.** is flying **2.** are starting **3.** is leaving **4.** are coming back **5.** are having **6.** is giving **7.** am taking

151. **1.** starts **2.** leaves **3.** meet, join **4.** takes place, is **5.** ends **6.** sees

152. Przy przewidywaniach lub opiniach dotyczących przyszłości używamy Future Simple.
1 C **2** A **3** A **4** C **5** B **6** B **7** C

153. **1.** come back, will talk **2.** go off, will take **3.** will select, have reviewed **4.** find out **5.** enter, will see **6.** will probably go, has completed **7.** read/have read, will change

154. **1.** b) will take, has taken **2** h) has heard, will excuse **3.** f) Will you let, you decide/have decided **4** a) have solved, will discuss **5** d) will go over, send **6** g) see, will you ask **7** c) will be, finds out

155. **1.** After we have learnt something about the history of ballet, we will start practical classes. **2.** We will discuss the situation once you have calmed down. **3.** Before the students take their exams in May, they will have a mock exam session. **4.** As soon as we get to the top of the mountain, we will have to set up the tents. **5.** When the delegation arrives, it will be greeted by the Ambassador. **6.** Will you call me after you have heard the results of the competition? **7.** When the plane lands, the band will start playing the welcome song. **8.** As soon as I meet the professor tomorrow, I will ask him to sign my student's book.

156. **1.** shall be **2.** shall not disappoint **3.** shall see **4.** shall explain **5.** shall not tolerate **6.** shall collect **7.** shall return

157. **1.** Shall I open the window? **2.** Shall I get you something to drink? **3.** Shall I help you? **4.** Shall I buy the tickets? **5.** Shall I talk to her? **6.** Shall I prepare the data (for you)? **7.** Shall we discuss this topic again?

158. **1.** are going – bo czynność jest zaplanowana **2.** OK **3.** OK **4.** are you girls going to watch/are you girls watching – bo pytamy o plany **5.** will/'ll finish – shall jest używane tylko w 1 os. l.p. i l.mn. **6.** OK **7.** is going to fall – na podstawie istniejących dowodów stwierdzamy oczywiste wydarzenie, które nastąpi w przyszłości **8.** Shall I offer – przy uprzejmych propozycjach używane jest shall, nie will

159. **1** C, C **2** A, A **3** C, B **4** C, C **5** B, A

160. **1** C Present Continuous podkreśla irytację mówcy na powtarzającą się czynność/sytuację.
2 A **3** C **4** B Forma *going to* w Past Continuous określa niezrealizowany zamiar. **5** C **6** A **7** B **8** C **9** C **10** B

161. **1.** has recently moved up **2.** were **3.** had developed **4.** was gradually vanishing **5.** has now ceased **6.** wears **7.** survive **8.** has been facilitated **9.** has reduced **10.** predict **11.** will be coming **12.** reach/have reached **13.** will be **14.** will never forget

MODAL VERBS

A. EXPRESSING ABILITY, POTENTIAL AND GENERAL CHARACTERISTICS

CAN/COULD/COULD HAVE

162. ☺ Uzupełnij zdania odpowiednimi formami *can*.

1. When my brother was a little baby, he _____ actually be quite cute.
2. Is it true that our English teacher _____ also speak Russian and Japanese?
3. Why are you making so much noise?! _____ you see I'm working?
4. The speaker's voice was shaking, so the audience _____ hear very clearly how nervous he was.
5. _____ you pass me the salt please? It's right next to your plate.
6. Why don't we go to the concert tonight; my husband _____ pick us up afterwards.
7. Work at the factory _____ be very strenuous sometimes, but none of the workers complained, since it was difficult to find any employment at all.
8. The autumn in Poland _____ be very warm and sunny, but usually the weather is gloomy and wet.
9. It's better for Peter to stay in the port while we sail to the village for some food. The sea is rough today and he _____ swim.
10. When Lucy announced she was moving to Greenland, her friends _____ understand her decision at first.

163. ☺☺ Wybierz poprawną wersję poniższych zdań.

1. We're looking for someone who is not only an excellent manager, but <u>can also create/could have also created</u> a true team-spirit among his staff.
2. It's a shame that the customer has decided not to buy the car. Perhaps we <u>could offer/could have offered</u> him a higher discount.
3. When Robert was still a practising acrobat, he <u>could do/could have done</u> five summersaults in a row without pause.
4. I really don't know how you <u>could bump/could have bumped</u> into that tree. <u>Couldn't you see/Couldn't you have seen</u> that it was right in front of you?!
5. Chinese folk music, although generally gentle and cheerful, <u>can sometimes surprise/could sometimes surprise</u> the listener with its abrupt changes of mood.
6. In medieval times, the heir to the throne <u>could only marry/could have only married</u> a girl from an approved aristocratic family.
7. I guess we <u>could plan/could have planned</u> the conference for a different weekend.

8. The publicity that film stars attract <u>can be/could have been</u> tiring and stressful, but I still think I would enjoy it.

164. ☺☺☺ Skomentuj treść poniższych zdań, używając formy *could+perfect infinitive* oraz czasowników podanych w nawiasach.

Wzór: You knew that the classes were cancelled, but you didn't tell me. (TELL)
You *could have told me that the classes were cancelled.*

1. Gary knew how to fix the tap, but none of us told him that we needed help. (HELP)
Gary _____

2. The guard knew where the exit was, but the visitors didn't ask him about it. (SHOW)
The guard _____

3. The party was quite good, but the host didn't buy enough food. (BUY)
The host _____

4. The two countries went to war, because their governments didn't do enough to prevent it. (DO)
The governments _____

5. It's a shame that you didn't warn me that the hotel manager was so short-tempered. (WARN)
You _____

6. It's a pity that the band played so few songs from their last album during the concert. (PLAY)
The band _____

7. I must say that I didn't put too much effort into this essay. (PUT)
I _____

CAN/BE ABLE

165. ☺ Uzupełnij poniższe zdania odpowiednią formą wyrażenia *be able* oraz jednym z czasowników podanych w ramce.

> fix   (not) find   register   prevent   buy   (not) contact   return   make

1. Fred hopes that next year he _____ a bigger house for his family.
2. The mechanic should _____ my car.
3. This article is about Polish people who _____ a career abroad and are now famous all around the world.
4. Those users who _____ on time, will receive a special bonus program.
5. The fog was thick, but the captain _____ the ship safely to the harbour.
6. I am sorry, Sir, but I _____ the Embassy so far, as you asked.
7. Scientists _____ a cure for this disease yet.
8. Hopefully the government _____ the bad news from spreading, before people start panicking.

166. ☺☺ Zastąp czasownik podany w nawiasie odpowiednią formą wyrażenia *be able*.

1. If you finish the last chapter of your book today, we (can) _____ to send it to the publisher before the end of the month.

2. Ever since he came from the hospital, the boy (cannot) _____ to catch up with the learning material at school.

3. Before she went to her job interview at the shoemaking company, Doris had read a lot about the history of shoe fashion, because she wanted (can) _____ to impress her employer with her knowledge of that industry.

4. After the introductory course in French, the students should (can) _____ to formulate at least the basic questions and answers in that language.

5. If the Manager gave his employees some tips on how to improve their performance, they would (can) _____ to achieve the targets he had set for them at the beginning of the year.

6. I'm afraid that we (cannot) _____ to announce the final results of the tender until all the participating companies have submitted their bids.

7. Owing to its skilful diplomacy and strategic thinking, the present government (can) _____ to solve many problems in our country and bring about the prosperity that we enjoy today.

8. It's quite funny to see people who first pretend (can) _____ to speak a given language and then in fact just smile and nod and produce some unintelligible sounds.

167. ☺☺ *Can* czy *be able to*? Zdecyduj, której formy użyć w poniższych zdaniach.

1. It seemed that the conflict between the two ministers was inevitable, but luckily they could/were able to reach a compromise.

2. During WWII, people who were helping the resistance movement could/were able to face serious repercussions.

3. The teacher forgot to bring her glasses to the test, so she couldn't/wasn't able to see very clearly if her students were cheating.

4. My nephew is a truly restless child who just can't/isn't able to stay still for more than 5 minutes.

5. During her farewell party, your fiancée was constantly surrounded by her girlfriends. Could you/Were you able to find some time for each other?

6. As a young girl, the actress could/was able to spend hours sitting in an empty theatre, dreaming that one day she would act on its stage.

7. Jimmy broke his mom's favourite vase, but luckily he could/was able to clean the glass up before she came back from work.

8. I'm very happy that I could/was able to take so many photos of my class during high-school re-union.

B. EXPRESSING OBLIGATION, ADVICE AND RECOMMENDATION

MUST/HAVE TO/NEED TO

168. ☺☺ Uzupełnij poniższe zdania czasownikiem *must* lub *have to*.

1. I live on the outskirts of Warsaw and _____ to get up at 5 every day to get to my office in the town centre.
2. You won't believe what happened at school today! I _____ talk to you right away!
3. The notice on the board says: 'All students wishing to take their Norwegian oral exams in June _____ report to the Head of Norwegian Studies by the end of this week'.
4. Have you heard that the people who want to take their Norwegian oral exams in June _____ report it by the end of this week? That doesn't give us much time to decide what to do, does it?
5. Reviews of this film have been quite promising. I _____ see it at the weekend!
6. Tony can't come to the poker game tonight, because he _____ stay at home with the kids. His wife is away on business.
7. Patricia has failed my course again. Please tell her that she _____ see me during my office hours tomorrow.
8. As a company devoted to providing the highest quality, we _____ constantly try to improve our methods and procedures.
9. The annual financial statements _____ be submitted to the Revenue Office by 10 February at the latest.
10. You _____ be a bit more careful about what you say to your mother. She has called me again asking if you were in trouble.
11. The school _____ cancel yesterday's auction due to bad weather forecasts. The auction will probably take place next week, unless the weather doesn't improve and the whole event _____ be rescheduled again.
12. Our last biology lecture was surprisingly interesting, I _____ say. I'd never thought there were so many interesting insects.

169. ☺☺☺ Przekształć poniższe zdania, używając *have to* lub *need to*.

Wzór:
Lucy's computer broke down and now she <u>is forced to use</u> a typing machine instead.
Lucy's computer broke down and now she has to use a typing machine instead.

1. <u>It is necessary for the City Mayor to do</u> something about the traffic in our town, if he wants to be re-elected!

_____

2. Every student of veterinary science who has completed his third year <u>is obliged to get</u> a four-week training at an animals' clinic.

_____

3. Is it necessary that we fill in the questionnaire in black ink? Can't we use a pencil instead?

   _____

4. I never remember my dentist's surname, so whenever I call him it is necessary for me to look it up in my address book.

   _____

5. If the revenues of the shop don't go up next year, it will be forced to close down.

   _____

6. According to this agreement, the borrower is obliged to repay the loan in regular instalments.

   _____

7. The tourists have just missed the last train to Warsaw and are forced to stay at the railway station over the night.

   _____

8. This course is designed to prepare you for your oral English exam and teach all the tricks that you are obliged to know.

   _____

170. ☺ Przekształć poniższe zdania, używając podanych czasowników oraz konstrukcji *need + -ing*.

1. The TV set is broken.
   (MEND) _____
2. The battery has run out.
   (RECHARGE) _____
3. One of the car tyres has gone flat.
   (REFILL) _____
4. The pencil is blunt.
   (SHARPEN) _____
5. Flowers in your garden look dry.
   (WATER) _____
6. One of the issues in this report is unclear.
   (CLARIFY) _____
7. The windows in the living-room are covered with finger smudges.
   (CLEAN) _____
8. My dancing shoes are not shiny.
   (POLISH) _____

MUSTN'T/DON'T HAVE TO/DON'T NEED TO

171. ☺ Uzupełnij poniższe wypowiedzi, używając *mustn't* i wyrazów podanych w nawiasach.

1. This glass comes from the 17th century and is a gift from the Queen of France. (not break it)
   You _____
2. It's a secret that Hilary won this year's 'Pop Idol' contest. (not tell anyone)
   You _____

3. I will now hand out the tests, but don't look at them before I say you can. (not turn them around yet)
   You _____

4. There are some customers waiting outside the shop. Please tell them that we open late today! (not enter the shop yet)
   They _____

5. Please tell Susan that I am allergic to her perfume. (not use that fragrance anymore)
   She _____

6. I have problems falling asleep at night. (not drink so much coffee)
   I _____

7. Look, there is a non-smoking sign right above our table. (not smoke here)
   We _____

8. It's a shame that the project has failed, but Beth really did her best to save it. (not blame her for what has happened)
   We _____

172. ☺ *Mustn't* czy *don't have to/don't need to*? Wybierz poprawną wersję poniższych zdań.

1. Vanessa's husband gave her a new Porsche for her birthday, so she mustn't/doesn't have to walk to work anymore.

2. There are many places where we can go for holiday, so we mustn't/don't need to decide now. We may still wait and see if there are any interesting last-minute bargains available.

3. You mustn't/don't have to be so rude to your younger sister. Look, you have made her cry again!

4. I believe that the dress code at our company is too liberal. People mustn't/don't have to be allowed to walk around in jeans and T-shirts. After all, we are a reputable insurance company and not some fashion agency!

5. Yes. I do remember that I still have 5 tests in this exam session. You really mustn't/don't need to remind me!

6. There is still some hope for us to succeed in the competition. We mustn't/don't have to give up yet!

7. If things go as smoothly as I have planned, I mustn't/won't need to work for the rest of my life!

8. Please tell your daughter that she mustn't/doesn't need to shout at me while I am trying to help.

173. ☺☺ Przekształć podkreślone części zdania, używając wyrażeń *don't need to/don't have to*.

1. It is not your obligation to hand in your passport to the border guard; it's enough if he looks at it while you hold it.

   _____

2. It is not necessary for me to take my ballet shoes to the shoemaker; my mom has already done it for me.

   _____

3. It is not our parents' obligation to give us pocket money, but it seems that they want to teach us some responsibility.

   _____

4. It's a rule at our company that the employees who have worked 10 hours overtime in one week are not obliged to come to work on Fridays.

   _____

5. Fortunately, it is not necessary for me to worry about my holidays this year, because my boss has already promised me 3 weeks in July. And I have it on paper, too!

   _____

6. Since Ben had already done Latin in high school, <u>it wasn't necessary for him to</u> take a Latin course at college.

_____

7. <u>It is not necessary for us to</u> go to the tax office today, if we don't have all the papers ready yet. The deadline for the tax returns is only next Friday.

_____

8. I advise all of you to do as much work on your project as possible now, so that <u>it won't be necessary for you to</u> work on it at the weekend.

_____

DON'T NEED TO/NEEDN'T

174. ☺☺ Uzupełnij poniższe zdania czasownikiem *don't need to* lub *needn't*.

1. From what I have read in the press, Polish people travelling to other EU countries _____ take their passports with them. A valid ID card is sufficient.
2. Those of you who have handed in all their homework assignments _____ come to my last lecture next week.
3. Our bank will take care of all the formalities for you, Sir, so you _____ worry about anything.
4. Cactuses are very convenient plants for people who tend to be forgetful, as they _____ be watered more than once every few weeks.
5. Tell Paul that I have already fixed the satellite cable, so he _____ call the emergency service.
6. My grandparents, who live in the country, _____ buy milk in the shop, because they have a cow or two of their own.
7. Barbara, an experienced attorney, has obviously had her professional failures in the past, which we _____ discuss here.
8. One of the advantages of being a freelance translator is that you _____ go to the office every day and can do most of your work at home.
9. Let me give you a piece of advice: even when you have known somebody for a long time, you _____ assume that he or she has been honest with you at all times.
10. The new book by Mary Johnson is an example of a travel journal at its best. You _____ be a fan of this type of novels to let yourself be swept away by her style.

175. ☺☺ Przeczytaj poniższe zdania, a następnie utwórz komentarze z użyciem konstrukcji *needn't* + **perfect infinitive**.

Wzór:
Lucinda brought her car to a garage for a check. There was nothing wrong with it.
Lucinda *needn't have brought her car to the garage for a check* .

1. I worried about the results of my exam. I got an A.
   I _____
2. The girls took playing cards with them on the school trip. The boys didn't want to play with them.
   The girls _____

3. Calvin hurried to make it for the bus. The bus came 10 minutes late.
   Calvin _____

4. The guest shouted at the waitress. In fact it wasn't her fault that the soup was cold.
   The guest _____

5. Agnes dressed up for the party as a princess. The party was not a fancy-dress ball and everybody else was wearing normal clothes.
   Agnes _____

6. We booked the tickets for the concert long in advance. A few days before the concert there were still plenty of tickets left.
   We _____

7. The accused told the prosecutor about a silly event in the past. During the trial the prosecutor used it against him.
   The accused _____

8. I took an umbrella with me to the horse race. It didn't rain.
   I _____

9. My mom prepared a three-course dinner for us. We had just eaten a Chinese take-away.
   My mom _____

176. ☺☺ Połącz poniższe zdania w pary, uzupełniając je konstrukcjami z *don't need to* lub *needn't.*

1. I'm not going to need this book at the moment.
2. The student passed his final exam.
3. The classes were cancelled, which we didn't know about.
4. The Queen's servants take care of all her needs.
5. Luckily for us the teacher forgot to bring the tests with him.
6. Half of the guests didn't turn up.
7. My dentist said I had perfectly healthy teeth.
8. My boss announced that the company Christmas party was obligatory for most the staff.

a) She (even know) _____ how to brush her teeth.
b) He (resit) _____ it.
c) You (return) _____ it until next week.
d) We (write) _____ the test that day.
e) The host (buy) _____ so much food.
f) He also said I (come) _____ for another visit until next year.
g) We (come) _____ to school that day.
h) Lucinda was among the lucky few who (go) *didn't have to go.*

EXPRESSING OBLIGATION

177. ☺ Uzupełnij poniższe zdania konstrukcją *be to* oraz czasownikami podanymi w nawiasach.

1. Today, all students (report) _____ to their mentors after their last lesson.
2. We couldn't go to the party, because we had to work on our history assignment, which (be handed in) _____ the following morning.

3. The concert (start) _____ at 9 pm, but it was delayed because of some technical problems.
4. Our honeymoon (be) _____ the journey of our lives, but it turned out a complete disaster.
5. We have an official inspection from the Tax Office tomorrow, so all staff (arrive) _____ to work on time and behave properly.
6. Why isn't the end-of-year report ready yet? Who (prepare) _____ it?
7. The meeting (begin) _____ at 5 pm, but with our boss coming 2 hours late it had to be postponed until next week.
8. Horrifying news awaited me in my office: I (see) _____ the manager immediately.

178. ☺☺ Uzupełnij poniższe zdania właściwym czasownikiem modalnym, wybierając odpowiedź A, B lub C.

1. There are many problems that foreigners _____ in another country before they truly settle in.
   A. must solve   B. have to solve   C. need solving
2. I will not accept any essays after the deadline. They _____ handed in on Friday.
   A. need be   B. have to be   C. must be
3. Chris _____ in the school race, but unfortunately he fell ill the day before.
   A. was to start   B. was to have started   C. had to start
4. Peter couldn't decide which tie to buy, so he _____ the salesman for help.
   A. must ask   B. had to ask   C. must have asked
5. Thank you for returning this book on time, but you _____, really. We have more of these on stock, so you could have kept it for another week.
   A. mustn't   B. needn't have   C. didn't need to
6. Only because you are the best student in your group, doesn't mean you _____ treat the others like fools. You _____ act like you are better than them in some way!
   A. have to, mustn't   B. mustn't, mustn't   C. have to, have to
7. There are still some serious mistakes in your book, but we _____ discuss them now. We will have some time for such discussions later.
   A. don't have to   B. mustn't   C. needn't
8. Madeleine has agreed to swap shifts with me at the weekend, so I _____ work on Sunday morning.
   A. needn't   B. mustn't   C. don't need to
9. Patients with high blood pressure _____ smoke or drink much coffee and should get regular exercise.
   A. mustn't   B. don't have to   C. needn't
10. Nobody appreciated my help. I guess _____ so hard to please them!
   A. had to try   B. mustn't try   C. needn't have tried

179. ☺☺☺ Uzupełnij poniższe zdania właściwym czasownikiem modalnym, wybierając odpowiedź A, B lub C.

1. The author _____ the book by Monday, but he called his publisher at the weekend to ask for a little more time.
   A. had to finish   B. was to have finished   C. was to finish
2. Tell your Andy that he _____ return the money now, if he hasn't got enough cash. I can manage without for another week or two.
   A. mustn't   B. needn't   C. doesn't need to

3. 'How was your English lesson yesterday?'
   'Oh, luckily my teacher called me and said that she wasn't feeling too well, so
   I _____!'
   A. didn't have to go   B. needn't have gone   C. wasn't to have gone
4. Don't be late for your karate training, honey! Remember that you _____ there
   at 10 o'clock sharp in order to get a clean outfit!'
   A. must be   B. have to be   C. need being
5. If my suspicions are true and somebody has really broken into our computer system, we
   _____ access passwords for the entire company.
   A. must change   B. will have to change   C. are to change
6. 'The applicants invited to the interview _____ bring their CVs with them, as
   they will be provided with special forms to fill out. They should, however, prepare a
   short speech on their past experience in the banking industry and, obviously,
   _____ come late'.
   A. mustn't, needn't   B. are not to, needn't   C. needn't, mustn't
7. I'm really sorry, but I can't go to the cinema with you tonight. I _____ home
   at six for my father's birthday dinner.
   A. will have to be   B. am to be   C. must
8. Owen and I _____ about which one of us will invite Marilyn to the prom,
   because in the end she decided to go with her swimming instructor.
   A. needn't have argued   B. didn't need to argue   C. mustn't argue
9. According to the newest statistics of the Ministry of Environment, public awareness of
   environmental issues still _____.
   A. must improve   B. needs improving   C. was to improve
10. My secretary is on maternity leave from next week onward, which should be an
    interesting experience for me. I _____ my own coffee for about a year now.
    A. mustn't make   B. needn't have made   C. haven't had to make

SHOULD/OUGHT TO/'D BETTER

180. ☺ Przekształć poniższe zdania, zastępując podkreślone części zdań wyrażeniami
z czasownikiem *should*.

Wzór: The Australian author is extremely popular, so we <u>expect that her new book
will become another bestseller.</u>
*The Australian author is extremely popular, so her new book should become
another bestseller.*

1. Right now the situation on the poultry market is rather shaky, but <u>it is expected to
   improve</u> next year.

   _____

2. Our project is running quite smoothly, so <u>it is likely to be ready</u> by next week.

   _____

3. Monica has taken extra lessons to prepare for her driving exam, so <u>I don't expect that she
   will have any problems</u> passing it.

   _____

4. Because Tuesday is a holiday, <u>the management is likely to give us</u> Monday off as well.

_____

5. After completing the course<u> the participants are expected to be able to operate</u> the system.

_____

6. The controversial paper by Professor Johnson, to be read at the Annual Globalisation Conference, <u>is likely to stir a lot of discussion</u> among conference participants.

_____

7. The results of the Miss World Contest <u>are expected to be announced</u> any minute now.

_____

181. ☺ Przeczytaj poniższe zdania i utwórz stosowne porady, używając *should/ought to* oraz wyrazów podanych w nawiasach.

Wzór: You look very pale and have little energy. (DAY OFF)
You *should take a day off.*

1. Norbert told Betty's sister that she should go on a diet. (APOLOGISE)
Norbert _____

2. My children's typical meal consists of fried sausages and chips, followed by some ice-cream for dessert. (FRUIT AND VEGETABLES)
My children _____

3. Our car's engine has been working rather loud lately. (GARAGE)
We _____

4. My wife complains that I work too much and spend too little time with our family. (TIME)
I _____

5. Sandra's hairstyle is slightly outdated, which many people make fun of. (HAIRDRESSER'S)
Sandra _____

6. Not all students in our class will be able to pay for the school trip to Egypt. (CO-FINANCE)
The school _____

7. Grandpa's backache has got much worse in the past few days. (DOCTOR)
Grandpa _____

182. ☺☺ Używając wyrażenia z *had better* (*'d better*), dopisz komentarz do poniższych wypowiedzi.

Wzór:

The material from today's lecture is likely to come up in the exam. (I should take notes.)
I'd better take notes.

1. The fact that Greg is joining a monastery will be a shock to everybody. (I should keep quiet about it.)

_____

2. I'm not sure if you are allowed to use the company car for private trips. (You should ask your boss's permission first.)

_____

3. Buying a flat is basically a life-long investment. (We should ask a real estate agent for help.)

_____

4. The guests are about to arrive and Jack has gone to fetch the drinks. (It's better for him to be here on time.)

_____

5. I've heard that my daughter's roommate cannot stand the mess she makes in the kitchen. (She should start looking for new accommodation.)

_____

6. The party upstairs is getting louder and louder. (We should call the police.)

_____

7. I'm not sure how to spell this word. (I should look it up in a dictionary before printing my essay.)

_____

SHOULD – OTHER USES

183. ☺ Przyjrzyj się poniższym postulatom wobec Rady Miasta i ułóż zdania, używając podanych czasowników oraz *should*.

Wzór: Open a new library in town.
              The protesters demand *that the City Council should open a new library in town.*

1. Donate more money to charity.
The protesters request _____
2. Take care of public parks.
The protesters order _____
3. Organize open-air fairs and festivals in the summer.
The protesters insist _____
4. Build an open-air ice-skating rink.
The protesters stipulate _____
5. Invite famous people to hold lectures at the City Hall.
The protesters demand _____
6. Solve the problem of people being mugged in the streets.
The protesters request _____
7. Introduce stricter controls of public expenditure.
The protesters insist _____
8. Take steps towards reducing air pollution in the city centre.
The protesters postulate _____

184. ☺☺ Uzupełnij poniższe zdania, używając czasowników podanych w ramce oraz *should*.

eliminate   spend   gain   become   sign   get   volunteer   want

1. It is surprising that Donald _____ to help with Christmas dinner preparations.
2. It is suspicious that this company _____ such large amounts on waste and sewage disposal.
3. It is important that you _____ accustomed to speaking in front of large groups of people.
4. It is vital that the government _____ bribery at public institutions.
5. It's encouraging to see that so many people _____ for our 'Save the Earth' project.
6. It is odd that he _____ suddenly _____ interested in my personal life.

98

7. It is necessary that you _____ a lot of practical experience while you are still at university.

8. It is doubtful that the President _____ this regulation.

185. ☺☺☺ Przekształć poniższe zdania, używając wyrażeń podanych w nawiasach oraz *should*.

Wzór: I'll take a map on our cycling tour, because we might get lost.
(in case) *I'll take a map on our cycling tour with me, in case we should get lost.*

1. David took his CV to the job interview, because he thought that someone might want to see it.
(in case) _____

2. You must not report the accident to the Management if you are not absolutely certain who is responsible.
(unless) _____

3. We must work harder. Then we will be able to achieve better results next year.
(so that) _____

4. The speaker had some official statistics to support his argument if somebody doubted his conclusions.
(in case) _____

5. Please ensure that all exits are properly secured. We must be certain that no one enters or leaves the building during the ceremony.
(so that) _____

6. You are not to tell the rest of the team about our plan. Otherwise they will try to stop us.
(lest) _____

SHOULD, OUGHT TO + PERFECT INFINITIVE

186. ☺☺ Przekształć poniższe podkreślone części zdań, używając *should+perfect infinitive*.

Wzór:
It takes two hours to get to London by plane, so <u>I expect that Albert has already arrived</u>.
It takes two hours to get to London by plane, so *Albert should have already arrived.*

1. I will put you through to the manager, because <u>I believe that the meeting has finished by now</u>.
I will put you through to the manager _____

2. It's nearly July, so <u>I expect that most people have already booked their holidays</u>.
It's nearly July, _____

3. The wedding is just days away, so <u>the bride and the groom have probably sent off all the invitations by now</u>.
The wedding is just days away, _____

4. Don't worry, public transport in Poland is very reliable, so <u>your parents are likely to have made it to the airport on time</u>.
Don't worry, public transport in Poland is very reliable _____

5. I've heard that the theatre wasn't very full last night, so <u>I believe that Stacy was able to get some last-minute tickets for the show</u>.
I've heard that the theatre wasn't very full last night _____

6. Our neighbours have just returned from the summer 'Work and Travel' programme. They both worked in a casino, so <u>I expect that they have earned a lot of money</u>.
They both worked in a casino _____

7. If you are looking for cheap clothes, try 'Chester's'. They are closing down, so <u>they have probably put most of their goods up for sale</u>.
They are closing down _____

187. ☺☺ Uzupełnij poniższe zdania, używając czasowników podanych w ramce oraz konstrukcji *should + perfect infinitive*.

study take trust tell react happen think book

1. I'm sorry, but I have thrown today's paper away. If you wanted to look through job advertisements, you _____ me about it in the morning!

2. Adam has failed his math exam, which was apparently very difficult. Honestly, he _____ harder.

3. Buying the washing machine has made housework much easier for all of us. We _____ of it a long time ago!

4. Our garage is extremely sorry for losing Mr. Johnson's car keys. This _____ never _____!

5. I gave Martha the love letters from my boyfriend, thinking that she was my friend, and she published them in the school magazine! I _____ never _____ her.

6. It's too late now to prevent the strike at the car factory. The government _____ earlier.

7. It's a shame that tickets for the football game are already sold out. Our sports club _____ some in advance.

8. The bouncers at the night club thought that Albert's driving license was fake and didn't let him in. He _____ his ID card with him.

188. ☺☺ *What should have been done in the situations below?* Odpowiedz, uzupełniając zdania konstrukcją *should + perfect infinitive*.

Wzór:　　I didn't listen to my parents, but it turned out that they were right.
　　　　I should have listened to my parents.

1. The wedding guests couldn't dance, because nobody had brought any music equipment.
Somebody _____

2. I couldn't enjoy the theatre play because I was very hungry. I hadn't eaten anything before going to the theatre.
I _____

3. The waitress wasn't careful carrying the tray and spilled all the drinks.
The waitress _____

4. The patient wasn't given the right medicine and his condition didn't improve.
The patient _____

5. The family couldn't move into their new flat, because the builder forgot to hand over the keys.
The builder _____

6. The shoes that Marjorie bought at the summer sale turned out to be several sizes too small. She hadn't tried them on in the shop.
She _____

7. Mike lent his car to his son at the weekend, who somehow managed to break the steering wheel off.

Mike _____

8. The school board didn't plan the end-of-year party too well and the entire event was a failure.

The school board _____

C. EXPRESSING PERMISSION

MAY/MIGHT

189. ☺ Ułóż zdania z podanych wyrazów.

For my seventh birthday, my parents took me to the ZOO. (1. not, the porcupine, feed, may, visitors) '_____', said a sign on one of the cages. I had a pack of biscuits with me. So I went up to a guard standing nearby and asked: (2. speak, I, the ZOO manager, may, to) '_____, please, sir?' (3. you, of, may, course) '_____, young man,' the guard replied. He phoned the manager and gave me the phone. 'The porcupine looks hungry, sir. (4. with, may, biscuit, share, my, I, him) _____ _____?' I asked. (5. you, afraid, not, I'm, may) '_____ _____', answered the manager politely, 'He is on a diet. But (6. offer, one, to, may, you) _____ the guard'. (7. he, allowed, eat, is, to, biscuits) '_____ on duty?' I asked gravely. 'Certainly,' laughed the manager, 'One biscuit won't do him any harm!'

190. ☺☺ W zdaniach, w których jest to możliwe, zastąp wyrażenie *be allowed to* odpowiednią formą czasownika *may*.

1. The boy *is allowed to* do whatever he pleases! *I* am his guardian, not you.
2. Young people should *be allowed to* pursue their interests and develop their skills.
3. *Being allowed to* speak your mind is one of the blessings of democracy.
4. The Manager said that we *were* only *allowed to* have a coffee break twice a day. Call it what you will. I think it's exploitation!
5. In the early 20th century, all piano factories *were allowed to* use ivory for the production of keys.
6. I expect to *be allowed to* choose my research team myself.
7. It's the New Year's Eve today. The children *are allowed to* stay up till midnight.
8. I am sure everybody would like to *be allowed to* comment on the issue. But we have to reach a hasty decision. No time for hair splitting, gentlemen.

191. ☺☺☺ Zdecyduj, które wyrażenia są poprawne.

1. I am the owner of this lake. You *may/might* fish here as long as you don't use fishing nets or dynamite.

2. 'May I use your computer while you're away?' 'No, I'm afraid you *mayn't/may not*.'

3. 'Might I have a brief look at this document?' 'Yes, of course you *may/might*. Be careful, though. It's very old.'

4. I'm a special correspondent for the 'Warsaw News' daily. *May/Might* I ask you a few general questions?

5. 'Could I possibly borrow your hairdryer?' 'Yes, of course you *might/may*.'

6. In the past, women *might not/were not allowed to* study at universities.

7. A police officer *is allowed to/may* stop any person he suspects with reasonable cause of committing an offence.

8. These days, women *are allowed to/may* walk into a Catholic church bareheaded.

9. I was wondering if I *may/might* take another one of those delicious croissants...

10. I can't believe it! *Are we really allowed to/May we really* use the office phone for private conversation?

CAN/COULD VERSUS MAY/MIGHT

192. ☺ Przeczytaj opis sytuacji. Zastanów się, jakie pozwolenie stanowiłoby dla osoby A wybawienie z kłopotu. Wyraź je za pomocą czasownika *can*.

Wzór: A: I can't find any parking place! I'll be late for the meeting!
        B: Don't worry. *You can park in my garden.*

1. A: Does the library really close at 5 pm? What a pity! I haven't finished the book yet.
   B: Don't worry! _____

2. A: Oh no! My laptop keeps breaking down and I need it for the presentation!
   B: _____ I don't need it today.

3. A: Alice is not feeling well. Does she have to go to uncle Ben's birthday party?
   B: Of course not! _____

4. A: I must get in touch with my lawyer. It's urgent!
   B: Well, why don't you ring him? _____

5. A: Where have you bought this book? My daughter wanted to read it and I can't find it in the bookshops.
   B: _____ I have already read it twice.

6. A: Our neighbours are renovating their flat. I can't study to my final exams because of the noise!
   B: You absolutely need peace and quiet. _____

7. A (student): Sam Johnson is in New Zealand. He won't be here for the exam in June.
   B (teacher): Let me see... Well, _____

193. ☺☺ Wybierz właściwy czasownik. Użyj formy *may* wszędzie tam, gdzie pozwolenie wychodzi bezpośrednio od osoby mówiącej.

I met a curious man the other day. He was putting up a shabby tent on my beautiful lawn. 'You (1) *can/may/could* not camp here, sir,' I said politely. 'Oh, come on! Every citizen (2) *might not/could/can* use public spaces,' was his insolent reply. 'I'm sure everybody (3) *does/can/might*,' I admitted, 'but this is not public space. This is my own private lawn. You (4) *may/can/might* surely use the park lawn over there.' 'That's where the problem lies,' he continued, 'The park guard told me that I (5) *can't/couldn't/mightn't*.' I finally lost my temper. 'Oh, and that's why you came here, isn't it? Well, keep off my grass, (6) *will/can/ may* you?!' 'Are you aware of the fact that an insulted person (7) *may/can/might* sue the insulting party?' He talked like a lawyer! But I didn't give in. 'You (8) *may/can/might* sue me if you so wish,' I answered, 'I'm afraid you'll lose.' He must have reached the same conclusion for he took his tent down and walked away.

194. ☺☺☺ Wstaw *can* w odpowiedniej formie tam, gdzie jest to możliwe.

1. Excuse me! I'm afraid you *are not allowed to* eat or drink in the library.
2. I expect to *be allowed to* see my son!
3. Sheila's father said she *was allowed to* use the family car for our trip to Spain.
4. I'm sorry, sir. This is private area. You need my uncle's permission to *be allowed to* park here.
5. Let us forget the past! Young generations should *not be allowed to* take revenge for their parents' mistakes.
6. We wanted to eat at this fancy new restaurant but we *weren't allowed to* take our dog inside. So we chose the takeaway.
7. *Being allowed to* manifest your religious convictions is a basic right of free people.

COULD/WAS ALLOWED TO

195. ☺ Wstaw *was/were allowed to, could* lub *couldn't*. W niektórych punktach poprawne są dwie odpowiedzi.

1. I remember that wonderful day when I _____ cross the American border.
2. I was extremely naughty that day and so I _____ play with the other children.
3. The Sundays were free, so we _____ visit Aunt Agatha every weekend.
4. Sue had an Euro<26 card with her so she _____ enter the club for half price.
5. When the temperature fell below –25 degrees, the school children _____ _____ stay inside the building during the break.
6. The prices were always cheaper on the market so we _____ buy some sweets with our pocket money.
7. The pilot was my mother's old school friend so I _____ come to the cockpit.

196. ☺☺ Wybierz właściwą formę. W niektórych punktach poprawne są dwie odpowiedzi.

1. The road was blocked. Only the police _____ pass.
   a) could   b) was allowed to   c) were allowed to
2. You are kidding! You _____ enter because of your shoes?! Were you wearing rubbers or what?
   a) weren't allowed to   b) couldn't   c) can't
3. Thank you, Jeeves. You _____ leave when you have dusted the drawing room.
   a) might   b) may   c) could

4. There were times when the skins of rare animals _____ be traded without permission.
   a) might   b) were allowed to   c) could
5. When Mary turned 18, she _____ see her real parents.
   a) could   b) was allowed to   c) must
6. The Moscow-bound plane _____ land on the Frankfurt airport, owing to repeated turbulences.
   a) could   b) had to   c) was allowed to
7. _____ open the window? It's so awfully hot in here.
   a) Could I   b) Am I allowed to   c) Will

197. ☺☺☺ Wstaw do tekstu *was/were allowed to, could* lub *couldn't*.

We got on board the *Moonranger* at the crack of dawn. As usual, I brought a largish suitcase with me. This time, however, the crew (1) _____ take one spare spacesuit each. Of course, hunting spacecrafts (2) _____ carry too much weight – they had to be light and speedy. But this strict regulation came as a surprise. Even the captain himself (3) _____ take only one small suitcase! And we all knew that, according to Space Mission Regulations, captains (4) _____ have quite a lot of luggage. We could feel the tension growing.
Before leaving the Earth orbit we had our IDs checked. Everybody was on board legally and so we (5) _____ pass. It was a high priority mission. A group of tourists, who according to the Moon Act (6) _____ stay on the Moon for more than three months, had decided not to leave. They had threatened the authorities with violence. We had been sent to remove them.

REQUESTS FOR PERMISSION

198. ☺ Wybierz właściwą formę.

1. A: Barbara, could I borrow your pencil?
   B: Yes, of course you _____.
   a) might   b) can   c) shall
2. A: May I open the window? It's so stuffy in here.
   B: I'm _____ you may not. The paintings need a stable temperature.
   a) afraid   b) certain   c) sorry
3. Mum, _____ I turn on the TV? The Muppet Show is on right now.
   a) might   b) could   c) must
4. A: Dad, _____ I water the plants myself?
   a) can   b) might   c) shall
   B: Of _____ you can! But be careful with the cacti.
   a) pleasure   b) sure   c) course
5. A: Could I open an account at your bank?
   B: You _____ provided you are of age.
   a) could   b) might   c) can

6. A: Could I sit down for a minute?

   B: _____. There's a comfortable armchair in the corner.

   a) For certain   b) Certainly   c) With pleasure

7. _____ I ask a question, Your Honour?

   a) Will   b) Can   c) May

199. ☺☺ Wybierz odpowiedni czasownik. W niektórych punktach dwie z podanych odpowiedzi mogą być poprawne.

Son: Mum, (1. can, might, could) _____ I go for a ride on my new bike?

Mother: Of course you (2. might, can, could) _____, darling. Why do you ask? It's your birthday present, isn't it?

S: Oh, gosh, look, it's raining...

M: In that case you certainly (3. can't, may not, mightn't) _____. You might catch a cold.

S: But Mum! (4. couldn't, mightn't) _____ I just go twice round the house? Please?

M: I said no and I mean no.

Mother: (5. may, can't, might) _____ I ask you to eat up your dinner, young lady?

Daughter: (6. can, could) _____ I have a piece of my birthday cake afterwards?

M: Yes, you (7. may, might, can) _____. As long as there's anything left of it.

200. ☺☺ Wybierz odpowiedni czasownik. W niektórych punktach dwie z podanych odpowiedzi mogą być poprawne.

Employee: I wondered if I (1. can, might, could) _____ print out one page on your printer.

Manager: Yes, you (2. might, can, may) _____.

E: (3. Can I, Might I, Am I allowed to) _____ check my mail on your PC today? I've had some problems with my internet connection.

M: I'm afraid you (4. might not, can't, aren't) _____. There is some confidential data you could accidentally access.

E: Just one other question, if you please. Where should I store my old files and papers?

M: You (5. could, can, might) _____ keep them in the basement.

E: (6. may, might, could) _____ I possibly use the store room? That would spare me climbing the stairs...

M: Can't you see the sign on the door? It says: 'Senior staff only'. (7. May, Are you allowed to, Could) _____ enter it, then?

E: I suppose not. But (8. mightn't, couldn't, mayn't) _____ I just store them there while I'm moving to the other room?

M: No. Definitely not.

D. EXPRESSING POSSIBILITY

MAY/MIGHT/COULD – PRESENT TENSES

201. ☺ Wstaw *maybe, may be, maybe not, may not be.*

1. Michel Owen _____ the greatest football player in the history. I'm *quite* sure he is.
2. 'Don't you know radishes are good for you?'
   '_____ they are, but I hate their taste'.
   'Well, I agree they _____ especially tasty, but you should eat them for the vitamins anyway.'
3. There _____ another planet in the universe with an advanced civilization. Scientists think it's probable.
4. 'Do you think Fellini's film deserved such praise?'
   '_____, but there were no better films at the festival.'
5. The numerous accounts about UFO _____ true. However, some scientific evidence proves that UFO really exist.
6. Sue is absent today. She _____ ill.

202. ☺☺ Które z poniższych zdań wyrażają możliwość?

1. *May* the Force *be* with you!
2. Only a few minutes have passed since the robbery. The thieves *couldn't* be far away.
3. This *might be* our last meeting in Warsaw. I am moving to Bandar Seri Begawan.
4. You *could* at least *have asked* before you borrowed my phone.
5. Dogs *may not* be unleashed or un-muzzled in the park.
6. We *may not* go to Egypt after all. It seems to be fairly dangerous there after recent terrorist attacks.
7. In the past, more women *could knit*, crochet and embroider. They were more feminine.
8. Students *may consult* their notes but they are not supposed to communicate.
9. It's no use waiting for the drummer. We *might as well start* practising without him.
10. Beware! Any sudden movement *might be* your last!

203. ☺☺☺ Sparafrazuj podane zdania, używając *may, might* lub *could* oraz *may not, might not* lub *could not*. Zwróć uwagę na stopień prawdopodobieństwa wyrażony procentowo.
„/" oznacza, że możliwa jest więcej niż jedna poprawna odpowiedź.

1. It is possible (50%) that global warming is the result of the greenhouse effect.
   Global warming _____.
2. The Prime Minister admitted that it was possible (50%) that he would resign.
   The Prime Minister _____.
3. It is just possible (30%) that the weather will be nice tomorrow. But I doubt it.
   The weather _____.
4. Is it possible that our train is already standing at the platform?
   _____/_____?

5. Perhaps (30%) our course in philosophy will not be so boring after all.
   Our course in philosophy _____.
6. If you talked to him, perhaps (50%) he would change his mind.
   If you talked to him, _____/_____.
7. It is impossible that he will lie to her.
   He_____.
8. It is possible (50%) that our company will not profit from the transaction.
   Our company _____/_____.

MAY/MIGHT/COULD – PERFECT TENSES

204. ☺ Ułóż zdania z podanych wyrazów (a–h); dobierz odpowiedzi do poniższych pytań.

   a [suspense, might, they, the, enjoy]
   b [more, business, might, he, have, important, had]
   c [nervous, it, be, a, might, reaction]
   d [neighbour, our, have, moving, might, cupboards, been]
   e [a, they, have, might, had, falling-out]
   f [might, found, peaceful, location, they, have, more, a]
   g [be, she, might, the, beach, on, lying]
   h [looking, bargains, they, be, for, might]

   1. A: I wonder why Peter talks so much.
      B: _____
   2. A: I wonder why Sue was absent at Karen's party.
      B: _____
   3. A: I wonder why the president cancelled his visit to Vienna.
      B: _____
   4. A: I wonder what made them move house.
      B: _____
   5. A: I wonder why so many people spend so much time in the shops.
      B: _____
   6. A: I wonder why people watch thrillers.
      B: _____
   7. A: I wonder what Sue is doing now.
      B: _____
   8. A: What was the terrible noise last night?
      B: _____

205. ☺☺ Zdecyduj, które z podanych zdań jest poprawną parafrazą zdania podkreślonego.

   1. Jack: It is possible that J. S. Bach wrote many of the works attributed to his sons.
      a) J.S. Bach may've written many of the works that are attributed to his sons.
      b) J.S. Bach may have written many of the works that are attributed to his sons.
   2. Mary: Perhaps plagiarism wasn't censured then as much as it is today.
      a) Plagiarism may not have been as censured then as it is today.
      b) Plagiarism must have been censured then as much as it is today.

3. Jack: <u>It is also possible that he wanted his sons to make a decent career.</u>
   a) He can also have wanted his sons to make a decent career.
   b) He may also have wanted his sons to make a decent career.
4. Mary: <u>It is impossible that he deliberately wrote the pieces for them!</u> He had too much work himself to do *that*.
   a) He can't have written the pieces for them!
   b) He might not have written the pieces for them!
5. Jack: <u>Well, if he was so busy, perhaps he didn't notice that one or two preludes were missing.</u>
   a) He may not have noticed that one or two preludes were missing.
   b) He may have not noticed that one or two preludes were missing.
6. Mary: <u>It is possible that he didn't care.</u>
   a) It could have been all the same to him.
   b) It might not have been all the same to him.

206. ☺☺☺ Podkreśl właściwy czasownik.

1. It was a brilliant performance! She *might not/couldn't have* been more enchanting.
2. Many renowned scientists insisted that an enormous meteor hitting the Earth *may have/might have* caused the latest Ice Age.
3. You're kidding! Sue *may/can* hardly *have* gone to a Holy Mass. She is a declared atheist.
4. Andy *might not have/could not have* read that book, but you can't be sure. You'd better buy him some sweets for birthday.
5. Why did you drive so fast? You *may have/might have* caused an even greater accident!

207. ☺☺☺ Podkreśl właściwy czasownik.

A: I think the party was a great success! Do you think we (1) *can have/might have* done anything to make it even better?
B: Well, actually, I keep wondering why you took the wine away. You (2) *could have/may have* let it stand on the table for the whole night. The guests (3) *might not have/may have* been thirsty.
A: They (4) *could have/may have* told us if they were.
B: How (5) *could/might* they *have* known that you had ten bottles in the kitchen? Thank God you let the food stay. Otherwise the party (6) *may have/could have* turned out a disaster.

CAN

208. ☺ Zakreśl właściwy czasownik.

1. The road <u>might/can</u> be very slippery today. Be careful!
2. <u>Can/Might</u> ice contain salt?
3. Polish roads <u>can/may</u> be extremely dangerous.
4. Our lakes are full of fish. You <u>might/can</u> fish from dawn till dusk.
5. Beethoven <u>might/could</u> be very unsociable at times.
6. The exam <u>can/might</u> prove too difficult. We'll see when the results are out.
7. Take lots of warm clothes with you. Lapland <u>may/can</u> be very cold in winter.
8. They say this winter <u>could/can</u> be unusually mild.

209. ☺☺ Sparafrazuj pokreślone zdania, używając czasowników *can, could, couldn't (have)* lub *might not (have)*.

1. Sylvia was emotionally unstable in her teens. <u>It was possible for her to have a fit of the giggles without any reason at all.</u>
   She _____
2. <u>It is not possible that Laura and Phil moved to the city.</u> They are both great nature-lovers!
   Laura and Phil _____
3. <u>In winter, it sometimes happens that the whole Bay of Bothnia is covered by ice.</u>
   In winter, _____
4. <u>It is possible that Barbara does not have much teaching experience.</u> But she loves children and has the right touch with them.
   Barbara _____
5. <u>Perhaps Tom didn't notice the red light.</u> He always pays great attention to traffic regulations.
   Tom _____
6. <u>It is certainly possible for us to ski today.</u> It was snowing all night.
   We _____
7. <u>Sue might still be waiting on the platform.</u> We told her somebody would pick her from the station.
   Sue _____
8. <u>I suppose the new Douglas film won't be as boring as the last one.</u>
   The new _____
9. <u>Children are sometimes noisy.</u> But they must always be loved.
   Children _____

210. ☺☺☺ Połącz zdania z opisem funkcji, jaką pełni czasownik *can/could*.

a) Sharks *can* swim.
b) Water *can* freeze.
c) Children up to the age of 8 *can* take part in the competition.
d) *Could* Tyrannosaurus be 15 m long?
e) Your toy dinosaur *could* be in the laundry basket.
f) *Could* he be waiting for us outside the station?
g) *Could* I meet you at the platform?
h) Forget his stupid remark. He *could* have been tired.
i) When he worked in the bank, Andy *could* be very tired in the evening.

1. pytanie o możliwość w teraźniejszości
2. pozwolenie
3. umiejętność
4. stan, który zdarzał się w przeszłości
5. prośba o pozwolenie
6. pytanie o możliwość w przeszłości
7. teoretyczna możliwość
8. przypuszczenie o teraźniejszości
9. przypuszczenie o przeszłości

E. EXPRESSING DEDUCTION AND ASSUMPTION

MUST/CAN'T/COULDN'T

211. ☺ Wstaw *must* lub *can't*.

1. His accent is so strange. He _____ be a native speaker of English.
2. They didn't award the Nobel Prize for Peace? You _____ be serious!
3. The government's ratings have fallen sharply. The Prime Minister _____ be under a lot of pressure these days.
4. What? Nicole Kidman is going to re-marry Tom Cruise? You've got to be kidding. This simply _____ be true.
5. This _____ be the biggest stamp collection in the world!
6. I'm so sleepy. The air pressure _____ be terribly low.
7. Please, do change the channel. This _____ be the only interesting programme on TV tonight.
8. Well, if Aunt Agatha says that, it _____ be true. She never lies.
9. Oh, come on! It's Sunday afternoon. He _____ be at work now.

212. ☺☺ Zakreśl właściwy czasownik.

A: Look at the photograph. What can you see?
B: I can see an audience in a theatre. They are standing and clapping their hands. The performance (1.) *must have/can't have* finished a minute ago. The people in the stalls are smiling at the actors. They (2.) *must/can* be good actors, since they are getting a standing ovation. There are some children in the circle, who are already leaving. They (3.) *can't/must* be great fans of drama. They (4.) *must have/might have* been forced by a teacher to come to the theatre.
A: How do you think the actors are feeling?
B: Well, I guess they (5.) *can't/must* be tired. It (6.) *can't have/may have* been an easy task to learn their roles. But they look happy and relieved. They (7.) *must/can* be delighted by the response of the audience.
A: What kind of play do you think it was?
B: It (8.) *can't have/might have* been Shakespeare. The costumes are too modern. It (9.) *can have/might have* been a contemporary comedy. Or, perhaps, an adaptation of Shakespeare. I've heard classics (10.) *can/must* be good material for adaptation.

213. ☺☺ Do poniższych zdań wstaw *must*, *can't* lub *couldn't* oraz odpowiednią formę czasownika podanego w nawiasie.

1. This opera (write) _____ by Brahms. He never wrote any operas!
2. Andy has got a black eye. He (have) _____ a fight yesterday.

3. Jose (read) _____ *Quo Vadis* in the original two years ago. He only started learning Polish then.
4. Dig in! You haven't eaten for ten hours. You (be) _____ starving!
5. Listen to the music! This (be) _____ the rumba. It's way too fast.
6. Look at this fancy BMW! It (be) _____ the model James Bond is driving.
7. I can't find the keys in the drawer. You (put) _____ them somewhere else.
8. *Bitwa pod Grunwaldem* is a huge painting. It (take) _____ Matejko a lot of time to paint.
9. The attorney claimed that his client (be) _____ on the scene of the crime when the policeman was shot. He was at his country house at that time.

MUST/MAY/MIGHT

214. ☺ Wybierz właściwy czasownik modalny.

1. Anne *must/might* be Laura's twin sister. She looks her double.
2. You *can't/must* be hungry already! I gave you a double helping of potatoes for dinner.
3. A: Who could have stolen my necklace?
   B: It *might/must* have been anyone who entered the empty drawing room.
4. John *must/might* be a wonderful husband! He is so considerate and caring.
5. I'm afraid you've got pneumonia. It *might/must* be a result of your last bronchitis. But the X-ray may show another cause.
6. She *might/must* not drink milk! She is allergic to it.
7. You have read *War and Peace* in two days? This *can't/might not* be true!
8. All of a sudden the car started skidding. The road *must/might* have been covered with black ice. I can't see any other reason.
9. A: Try doing some exercise. It *may/must* help you concentrate better on your work.
   B: You *must/may* be joking! You know me! Exercise only makes me more distracted.

215. ☺☺ Wybierz właściwą odpowiedź.

Mark: You are an ardent fan of the Polish football team. Surely you (1.)_____ the match between Poland and Ecuador last night...
a) must have watched   b) may have watched
Janek: I stopped being their fan long ago. But I (2.)_____ the match. My father said it was my duty as a Pole.
a) must have watched   b) had to watch
Mark: It's a pity Poland lost. You (3.)_____ be disappointed.
a) may   b) must
Janek: I'm not at all surprised. But my neighbours seem down in the dumps. They (4.)_____ a better result.
a) might have expected   b) can have expected
Mark: What did your father say? He (5.)_____ very pleased.
a) can't have been   b) must have been
Janek: He said they (6.)_____ too little time training...
a) might have spent   b) may have spent

Janek: ...So I (7.)_____ to skip the last quarter.
a) could   b) was allowed to
Mark: What (8.)_____ the reason of their defeat, do you think?
a) can have been   b) may have been
Janek: Lack of practice. It (9.)_____ anything else.
a) can't have been   b) must not have been
Mark: What (10.)_____ happen next, do you think?
a) will   b) must
Janek: Obviously, they'll lose with Germany. After what happened, every Polish fan
(11.)_____ be aware of that.
a) might   b) must

216. ☺☺☺ Zakreśl właściwy czasownik.

1. The elderly lady next door *might/must/can* be very lonely. Nobody ever visits her.
2. A: A guy I've never seen before picked up Susan from the party.
   B: But she doesn't have any boyfriend! It *can/might/must* have been her brother.
3. Tony is never late without a reason. Something important *must/can/might* have held him back.
4. I've no idea who told Alice about my birthday. It *might/may/can* have been Maria, but I'm sure she didn't know about it herself.
5. She simply *must/can't/might* have seen the Mona Lisa in the Musee D'Orsay. It's on show in the Louvre.
6. How should I know who played in the latest Bond production? It *mustn't/might/can't* have been Connery, he's way too old.
7. What *might/must* have made him to write so desperate a letter? He *could/might/must* really be in need of our help.
8. Your weakness *might/must* be caused by the medicine you've taken. If so, it will soon pass.

WILL/SHOULD

217. ☺ Połącz w pary podane zdania.

1. Somebody is at the door.
2. It's too late to phone.
3. Go to the tailor.
4. Let's go to the greengrocer's.
5. We might drop in now.
6. What was the use of taking them to court?
7. I will call my secretary.

a) A fresh supply of vegetables should be there already.
b) Maisie should be at home making dinner.
c) That'll be the postman.
d) He will remember all the important data.
e) They'll be celebrating now, laughing at our lawyer's mistakes.
f) Everybody will be asleep by now.
g) Your suit should be ready by now.

218. ☺☺ Zaznacz znakiem „+" te zdania, w których czasownik *should* wyrażający przypuszczenie może zastąpić czasownik *will*.

Wzór: They started their journey at 10 am. They will be approaching Warsaw now. [+]

1. Don't call Bill today. He'll be busy and irritated. He's preparing for tomorrow's job interview. [ ]
2. Turn on the TV. The President will have started his State of the Union address. [ ]
3. Ask your friends at school for help. They will have some notes from the classes. [ ]
4. Let's take another road to avoid the city centre. The demonstration will have reached the government buildings. There might be some blockades on the way. [ ]
5. We shouldn't call on them just now. It's six o'clock. They'll be having dinner. [ ]
6. This is the perfect time to go to the beach. It will be empty and quiet now. [ ]
7. I wouldn't buy *The Agony and the Ecstasy* for him if I were you. He will have read it. Stone is his favourite writer. [ ]
8. Give your parents a call. They'll be expecting some message from you. [ ]

219. ☺☺☺ Wybierz właściwy czasownik.

A: I phoned Helen yesterday. She has gone to Costa del Sol for her holiday. She (1) *will/can* be lying on the beach now, listening to the waves... After all the stress she had gone through at work it (2) *will/must* be like a dream!
B: I rather doubt it. People on the beach (3) *can/will* be noisy and irritating, and she has always hated noise. She (4) *won't/mustn't* have chosen Spain herself.
A: You (5) *should/may* be right. She (6) *should/might* have been persuaded by her family.
B: In that case she (7) *will/should* have had hard time trying to reject their arguments. She finally gave in. She always does.
A: Poor creature! Well, our Elizabeth (8) *should/could* be thankful she doesn't have a mother like that! *(doorbell ringing)* Oh, that (9) *should/could* be the postman! I'm expecting a postcard from Elizabeth. She went for three weeks to Costa Brava! She (10) *must/will* have written a sweet little postcard to her mummy! I paid for her trip, you see. It was a birthday present.
A: But it (11) *must/should* have cost you a fortune!
B: Of course it did. That's why I expect her to be especially grateful. Although, to be honest, she never liked sunbathing and sand, she preferred the mountains.

F. DARE

220. ☺☺ Uzupełnij poniższe zdania czasownikiem *dare* i jednym z czasowników podanych w ramce. Niekiedy czasownika *dare* należy użyć w formie przeczącej.

ask	question	approach	correct	go	come	persuade	disturb

1. The girl was standing outside the dentist's office, but she _____ inside.
2. The army successfully repelled any enemy who _____ their borders.
3. I was curious why the teacher had green hair but I _____.

4. The President announced that strict punishments will be administered to anyone who _____ public order.

5. Whenever my mom set her mind on something, not even our father _____ her plans.

6. The history professor had such a fearful reputation among his students that hardly anyone _____ to his lectures unprepared.

7. The Manager's report was full of spelling mistakes, but his typist _____ them.

8. When Henry VIII announced that he wanted to establish a new church, none of his officials _____ him to the contrary.

221. ☺☺ Utwórz pytania, zaczynając od *How dare...* i wykorzystując wyrazy podane poniżej.

1. to me, you, like that, talk   *How dare you talk to me like that?*

2. diary, my, read, you   _____

3. my, in front of, me, insult, boss, she   _____

4. interrupt, she, conversation, our   _____

5. you, your, me, invite, wedding, to   _____

6. my, go through, he, stuff   _____

7. a way, treat, such, me, in, he   _____

8. you are, me, dare, than, think, you, better   _____

9. these, tell, she, everybody, lies   _____

222. ☺☺ Połącz właściwe połówki zdań, uzupełniając je konstrukcją *would never dare*.

Wzór: *My best friend would never dare to come between my boyfriend and me.*

~~My best friend~~	do anything against my mother's will
Most scientists	challenge our company's market position
The government	disturb the Queen at night
My father	tell their boss what they really think about him
Our competitors	introduce a ban on the Internet
Most girls	~~come between my boyfriend and me~~
The servants	question this scientific theory
Most employees	try bungee-jumping

1. _____

2. _____

3. _____

4. _____

5. _____

6. _____

7. _____

G. USED TO/WOULD

223. ☺☺ Przekształć poniższe zdania, używając konstrukcji *used to* lub *would*.

Wzór: At college, I came late to school every single day.
At college, I would come late to school every single day.
I was once very shy, but my job has made me much more outspoken.
I used to be very shy, but my job has made me much more outspoken.

1. My sister was very spoilt as a child, but she has matured a lot since then.
   _____

2. As a young man, James often got into trouble with the police.
   _____

3. Hector believed earlier that there was no such thing as destiny, but now he has changed his mind.
   _____

4. University education was once a luxury that not everyone could afford, but the situation is different today.
   _____

5. In ancient times, warriors decorated their swords and shields with jewellery.
   _____

6. I have accidentally found out that Keith was once a professional gambler.
   _____

7. Keith's wife has told me that on some nights he earned up to ten thousand dollars!
   _____

8. Whenever the ice-cream man came to our village, all children ran outside and waved.
   _____

9. Rick didn't smoke as a student, but he has given in to the pressure of his smoking colleagues at work.
   _____

10. When Mary was at university, she didn't go out to clubs or discos. Now she has become a true clubber.
    _____

224. ☺☺ Próbujesz porozmawiać z nowo poznaną osobą o jej dzieciństwie. Utwórz pytania z *used to*, wykorzystując podane wyrazy.

1. play, school football team   *Did you use to play in the school football team?*
2. fan, 'Star Wars' series   _____
3. play, 'Hide and Seek', friends   _____
4. take, English lessons   _____
5. have, many, pets   _____
6. learn, play, instruments   _____
7. go, shopping, supermarket, parents   _____

225. ☺☺☺ Dokończ dowolnie poniższe zdania, używając konstrukcji z *used to* lub *would*.

1. When I was in primary school   _____
2. Twenty years ago   _____

3. When my family lived in the USA   _____

4. When there was still no underground in our town   _____

5. Before the Internet was invented   _____

6. When my brother and I were little   _____

USED TO, BE/GET USED TO

226. ☺☺ Uzupełnij poniższe wypowiedzi odpowiednimi formami konstrukcji *used to, be used to* lub *get used to.*

   I. At first I didn't like my new flat, because I (1) _____ living in a house. Now I have to (2) _____ the fact that there are people living below and above me. It's not that easy, especially that the house in Blackpool, where I (3) _____ grow up as a kid, was particularly large and had its own garden. However, it seems that I am gradually (4) _____ bumping into strange people outside my door or to the noise of the elevator at night. I've realized that it doesn't disturb me now as much as it (5) _____.

   II. The company where I (1) _____ work has a peculiar idea of company dress code. Our clothes had to be as colourful and bright as possible. It was quite a shock to me, because I (2) _____ wearing something rather traditional and smart. It took me quite a while before I (3) _____ my colleagues looking like some circus artists! And I think I never quite (4) _____ my own horrible outfits that I was told to wear. Come to think about it, it's no wonder my children (5) _____ refuse to walk to school with me.

227. ☺☺ Zdecyduj, która z wypowiedzi, A lub B, jest bliższa znaczeniu poniższych zdań.

  1. I don't mind getting up early.
    A. I used to get up early.
    B. I'm used to getting up early.

  2. I've grown attached to my students.
    A. I used to be really attached to my students.
    B. I've really got used to my students.

  3. I was once a very eager polo player.
    A. I used to be a very eager polo player.
    B. I'm used to being an eager polo player.

  4. I will never come to terms with this situation.
    A. I will never get used to this situation.
    B. I will never be used to this situation.

  5. She knows that she will always get exactly what she wants.
    A. She is used to getting exactly what she wants.
    B. She used to get exactly what she wants.

  6. You have to accept the fact that you are no longer the youngest in the family.
    A. You have to be used to the fact that you are no longer the youngest in the family.
    B. You have to get used to the fact that you are no longer the youngest in the family.

7. It's hard to believe that in the past people travelled only by foot or on horseback.

    A. It's hard to believe that people used to travel only by foot or on horseback.

    B. It's hard to believe that people are used to travelling only by foot or on horseback.

8. We've been trying to get accustomed to the new procedures.

    A. We used to try to get accustomed to the new procedures.

    B. We've been trying to get used to the new procedures.

228. ☺☺ Zmieniłeś/łaś pracę. Wykorzystaj podane wyrażenia, aby wymienić pięć rzeczy, do których jesteś przyzwyczajony/a i pięć, do których musisz się przyzwyczaić.

~~work in the city centre~~	~~work long hours~~	use foreign languages
go on business trips	have new duties	have a woman for my boss
write long reports	use a different IT system	coordinate a team of people
have free weekends	arrange meetings	meet a lot of foreigners

1. *I am used to working in the city centre.*

2. _____

3. _____

4. _____

5. _____

6. _____

1. *I have to get used to working long hours.*

2. _____

3. _____

4. _____

5. _____

6. _____

H. MODAL VERBS: FURTHER PRACTICE

229. ☺☺☺ Uzupełnij poniższe zdania, wybierając właściwy czasownik modalny: A, B lub C.

1. It was reckless of Fred to drive his friend's racing car. He _____ killed!

    A. could be   B. could have been   C. may be

2. I think we can safely go back home now. It's almost 10 pm and our parents' guests _____.

    A. should have already left   B. may have already left   C. must have already left

3. Try as I _____ , I can't get Barbara to tell me her secret.

    A. should   B. will   C. may

4. You _____ stop chewing gum when talking to your teacher! It's simply rude!

    A. might   B. ought to   C. can

5. Before we attend the contract negotiations tomorrow, we _____ find out as much as possible about the other party.

    A. can   B. need to   C. would

6. A typical TV series for teenagers today _____ with such problems as love, friendship, alcohol and drugs.

    A. dare deal   B. could have dealt   C. will deal

7. In his youth, he _____ almost every weekend on the beach.
   A. may spend   B. would have spent   C. would spend
8. Lucy's essay was so well-written that the teacher knew immediately she _____ it by herself.
   A. must have written   B. couldn't have written   C. shouldn't have written
9. Our dog is a lamb now, but in the past, when it still worked for the police, it _____ very aggressive.
   A. must be   B. could be   C. will have been
10. The book was so fascinating that I _____ if there are any more by the same author available.
    A. must see   B. have to see   C. ought to see

230. ☺☺☺ Zdecyduj, która wypowiedź, A czy B, odpowiada znaczeniu poniższych zdań.

1. It's impossible that Doris was at the party last night: I saw her at the cinema.
   A. Doris may not have been at the party last night.
   B. Doris could not have been at the party last night.
2. It's possible that the school will not agree to the rock concert.
   A. The school could not agree to the rock concert.
   B. The school may not agree to the rock concert.
3. It's likely that they already know the results of the contest.
   A. They should already know the results of the contest.
   B. They must already know the results of the contest.
4. I've been told that it's not necessary that you fill in the application now.
   A. You don't need to fill in the application now.
   B. You mustn't fill in the application now.
5. You don't need to type your essays for me, I will accept hand-written versions.
   A. You needn't type your essays for me.
   B. You mustn't type your essays for me.
6. It's certain that Joe knew about our plan: all evidence suggests that.
   A. Joe must have known about our plan.
   B. Joe should have known about our plan.
7. It's important that you don't tell anyone about that situation.
   A. You couldn't tell anyone about that situation.
   B. You mustn't tell anyone about that situation.
8. It's impossible that Jerry has been promoted Deputy-Director.
   A. Jerry may have not been promoted to Deputy-Director.
   B. Jerry can't have been promoted to Deputy-Director.

231. ☺☺☺ Uzupełnij poniższy tekst odpowiednimi czasownikami modalnymi.

Visiting the town of Visoko in central Bosnia for the first time (1) _____ be quite a shock to anyone who traditionally associates pyramids with Egypt. Once you enter the Visoko valley, you see an extraordinary triangular hill rising above the town looking just like an ancient pyramid. It's a sight that (2) _____ puzzle any archaeologist. No wonder that so many enthusiasts of ancient history have begun their private excavations on site, claiming that the huge pyramid (3) _____ have been built even some 12,000 years ago. They point to its geometric shape and a network of tunnels inside, which, they argue, (4) _____ be a work of human hands. According to the experts, however, no pyramid (5) _____ have been constructed in Visoko at that time, even if the hill (6) _____ resemble one. The tribes that (7) _____ inhabit the region then were not very advanced technologically and (8) _____ live in little earthen huts. These arguments have not convinced the crew of Bosnian Indiana Joneses, however. As excavation work progresses, we (9) _____ be able to learn more about the actual structure of the hill.

KLUCZ

162. 1. could – służy do opisania pewnych cech ogólnych, charakterystycznych dla danej osoby/danego przedmiotu w przeszłości. **2.** can – służy do opisania zdolności, umiejętności. **3.** can't – wyraża brak zdolności, możliwości. **4.** could – służy do opisania możliwości w przeszłości. **5.** could – typowa forma grzecznościowa. **6.** can/could – zarówno *can*, jak i *could* wyrażają pewną możliwość w przyszłości, przy czym *could* wyraża wątpliwość, czy dana czynność na pewno nastąpi. **7.** could – jak w pkt. 1. **8.** can – służy do opisania pewnych cech ogólnych, charakterystycznych w teraźniejszości. **9.** can't **10.** couldn't

163. 1. can also create **2.** could have offered – wyraża niewykorzystaną możliwość w przeszłości. **3.** could do – opisuje ogólne zdolności, umiejętności w przeszłości. **4.** could have bumped; couldn't you see **5.** can sometimes surprise **6.** could only marry – opisuje ogólnie pewną możliwość w przeszłości, nie konkretne zdarzenie. **7.** could have planned – wyraża niewykorzystaną możliwość w przeszłości. **8.** can be

164. 1. Gary could have helped us to fix the tap. **2.** The guard could have shown the visitors where the exit was. **3.** The host could have bought more food for the party. **4.** The governments could have done more to prevent the war. **5.** You could have warned me that the hotel manager was so short-tempered. **6.** The band could have played more songs from their last album during the concert. **7.** I could have put more effort into this essay.

165. 1. will be able to buy **2.** be able to fix **3.** have been able to make **4.** are able to register **5.** was able to return **6.** haven't been able to contact **7.** haven't been able to find **8.** will be able to prevent

166. Odpowiednia forma wyrażenia *be able* zastępuje *can* w miejscach, gdzie brakuje odpowiedniej formy gramatycznej tego czasownika.
1. will be able **2.** hasn't been able **3.** to be able **4.** be able **5.** be able **6.** won't be able **7.** has been able **8.** to be able

167. 1. were able – oznacza konkretne osiągnięcie i faktyczne wykonanie danej czynności. **2.** could – opisuje ogólnie pewną możliwość w przeszłości, nie konkretne zdarzenie. **3.** couldn't – z czasownikami wyrażającymi postrzeganie zmysłowe, np. see, hear, feel, należy używać *could*. **4.** can't – służy do opisania pewnych cech ogólnych, charakterystycznych dla danej osoby/danego przedmiotu w teraźniejszości. **5.** Were you able – pytanie o konkretne zdarzenie. **6.** could – opisuje ogólnie pewną cechę charakterystyczną w przeszłości, nie konkretne zdarzenie. **7.** was able – oznacza konkretne osiągnięcie i faktyczne wykonanie danej czynności. **8.** was able – jak w pkt. 7.

168. 1. have to – służy do opisania stałego obowiązku lub zwyczaju. **2.** must – wyraża wewnętrzną potrzebę. **3.** must – używany w oficjalnych regulaminach, przepisach itp. **4.** have to – mówca odnosi się do nakazu/obowiązku narzuconego z zewnątrz; *must* oznaczałoby, że się z danym nakazem utożsamia. **5.** must – jak w pkt. 2. **6.** has to – wyraża zewnętrzny nakaz lub konieczność. **7.** must – mówca utożsamia się z danym nakazem. **8.** must – mówca utożsamia się z daną koniecznością. **9.** must – jak w pkt. 3. **10.** must – jak w pkt. 7. **11.** had to – to forma przeszła używana zarówno dla *must*, jak i *have to*; will have to – używa się w sytuacjach, gdy pewna konieczność będzie zależna od innych okoliczności. **12.** must – wyrażenie.

169. *Have to* i *need to* mają zbliżone znaczenie, przy czym *have to* jest raczej wyrażeniem pewnego obowiązku lub nakazu, a *need to* – konieczności.
1. The City Mayor *will have to/need to* do something about the traffic in our town, if he wants to be re-elected! **2.** Every student of veterinary science who has completed his third year *has to* get four-week training at an animals' clinic. **3.** Do we *have to/need to* fill in the questionnaire in black ink? **4.** I never remember my dentist's surname, so whenever I call him I *have to/need to* look it up in my address book. **5.** If the revenues of the shop don't go up next year, it *will have to* close down. **6.** According to this agreement, the borrower *has to* repay the loan in regular instalments. **7.** The tourists have just missed the last train to Warsaw and *have to* stay at the railway station over the night. **8.** This course is designed to prepare you for your oral English exam and teach all the tricks that you *have to/need to* know.

170. 1. The TV set needs mending. **2.** The battery needs recharging. **3.** One of the car tyres needs refilling. **4.** The pencil needs sharpening. **5.** Flowers in your garden need watering. **6.** One of the issues in this report needs clarifying. **7.** The windows in the living-room need cleaning. **8.** My dancing shoes need polishing.

171. 1. You mustn't break it. **2.** You mustn't tell anyone. **3.** You mustn't turn them around yet. **4.** They mustn't enter the shop yet. **5.** She mustn't use that fragrance anymore. **6.** I mustn't drink so much coffee. **7.** We mustn't smoke here. **8.** We mustn't blame her for what has happened.

172. 1. doesn't have to – wyraża brak przymusu. **2.** don't need to – wyraża brak konieczności. **3.** mustn't – wyraża zakaz/opinię mówcy. **4.** mustn't – wyraża zakaz/opinię mówcy. **5.** don't need to – oznacza brak zewnętrznej konieczności i jednocześnie naganę wyrażoną przez mówcę. **6.** mustn't – wyraża zakaz/opinię mówcy. **7.** won't need to – wyraża brak konieczności w przyszłości. **8.** mustn't/doesn't need to – *mustn't* wyraża zakaz/opinię mówcy, podczas gdy *doesn't need to* jest ironiczne.

173. *Don't have to* i *don't need to* mają zbliżone znaczenie, przy czym *don't have to* jest raczej wyrażeniem braku obowiązku czy nakazu, a *don't need to* – braku konieczności.
1. You *don't have to* hand in your passport to the border guard; it's enough if he looks at it while you hold it. **2.** I *don't need to* take my ballet shoes to the shoemaker; my mom has already done it for me. **3.** Our parents *don't have to* give us pocket money, but it seems that they want to teach us some responsibility. **4.** It is a rule at our company that the employees who have worked 10 hours overtime in one week *don't have to* come to work on Fridays. **5.** Fortunately, I *don't need to* worry about my holidays this year, because my boss has already promised me 3 weeks in July. **6.** Since Ben had already done Latin in high-school, he *didn't have to* take a Latin course at college. **7.** We *don't need to* go to the tax office today, if we don't have all the papers ready yet. **8.** I advise all of you to do as much work on your project as possible now, so that you *won't have to/need to* work on it at the weekend.

174. 1. don't need to – wyraża ogólny brak konieczności/nakazu. **2.** needn't – wyraża zwolnienie kogoś z danego obowiązku przez mówcę. **3.** needn't – mówca utożsamia się z brakiem danej konieczności. **4.** don't need to – wyraża ogólny brak konieczności/obowiązku. **5.** needn't – jak w pkt. 2. **6.** don't need to – jak w pkt. 1. **7.** needn't – jak w pkt. 3. **8.** don't need to – jak w pkt. 1. **9.** needn't – mówca utożsamia się z danym zakazem. **10.** don't need to – jak w pkt. 1.

175. 1. I needn't have worried about the results of my exam. **2.** The girls needn't have taken playing cards with them on the school trip. **3.** Calvin needn't have hurried to make it for the bus. **4.** The guest needn't have shouted at the waitress. **5.** Agnes needn't have dressed up as a princess for the party. **6.** We needn't have booked the tickets for the concert in advance. **7.** The accused needn't have told the prosecutor about a silly event in the past. **8.** I needn't have taken the umbrella with me to the horse race. **9.** My mom needn't have prepared a three-course dinner for us.

176. 1 c) needn't return **2** b) won't need to resit **3** g) needn't have come **4** a) doesn't even need to know **5** d) didn't need to write **6** e) needn't have bought **7** f) needn't come

177. 1. are to report – konstrukcja 'to be to' oznacza obowiązek, ustalenie, zobowiązanie. **2.** was to be handed in – jak w pkt. 1. **3.** was to have started – konstrukcja 'was/were+perfect infinitive' oznacza, że pewne ustalenia dotyczące przeszłości zawiodły. **4.** was to have been – jak w pkt. 3. **5.** are to arrive – jak w pkt. 1. **6.** was to prepare – jak w pkt. 1. **7.** was to have begun – jak w pkt. 3. **8.** was to see – jak w pkt. 1.

178. 1 B   **2** C   **3** B   **4** B   **5** B   **6** A   **7** C   **8** C   **9** A   **10** C

179. 1 B   **2** B   **3** A   **4** A/B   **5** B   **6** C   **7** B   **8** A   **9** B   **10** C

180. 1. Right now the situation on the poultry market is rather shaky, but it should improve next year. **2.** Our project is running quite smoothly, so it should be ready by next week. **3.** Monica has taken extra lessons to prepare for her driving exam, so she shouldn't have any problems passing it. **4.** Because Tuesday is a holiday, the management should give us Monday off as well. **5.** After completing the course the participants should be able to operate the system. **6.** The controversial paper by Professor Johnson, to be read at the Annual Globalisation Conference, should stir a lot of discussion among conference participants. **7.** The results of the Miss World Contest should be announced any minute now.

181. 1. Norbert should/ought to apologise to Betty's sister. **2.** My children should/ought to eat more fruit and vegetables. **3.** We should/ought to take our car to a garage. **4.** I should/ought to spend more time with our family. **5.** Sandra should/ought to go to the hairdresser's. **6.** The school should/ought to co-finance the school trip to Egypt. **7.** Grandpa should/ought to see a doctor.

182. 1. I'd better keep quiet about it. **2.** You'd better ask your boss's permission first. **3.** We'd better ask a real estate agent for help. **4.** He'd better be here on time. **5.** She'd better start looking for new accommodation. **6.** We'd better call the police. **7.** I'd better look it up in a dictionary before printing my essay.

183. 1. The protesters request that the City Council should donate more money to charity. **2.** The protesters order that the City Council should take care of public parks. **3.** The protesters insist that the City Council should organize open-air fairs and festivals in the summer. **4.** The protesters stipulate that the City Council should build an open-air ice-skating rink. **5.** The protesters demand that the City Council should invite famous people to hold lectures at the City Hall. **6.** The protesters request that the City Council should solve the problem of people being mugged in the streets. **7.** The protesters insist that the City Council should introduce stricter controls of public expenditure. **8.** The protesters postulate that the City Council should take steps towards reducing air pollution in the city centre.

184. 1. should want **2.** should spend **3.** should get **4.** should eliminate **5.** should have volunteered **6.** should suddenly become **7.** should gain **8.** should sign

185. 1. David took his CV to the job interview in case someone should want to see it. **2.** You must not report the accident to the Management unless you should be absolutely certain who is responsible. **3.** We must work harder so that we should be able to achieve better results next year. **4.** The speaker had some official statistics to support his argument in case somebody should doubt his conclusions. **5.** Please ensure that all exits are properly secured so that we should be certain that no one enters or leaves the building during the ceremony. **6.** You are not to tell the rest of the team about our plan lest they should try to stop us.

186. 1. I will put you through to the manager, because the meeting should have finished by now. **2.** It's nearly July, so most people should have already booked their holidays. **3.** The wedding is just days away, so the bride and the groom should have sent off all the invitations by now. **4.** Don't worry, public transport in Poland is very reliable, so your parents should have made it to the airport on time. **5.** I've heard that the theatre wasn't very full last night, so Stacy should have been able to get some last-minute tickets for the show. **6.** They both worked in a casino, so they should have earned a lot of money. **7.** They are closing down, so they should have put most of their goods up for sale.

187. 1. should have told **2.** should have studied **3.** should have thought **4.** should have never happened **5.** should have never trusted **6.** should have reacted **7.** should have booked **8.** should have taken

188. 1. Somebody should have brought some music equipment. **2.** I should have eaten something before going to the theatre. **3.** The waitress should have been more careful carrying the tray. **4.** The patient should have been given the right/a different medicine. **5.** The builder should have remembered/shouldn't have forgotten to hand over the keys. **6.** She should have tried them on in the shop. **7.** Mike shouldn't have lent his car to his son. **8.** The school board should have planned the end-of-year party better.

189. 1. Visitors may not feed the porcupine
    2. May I speak to the ZOO manager
    3. Of course you may
    4. May I share my biscuit with him
    5. I'm afraid you may not
    6. you may offer one to
    7. Is he allowed to eat biscuits

190. 1. may **2.** – (nie łączymy dwóch czasowników modalnych) **3.** – (czasowniki modalne nie posiadają formy ciągłej -ing) **4.** might (forma *may* byłaby niepoprawna, ponieważ mamy tu do czynienia z mową zależną) **5.** – (o pozwoleniu w przeszłości mówimy, używając *could* lub *be allowed to*; obie te formy są możliwe w podanym zdaniu) **6.** – (czasowniki modalne nie łączą się z przyimkiem *to*, forma *to may* jest niepoprawna!) **7.** may **8.** – (patrz pkt. 6)

191. 1. may (*might* nie używamy przy udzielaniu pozwolenia) **2.** may not (teoretycznie możliwa, forma skrócona nie jest stosowana) **3.** may (patrz pkt. 1) **4.** may/might **5.** may (możliwe nawet wtedy, gdy prośba o pozwolenie została wyrażona za pomocą czasownika *could*) **6.** were not allowed to (*might* dotyczy teraźniejszości lub przyszłości) **7.** may (dotyczy zasad prawnych lub reguł gry dających komuś prawo/władzę robienia czegoś) **8.** are allowed to (mowa o ogólnym przyzwoleniu, które nie wymaga już konkretnego pozwolenia) **9.** might **10.** Are we really allowed to (patrz pkt. 8)

192. 1. You can take the book home for the weekend.
2. You can borrow mine.
3. She can stay at home./She can go to bed immediately.
4. You can use my phone./You can use my phone card.
5. You can give it to her.
6. You can stay at our place./You can come and study at our place.
7. he can take the exam later.

193. 1. may **2.** can **3.** can **4.** can **5.** couldn't (mowa zależna) **6.** will you (*question tag* dla formy rozkazującej, patrz 91.10) **7.** may (zasady prawne dające prawo/władzę do konkretnych prawnych posunięć) **8.** may

194. 1. cannot **2.** – (czasowniki modalne nie łączą się z przyimkiem *to*) **3.** could (forma *can* byłaby niepoprawna, ponieważ mamy tu do czynienia z mową zależną) **4.** – **5.** – (nie łączymy dwóch czasowników modalnych) **6.** couldn't **7.** – (czasowniki modalne nie posiadają formy ciągłej)

195. 1. was allowed to **2.** couldn't/wasn't allowed to **3.** could **4.** was allowed to **5.** could/were allowed to **6.** could **7.** was allowed to

196. 1. a/c (rzeczownik *police* wymaga czasownika w liczbie mnogiej) **2.** a/b **3.** b **4.** c **5.** b **6.** b/c **7.** a

197. 1. were allowed to **2.** couldn't **3.** was allowed to **4.** could (ogólne przyzwolenie, które zostało udzielone w przeszłości) **5.** were allowed to **6.** couldn't

198. 1. b **2.** a **3.** b (*might* zbyt formalne) **4.** a, c **5.** c **6.** b **7.** c

199. 1. can/could **2.** can **3.** can't (*may not* jest dopuszczalne, ale mało naturalne) **4.** couldn't (forma przecząca *can* lub *could* podkreśla chęć uzyskania pozytywnej odpowiedzi) **5.** may/might **6.** can/could **7.** can/may

200. 1. might/could (*can* zbyt nieformalne, zwłaszcza w połączeniu z *I wondered*)
2. may/can (ani *could*, ani *might* nie używamy w twierdzących zdaniach wyrażających pozwolenie)
3. Can I/Might I (*Am I allowed to* byłoby pytaniem o ogólne pozwolenie, a tu chodzi o konkretną sytuację)
4. can't
5. can (patrz pkt. 2)
6. could (połączenie *can/could I possibly* to forma uprzejmej prośby o pozwolenie)
7. Are you allowed to (patrz pkt. 3)
8. couldn't (sugeruje chęć uzyskania pozytywnej odpowiedzi)

201. 1. may be **2.** maybe; may not be **3.** may be **4.** maybe not **5.** may not be **6.** may be

202. Możliwość wyrażają zdania nr 3, 6 (jest to możliwość negatywna) oraz 10.

203. 1. Global warming may be the result of the greenhouse effect.
2. The Prime Minister admitted that he might resign.
3. The weather might be nice tomorrow.
4. Might/Could our train already be standing at the platform? (*may* nie używamy na początku pytania o stopień prawdopodobieństwa)
5. Our course in philosophy might not be so boring after all.
6. If you talked to him, he might/could change his mind.
7. He couldn't lie to her.
8. Our company may/might not profit from the transaction.

204. 1. c: It might be a nervous reaction. **2.** e: They might have had a falling-out. **3.** b: He might have had more important business. **4.** f: They might have found a more peaceful location. **5.** h: They might be looking for bargains. **6.** a: They might enjoy the suspense. **7.** g: She might be lying on the beach. **8.** d: Our neighbour might have been moving cupboards.

205. 1. b (forma skrócona *may've* jest niepoprawna **2.** a **3.** b **4.** a (*can't have* wyraża brak możliwości lub umiejętności) **5.** a (*not* musi stać bezpośrednio po czasowniku modalnym) **6.** a

206. 1. couldn't have **2.** might have **3.** can have gone **4.** might not have **5.** might have (dla rzeczy, które mogły się zdarzyć, ale się nie zdarzyły)

207. 1. might have (*can have done sth* jest formą niepoprawną) **2.** could have **3.** may have **4.** could have **5.** could they have **6.** could have (trzeci tryb warunkowy, patrz ćw. nr 255–257)

208. 1. might (przypuszczenie dotyczące konkretnej sytuacji w teraźniejszości lub przyszłości) **2.** Can (mowa o teoretycznej możliwości) **3.** can (mowa o teoretycznej możliwości) **4.** can (mowa o teoretycznej możliwości) **5.** could (mowa o typowym zachowaniu) **6.** might (przypuszczenie dotyczące konkretnej sytuacji w teraźniejszości lub przyszłości) **7.** can (mowa o teoretycznej możliwości) **8.** could (wyraża możliwość w przyszłości)

209. 1. could have a fit of the giggles without any reason at all. **2.** couldn't have moved to the city. **3.** the whole Bay of Bothnia can be covered by ice. **4.** might not have much teaching experience. **5.** might not have noticed the red light. **6.** can surely ski today. **7.** could still be waiting on the platform. **8.** might not be as boring as the last one. **9.** can be noisy.

210. a 3 b 7 c 2 d 6 e 8 f 1 g 5 h 9 i 4

211. 1. can't **2.** can't **3.** must **4.** can't **5.** must **6.** must **7.** can't **8.** must **9.** can't

212. 1. must have **2.** must **3.** can't **4.** must have **5.** must **6.** can't have **7.** must **8.** can't have **9.** might have **10.** can (możliwość teoretyczna)

213. 1. can't/couldn't have been written **2.** must have had **3.** can't/couldn't have read **4.** must be **5.** can't be **6.** must be **7.** must have put **8.** must have taken **9.** couldn't have been (*can't* niemożliwe ze względu na mowę zależną, patrz ćw. nr 273–275)

214. 1. must **2.** can't **3.** might **4.** must **5.** might **6.** must (*must not* znaczy *nie wolno*) **7.** can't **8.** must **9.** may (możliwość); must

215. 1. a **2.** b **3.** b **4.** a **5.** a **6.** a **7.** b **8.** b **9.** a **10.** a **11.** b

216. 1. must **2.** might **3.** must **4.** might **5.** can't **6.** can't **7.** might; must **8.** might

217. 1. c **2.** f **3.** g **4.** a **5.** b **6.** e **7.** d

218. 1. [–] **2.** [+] **3.** [+] **4.** [–] **5.** [–] **6.** [+] **7.** [–] **8.** [+]

219. 1. will **2.** must **3.** can **4.** won't **5.** may **6.** might **7.** will **8.** should **9.** should **10.** will **11.** must

220. Czasownik *dare* może się zachowywać jak czasownik modalny, a więc nie przybierać *to* w połączeniu z innymi czasownikami. Jednak takie jego użycie ma dziś nieco archaiczne i podniosłe brzmienie. Ilustrują to przykłady 2, 4, 5, 6 i 8.
1. didn't dare to go insid **2.** dared to approach/dared approach **3.** didn't dare to ask **4.** dared to disturb/dared disturb **5.** dared to question/dared question **6.** dared to come/dared come **7.** didn't dare to correct them **8.** dared to persuade/dared persuade

221. 2. How dare you read my diary? **3.** How dare she insult me in front of my boss? **4.** How dare she interrupt our conversation? **5.** How dare you invite me to your wedding? **6.** How dare he go through my stuff? **7.** How dare he treat me in such a way? **8.** How dare you think that you are better than me? **9.** How dare she tell everybody these lies?

222. 1. Most scientists would never dare to question this scientific theory. **2.** The government would never dare to introduce a ban on the Internet. **3.** My father would never dare to do anything against my mother's will. **4.** Our competitors would never dare to challenge our company's market position. **5.** Most girls would never dare to try bungee-jumping. **6.** The servants would never dare to disturb the Queen at night. **7.** Most employees would never dare to tell their boss what they really think about him.

223. Zarówno *used to*, jak i *would* używane są w odniesieniu do nawyków/powtarzających się czynności w przeszłości, przy czym *used to* podkreśla fakt, że dana sytuacja jest nieaktualna w teraźniejszości.
1. My sister used to be very spoilt as a child, but she has matured a lot since then. **2.** As a young man, James would often get into trouble with the police. **3.** Hector used to believe that there was no such thing as destiny, but now he has changed his mind. **4.** University education used to be a luxury that not everyone could afford, but the situation is different today. **5.** In ancient times, warriors would decorate their swords and shields with jewellery. **6.** I have accidentally found out that Keith used to be a professional gambler.

7. Keith's wife has told me that on some nights he would earn up to ten thousand dollars! **8.** Whenever the ice-cream man came to our village, all children would run outside and wave. **9.** Rick didn't use to smoke as a student, but he has given in to the pressure of his smoking colleagues at work. **10.** When Mary was at university, she didn't use to go out to clubs or discos.

224. **2.** Did you use to be a fan of the 'Star Wars' series? **3.** Did you use to play 'Hide and Seek' with your friends? **4.** Did you use to take English lessons? **5.** Did you use to have many pets? **6.** Did you use to learn to play any instruments? **7.** Did you use to go shopping in the supermarket with your parents?

225. Propozycje zdań:

1. When I was in primary school I would spend every holiday at the seaside. **2.** Twenty years ago mobile phones didn't use to be that popular. **3.** When my family lived in the USA we would often eat at a fast-food restaurant. **4.** When there was still no underground in our town it would take 2 hours to get from one end to the other. **5.** Before the Internet was invented, communication across the globe used to be much more difficult. **6.** When my brother and I were little, my parents would spend a lot of time with us talking and reading.

226. **I.** (1) was used to (2) get used to (3) used to (4) getting used to (5) used to **II.** (1) used to (2) was used to (3) got used to (4) got used to (5) used to

227. 1 B   2 B   3 A   4 A   5 A   6 B   7 A   8 B

228. Propozycje zdań:

2. I am used to using foreign languages. **3.** I am used to going on business trips. **4.** I am used to having a woman for my boss. **5.** I am used to writing long reports. **6.** I am used to coordinating a team of people. **2.** I have to get used to having new duties. **3.** I have to get used to using a different IT system. **4.** I have to get used to having free weekends. **5.** I have to get used to arranging meetings. **6.** I have to get used to meeting a lot of foreigners.

229. 1 B   2 A   3 C   4 A   5 B   6 C   7 C   8 B   9 B   10 A

230. 1 B   2 B   3 A   4 A   5 A   6 A   7 B   8 B

231. (1) may/could/might (2) will/may/might (3) could/may/might (4) must (5) could/can (6) may (7) used to (8) would/used to (9) should/might

PASSIVE VOICE

PASSIVE: PRESENT AND FUTURE

232. ☺☺ Wybierz właściwą formę czasownika.

1. My novel <u>is not being finished/has not been finished</u> yet.
2. At the exam you <u>will be given/are being given</u> an answer sheet.
3. This kind of soup <u>is making/is made</u> only for special occasions.
4. The seeds <u>are planted/are being planted</u> in early April.
5. Every year, more people <u>are being diagnosed/have been diagnosed</u> with allergy.
6. Congratulations, your task <u>is being done/has been done</u> perfectly.
7. Our summer house <u>is being renovated/has been renovated</u> at the moment.

233. ☺☺☺ Sformułuj podane zdania w stronie biernej.

1. The children's mother is mending their clothes.
   The children's clothes _____.
2. I am going to finish my research by September next year.
   By September next year _____.
3. They have sent Stan on a diplomatic mission to Peru.
   Stan _____.
4. Children are chasing puppies round the meadow.
   Puppies _____.
5. They close the shop and then they count the money.
   The shop _____ and then the money _____.
6. They have been excavating artifacts in our garden all summer.
   Artifacts _____.
7. Lester has shown Charlene all the tricks of the trade.
   All the tricks of the trade _____.

234. ☺☺ Zdecyduj, które z poniższych zdań można sformułować w stronie biernej.

1. They ask us not to shout.   (YES/NO)
2. French scientists are doing important research.   (YES/NO)
3. The thieves talked quietly.   (YES/NO)
4. Will somebody look after the baby?   (YES/NO)
5. I love chocolate.   (YES/NO)
6. Very few people read poetry nowadays.   (YES/NO)
7. Someone is coming up the path.   (YES/NO)

A teraz sformułuj wybrane zdania w stronie biernej.

PASSIVE: PAST

235. 😊😊 Sformułuj podane zdania w stronie biernej.
1. Magellan discovered the strait linking the Atlantic and Pacific oceans in 1520.
   The strait linking the Atlantic and Pacific oceans _____ in 1520.
2. They gave me a basket of apples.
   I _____ a basket of apples.
3. The police fined the reckless driver for speeding.
   The reckless driver_____ for speeding _____.
4. Someone broke into the City Hall and stole important documents.
   The City Hall _____ and important
   documents _____.
5. They had cooked the meat for three days and three nights before it was ready.
   Before it was ready, the meat _____.
6. Louis Pasteur administered the first vaccine against rabies on 6th July 1885.
   The first vaccine against rabies _____ on 6th July 1885.
7. A rabid dog had bit a nine-year-old boy, but Louis Pasteur saved his life.
   A nine-year-old boy _____ by a rabid dog, but his life
   _____ by Louis Pasteur.

236. 😊😊😊 Przetłumacz podane zdania.

POLISH	ENGLISH
1. To ciasto robi się na Boże Narodzenie.	_____
2. _____	Berries were picked by whole families.
3. Podano do stołu!	_____
4. _____	The text will have been finished by May.
5. Dzban rozbito na trzy części.	_____
6. _____	This can't be done.
7. Mięso i warzywa kroi się w kostkę.	_____
8. _____	The cathedral was built in the 17th century.
9. Mecz rozpoczyna sędzia.	_____

IT IS SAID THAT...

237. 😊😊 Połącz połówki zdań, które najlepiej do siebie pasują.

1. Terrible frost, isn't it? It is said that...
2. I've got some bad news. It is said that...
3. Old Mr Pearson is very ill. It is said that...
4. Jason failed three out of four exams. It is said that...
5. A plane has crashed outside town. It is said that...
6. Have you heard that Gloria sold her house? It is said that...

a) ...he may not live much longer.
b) ...over three hundred people have been killed in that accident.
c) ...she is moving to the North.
d) ...tonight is going to be the coldest night this winter.
e) ...he will have to repeat the year.
f) ...our favourite restaurant is getting closed.

238. ☺☺ Utwórz zdania w stronie biernej, zaczynające się od *It is...*

1. They say that the castle is going to be sold.
   It is _____.
2. There is a rumour that the lead actor is going to be changed.
   It is _____.
3. They say that blood is thicker than water.
   It is _____.
4. There is a proverb 'A bird in the hand is worth two in the bush'.
   It is _____.
5. There is a rumour that the government is about to raise taxes.
   It is _____.
6. They say the guardians of the collection forgot to lock the door.
   It is _____.

239. ☺☺☺ Zamień stronę czynną na stronę bierną tam, gdzie to możliwe.

Many people believe that Christopher Columbus discovered America. But according to Norse sagas, the Vikings visited North America first. When about the year 986 AD a storm blew Bjarni Herjulfsson's ship westward, Bjarni and his crew became the first Europeans to see mainland America. After they safely returned to Greenland, they began to tell stories of the rich land in the west. About the year 1000 Leif Eriksson sailed westward to find the land which Bjarni had discovered. His Vikings landed in a wooded area in the west and named it Vinland.

The Vikings lived in Vinland for about thirteen years. Then they abandoned the settlement because of a war with the natives. Later, medieval texts mentioned Vinland several times. In 1963 archaeologists discovered the remains of houses and other Viking objects in north Newfoundland. They proved that they date from about the year 1000.

CAUSATIVE HAVE

240. ☺☺ Popraw zdania z kolumny B zgodnie z sytuacjami opisanymi w zdaniach z kolumny A.

A.
1. Jane paid someone to paint the fence.
2. Someone will clean Anna's room.
3. A hairdresser is dyeing Charlotte's hair.
4. Someone irons Ted's shirts.
5. A tailor has made this suit for John.
6. Ronald will hire somebody to mow the lawn.
7. The fridge we bought is too heavy for us to carry.

B.

1. Jane painted the fence.
2. Anna will be cleaning her room.
3. Charlotte is dyeing her hair herself.
4. Ted irons his shirts.
5. John has bought this suit in a shop.
6. Ronald will be mowing the lawn.
7. We will carry the fridge in ourselves.

241. ☺☺ Połącz odpowiednie części wypowiedzi.

1. The bathroom tap is leaking. Its dripping is driving me mad.
2. The Headmaster's computer is not working.
3. A lot of tiles have fallen off the roof.
4. One of the blinds is hanging by one hinge.
5. Mary's wedding dress is way too long.
6. Lindsay says he hates the colour of his sitting-room.
7. There is a pile of rubbish bags in front of our gate.

a) He is going to have its walls painted green.
b) We must have them taken away tomorrow.
c) I need to get the tap repaired as soon as possible.
d) She should have it shortened.
e) The concierge must get the other hinge reattached.
f) We must have the roof re-tiled.
g) He asked his secretary to have it repaired.

242. ☺☺ Zaproponuj rozwiązania problemów, używając *causative have*.

What do you do when...

a) there is a dead tree in your yard? _____
b) a jacket no longer fits you well? _____
c) you buy a piece of antique furniture? _____
d) you break a heel in your best shoes? _____
e) your car still has winter tyres in May? _____
f) you no longer like your hair colour? _____

KLUCZ

232. 1. has not been finished **2.** will be given **3.** is made **4.** are planted **5.** are being diagnosed **6.** has been done **7.** is being renovated

233. 1. The children's clothes are being mended by their mother.

2. By September next year my research will have been finished.

3. Stan has been sent on a diplomatic mission to Peru.

4. Puppies are being chased by children round the meadow.

5. The shop is closed and then the money is counted.

6. Artifacts have been excavated in our garden all summer.

7. All the tricks of the trade have been shown to Charlene by Lester. (Zdania z dopełnieniem bliższym i dalszym można w stronie biernej sformułować dwojako. Zdanie: *Charlene was shown all the tricks of the trade by Lester.* ma to samo znaczenie.)

234. Zdania w stronie biernej można tworzyć tylko z czasownikami posiadającymi dopełnienie (**transitive verbs**).

1. YES – We are asked not to shout.

2. YES – Important research is being done by French scientists.

3. NO – w zdaniu brak dopełnienia.

4. YES – Will the baby be looked after?

5. NO – niektóre typy zdań nie występują w stronie biernej nawet mimo tego, że posiadają dopełnienie.

6. YES – Poetry is read by very few people nowadays.

7. NO – w zdaniu brak dopełnienia.

235. 1. The strait linking the Atlantic and Pacific oceans was discovered by Magellan in 1520.

2. I was given a basket of apples. (Zdania z dopełnieniem bliższym i dalszym można w stronie biernej sformułować dwojako. Każde z dopełnień może stać się podmiotem zdania w stronie biernej. Zdanie: *A basket of apples was given to me.* ma to samo znaczenie.)

3. The reckless driver was fined for speeding (by the police). (Strona bierna podkreśla samo wydarzenie, wykonawca czynności schodzi na drugi plan, dlatego często można go opuścić.)

4. The City Hall was broken into and valuable documents were stolen.

5. Before it was ready, the meat had been cooked for three days and three nights.

6. The first vaccine against rabies was administered by Louis Pasteur on 6th July 1885.

7. A nine-year-old boy had been bitten by a rabid dog, but his life was saved by Louis Pasteur.

236. 1. This cake is made for Christmas. (Typowy błąd: ☺*This cake is making for Christmas.*)

2. Jagody zbierano całymi rodzinami. (Strona bierna w języku angielskim często odpowiada polskim formom nieosobowym kończącym się na *–o.*)

3. Dinner has been served! (Trzeba dodać nazwę posiłku.)

4. Tekst będzie ukończony do maja.

5. The jug was broken into three pieces. (Użycie strony biernej sugeruje, że dzban rozbito intencjonalnie; strona czynna oznaczałaby, że stało się to przypadkiem.)

6. Tego nie da się zrobić.

7. Meat and vegetables are diced. (Strona bierna w języku angielskim często odpowiada polskim formom nieosobowym z *się.*)

8. Katedrę zbudowano w XVII w.

9. The match is commenced by the referee. (Zdania, które po polsku mają stronę czynną, lecz dopełnienie na początku, w języku angielskim występują w stronie biernej.)

237. Konstrukcji *It is said/It is believed/It is rumoured that...* używamy, relacjonując pogłoski i plotki, a także przysłowia i powiedzenia.

1. d **2.** f **3.** a **4.** e **5.** b **6.** c

238. 1. It is said that the castle is going to be sold.

2. It is rumoured that the lead actor is going to be changed.

3. It is said that blood is thicker than water.

4. It is said that a bird in the hand is worth two in the bush.

5. It is rumoured that the government is about to raise taxes.

6. It is said that the guardians of the collection forgot to lock the door.

239. It is believed (by many people) that America was discovered by Christopher Columbus. But according to Norse sagas, North America was visited first by the Vikings. When about 986 AD Bjarni Herjulfsson's ship was blown by a storm westward, Bjarni and his crew became the first Europeans to see mainland America. After they safely returned to Greenland, they began to tell stories/stories began to be told of the rich land in the west. About the year 1000 Leif Eriksson sailed westward to find the land which had been discovered by Bjarni. A wooded area in the west, where his Vikings landed, was named Vinland (by them).

The Vikings lived in Vinland for about thirteen years. Then the settlement was abandoned because of a war with the natives. Later, Vinland was mentioned several times by medieval texts. In 1963 the remains of houses and other Viking objects were discovered (by the archaeologists) in north Newfoundland. It was proved that those remains date from about the year 1000.

240. Konstrukcji *have something done* (causative have) używamy, mówiąc o pracy, której wykonanie komuś zlecono, czyli którą wykonuje dla zleceniodawcy ktoś inny.

1. Jane had the fence painted.

2. Anna will have her room cleaned.

3. Charlotte is having her hair dyed.

4. Ted has his shirts ironed.

5. John has had this suit made for him.

6. Ronald will have the lawn mowed.

7. We will have the fridge carried in.

241. 1. c (*get something done* stosuje się w mowie potocznej) **2.** g **3.** f **4.** e **5.** d **6.** a **7.** b

242. Możliwe odpowiedzi:

    a) I have the tree cut.

    b) I have the jacket altered.

    c) I have the piece of furniture renovated.

    d) I have the heel mended.

    e) I have the tyres changed.

    f) I have my hair dyed.

CONDITIONALS

ZERO CONDITIONAL

243. ☺ Połącz zdanie warunkowe z właściwym zdaniem wynikowym.

1. Whenever Bess is having a good time,
2. If you have any common sense,
3. Whenever my father drinks too much,
4. When Lilla has to speak in public,
5. When I think about my first boyfriend,
6. Whenever we go to the cinema,

a) ...I always wonder how I could be blind enough to love him.
b) ...someone tall sits down in front of me.
c) ...she dances on the table.
d) ...she grows nervous and stutters.
e) ...he gets aggressive.
f) ...you don't offend your teachers.

244. ☺ Wstaw podane czasowniki w odpowiedniej formie, tak by tworzyły zerowy tryb warunkowy.

1. If you take a snowball home, it (melt)_____.
2. When iron gets wet, it (rust) _____, and when wood gets wet, it (rot) _____.
3. Children (grow) _____ fat if they eat a lot of hamburgers.
4. If you leave water in a glass, it (evaporate) _____ eventually.
5. If they work too hard, people (fall) _____ ill.
6. When a wasp gets irritated, it (sting) _____.
7. Bacteria which cause salmonella (die) _____ if you expose them to temperature of 100°C.
8. The harvest (be) _____ poor if the winter is wet and cold.

245. ☺☺ Wykorzystaj podane słowa, by utworzyć zdania w zerowym trybie warunkowym.

Wzór: (boil, water, 100°C, heat)   *If you heat water to 100°C, it boils.*

1. (drop, shirt, blueberries, stain)

_____

2. (rot, meat, sun, leave)

_____

3. (step on, bite, viper)

_____

4. (watch for, too long, eyes, TV, tired)

_____

5. (leave, laundry, rain, wet, hang)

_____

6. (hot, wash, woollen, shrink, water, clothes)

_____

FIRST CONDITIONAL

246. ☺ Połącz połówki zdań.

1. If you stumble,
2. If this old tree falls,
3. We won't get any sleep
4. If Mary doesn't stop behaving like that,
5. Luke is not going to help us
6. If you buy pasta,
7. I can give you another book

a) we will have it for dinner.
b) you will fall all the way to the bottom of the ravine.
c) if this one is too difficult for you.
d) she will not go to Eurodisneyland with her sisters.
e) if the thunderstorm comes in the night.
f) if we don't to pay him.
g) it will damage the house.

247. ☺☺ Wstaw podane czasowniki w odpowiedniej formie, tak by utworzyć zdania w pierwszym trybie warunkowym (*Conditional 1*).

1. If you (keep) _____ talking, father (get) _____ angry.
2. If Joanna's party (be/not) _____ cancelled, I (buy) _____ that dress my boyfriend liked so much.
3. You (may) _____ go home if you (finish) _____ your essay.
4. If Tess (go) _____ out tonight, I (not/call) _____ her. It would be pointless, wouldn't it?
5. Jane (must) _____ have very swollen eyes if she (cry) _____ all night.
6. If Leslie Vaughan (keep) _____ on driving like this, sooner or later he (have) _____ an accident.
7. If Maddy (come) _____ to the party, I (leave) _____.
8. If anything (happen) _____ to me, please (look) _____ after my mother.
9. If Dr Bailly (can) _____ save my son's life, please (pay) _____ him as much as he asks.
10. If his beloved daughter (win) _____ the piano contest tomorrow, the old man (achieve) _____ all he ever wanted in life.
11. If you (plan) _____ to leave, (do) _____ it now.
12. He (ought to) _____ phone you if he (win) _____ the contest.

13. If it (rain) _____ all night, the race (be) _____ called off.
14. You (may) _____ watch the film with us if you (can) _____ stay awake until midnight.
15. If you (be) _____ in Singapore again, you (must) _____ visit us.

248. ☺☺☺ Przekształć zdania, rozpoczynając je od podanych słów.

1. If it does not rain soon, the harvest is going to be very poor.
   Unless _____.
2. If there is a thunderstorm, close all the windows.
   In case of _____.
3. What shall we do if the car breaks down?
   Supposing _____.
4. What if the valley gets flooded?
   Suppose _____.
5. You may play with the neighbour's puppy if you never bring it home.
   Provided that _____.
6. He is quite a nice person when he stops complaining.
   Providing _____.
7. There can't be any mushrooms yet, but I will go for a walk in the forest anyway.
   Even though _____.
8. It doesn't matter if you want to or not, you will drink this medicine.
   Even if _____.

SECOND CONDITIONAL

249. ☺☺ Połącz zdanie warunkowe z właściwym zdaniem wynikowym.

1. If Jill had to share her room with her sister,
2. If Gertie were less shy,
3. If the Headmaster were more lenient,
4. If I were Stan,
5. If Sue moved to China,
6. If the door got jammed,
7. If Colin had any common sense,

a) the guests would have to climb through the window.
b) he would stop complaining so much at work.
c) they would quarrel even more than they already do.
d) he would allow us to smoke in the corridors.
e) I would have a serious talk with his older boy.
f) she could take part in school theatre performances.
g) she would get a much better job.

250. ☺☺ Utwórz zdania w drugim okresie warunkowym (*Conditional 2*), tak by uzupełnić poniższe wypowiedzi.

1. Martha doesn't have a computer, so she can't surf the Internet at home.
   'If _____. I wouldn't have to pay so much at the Internet cafés.'
2. Rena is working on Sundays, so she can't go out with her boyfriend.
   'If _____. Every sunny Sunday we would go for a long walk!'
3. Mark is very short-sighted, so he can't practise archery, the sport he is dreaming of.
   'If _____. I would learn to use a bow like Legolas.'
4. Bob isn't well organised, so he doesn't have any free time.
   'If _____. Then I could hang out with you folks more.'
5. Jennifer lives in a small flat, so she can't throw big parties.
   'If _____. Wouldn't that be fun!'
6. Tina has very strict parents, so she has to be home by 10 pm.
   'If _____. From time to time I could go to the students' club with you.'

251. ☺☺☺ Przepisz podane zdania warunkowe, używając inwersji. Rozpocznij zdania od podanych wyrazów.

1. Everyone would be able to write a novel if it were so simple.
   Were _____.
2. If you change your mind, do let me know.
   Should _____.
3. If I were to tell him the truth, how should I start?
   Were _____.
4. If the President should decide to attend the conference, security would have to be tightened.
   Should _____.
5. If the system were to collapse, a social revolution would be inevitable.
   Were _____.

FIRST OR SECOND CONDITIONAL?

252. ☺☺ Zaznacz, która osoba wypowiedziała dane zdanie.

1. 'If I had a three-month holiday, I would go to India.'
   a) a student
   b) a busy professional
2. 'If I go to the Shetlands, I will bring you a real Shetland sweater.'
   a) a traveller who may go to the Shetlands
   b) a traveller who will probably not go to the Shetlands

3. 'If I had a horse, I would go riding in the forest.'

   a) a person who plans to buy a horse

   b) a person who dreams of having a horse

4. 'If I got this job, I would get a mortgage and buy a flat.'

   a) a person who has a chance of getting the job

   b) a person who doesn't have much chance of getting the job

5. 'If I get the weekend off, I will go to Florence.'

   a) a person who is likely to get the weekend off

   b) a person who will probably not get the weekend off

6. 'If I had a moment's peace, I would rearrange my office.'

   a) a person who may get a chance to rearrange his office

   b) a person who is too busy to rearrange his office

7. 'If I were able to, I would write a sonnet.'

   a) an aspiring sonneteer

   b) a successful poet

253. ☺☺ Wybierz właściwą formę czasownika.

1. I've never met John, but I've heard so much about him that if I meet/met/will meet him, I recognise/recognised/would recognise him immediately.

2. Look, the sky is getting grey. If it rains/rained/would rain, our excursion was/would be/will be ruined.

3. Can you help me? If the cookies are/were/will be ready, please take/took/will take them out of the oven.

4. I hate liver. If I have to/had to/will have to swallow some, I think I will be/would be/am sick. Fortunately, nobody asks me to eat it.

5. Please be on time! If you be/are/were late, I am/was/will be very angry with you.

254. ☺☺ Napisz zdanie, jakie wypowie dana osoba.

1. **a tired housewife:** 'I look like a scarecrow! If I (have) _____ more free time, I (go) _____ to a hairdresser's.'

2. **a successful actress:** 'I am sure the film we are making now is going to be a success. And when it (be) _____ a hit, I (receive) _____ many interesting proposals of new roles.'

3. **a rich businessman:** 'When we (close) _____ this deal, our company (make) _____ twice as much money as last year.'

4. **a lazy student:** 'If I somehow (manage) _____ to pass the tests this term, I (study) _____ much harder next term. Having a little more free time is not worth all the worry.'

5. **a little girl:** 'I (be) _____ a nurse when I (grow up) _____.'

THIRD CONDITIONAL

255. ☺☺ Wstaw podane czasowniki w odpowiedniej formie, tak by tworzyły trzeci tryb warunkowy (*Conditional 3*).

1. Stella has a gift for music, but she no longer plays the violin.
   'If I (practise) _____ the violin more, I (go) _____to the Conservatory. But I found it far too boring.'

2. Paul is a lawyer, although he always dreamed of being an artist.
   'If I (be) _____ more courageous, I (tell) _____ my father I didn't want to inherit his legal firm. Perhaps I would be happier now.'

3. Bronka married an Englishman and emigrated from Poland.
   'If I (not/marry) _____ William, I (not/leave) _____ Poland. I would still be living in Tarnów.'

4. Margaret cooked a wonderful wedding feast for a friend. Among the guests there was a millionaire, and Margaret got a job in his residence.
   'I'm glad I had agreed to cook at Maisie's wedding. If I (not/agree) _____, Mr Wellborn (not/employ) _____ me as his cook.'

5. Becky's mother thought horses were dangerous, so Becky learnt to ride only after she had moved out.
   'I (learn) _____ to ride much earlier than I actually did if my mother (not/afraid) _____ of horses so much. I lost a lot of time because of her!'

256. ☺☺ Wstaw podane czasowniki w odpowiedniej formie, tak by tworzyły trzeci tryb warunkowy (*Conditional 3*). Następnie połącz odpowiednie połówki zdań.

1. If I (not/gossip) _____ with Yolande,
2. If you (not/crib) _____,
3. What a pity I lost touch with Jeanne. If I (write) _____ to her as regularly as she wrote to me,
4. If you (not/criticise) _____ Luke so severely in front of everyone,
5. It's a shame I lost Mhairi's address. If I (not/lose) _____ it,
6. It's your fault you didn't get the scholarship. If you (send) _____ the application form on time,

a) the examiners (not/throw) _____ you out of the room. It's your own fault.
b) he (not/split up) _____ with you. You have only yourself to thank for it.
c) you (have) _____ a real chance of getting it.
d) she (not/get) _____ offended.
e) she (not/tell) _____ my secret to everyone. But I had, and now it's all over town.
f) I (can/visit) _____ her when I was in Inverness.

257. ☺☺☺ Przepisz podane zdania warunkowe, używając inwersji. Rozpocznij zdania od podanych wyrazów.

1. Larry wouldn't have left Tess if she had been wiser.
   Had _____.
2. If I had known there would be so many mosquitoes in that villa, I would've taken a repellent.
   Had _____.
3. If the general had been more cautious, the decisive battle would not have been lost.
   Had _____.
4. They would have realised what mistake they made if they had listened to our arguments.
   Had _____.
5. If Leslie's had not made this ill-timed remark, Professor Walton would have cancelled the exam.
   Had _____.

SECOND OR THIRD CONDITIONAL?

258. ☺☺ Wybierz właściwą formę czasownika.

1. If Leslie <u>didn't buy/hadn't bought</u> some bread, we <u>didn't have/wouldn't have/wouldn't have had</u> anything to eat for supper.
2. If you <u>told/had told</u> me of your problem last week, I <u>was able/had been able/would have been able</u> to get that book for you.
3. What <u>do you say/would you say</u> if the boss <u>sent/would sent</u> you to Paris for the negotiations?
4. Why didn't you tell me? If I <u>knew/had known</u> about your illness, I <u>would not make/wouldn't have made</u> that remark.
5. If you <u>stop thinking/stopped thinking/would stop thinking</u> about your headache, it <u>would go/would have gone</u> away.

259. ☺☺ Wybierz właściwą wypowiedź.

1. Amanda is angry with Madeleine for forgetting to tell her that the meeting had been cancelled.
   a) 'If you remembered to tell me, I wouldn't stay at the office until six!'
   b) 'If you had remembered to tell me, I wouldn't have stayed at the office until six!'
2. Bess is dreaming of changing her job.
   a) 'If I worked freelance, I could get up late and work till midnight.'
   b) 'If I had worked freelance, I could have got up late and have worked till midnight.'
3. Miriam is rather critical of Andy's behaviour at the party last night.
   a) 'If you didn't get drunk, you wouldn't ruin Tom's sitting-room! How could you!'
   b) 'If you hadn't got drunk, you wouldn't have ruined Tom's sitting-room! How could you!'
4. Martin is sorry he acted wrongly.
   a) 'If I told the boss I lost the letter, the whole embarrassment could be avoided.'

b) 'If I had told the boss I lost the letter, the whole embarrassment could have been avoided.'
5. Nellie wants to learn to knit.
a) 'If I learnt to knit, I would make a warm sweater for my boyfriend.'
b) 'If I had learnt to knit, I would have made a warm sweater for my boyfriend.'
6. Bill wants to give Alison some advice.
a) 'If you spent less on expensive clothes, you would have enough money to pay your mortgage.'
b) 'If you had spent less on expensive clothes, you would have had enough money to pay your mortgage.'

260. ☺☺☺ Zaczynając od podanych słów, sformułuj zdania, tak aby sens wypowiedzi pozostał niezmieniony.

1. Robert didn't take his wallet with him and he had to ask Jill to lend him some money.
Robert wouldn't _____.
2. Andrew helped me with physics and that's why I passed the final test.
If Andrew _____.
3. Without a rope you cannot climb this rock.
Provided _____.
4. Your eyes hurt because you play too much computer games.
If you _____.
5. If you visit Edinburgh, you must see the Museum of Scotland.
Should _____.
6. If you ate less fatty foods, you would feel better.
Unless _____.
7. The dog tried to bite Maureen, but she climbed a tree.
If Maureen _____.

MIXED CONDITIONALS

261. ☺☺ Wstaw podane w nawiasach czasowniki w odpowiednich formach, tak aby po *if* pojawił się trzeci okres warunkowy, a w zdaniu wynikowym – drugi.

1. If I (read) _____ more as a child, I (not/know) _____ now _____ so much less than my friends do.
2. If Tim (study) _____ French irregular verbs during the weekend instead of going to a party, he (not/have) _____ to re-sit the French grammar exam in September.
3. If I (devote) _____ more time to my fiancée than to museums when we were in Venice, she (be) _____ my wife now.
4. If Adrienne (dare) _____ to refuse the offer to move to the company's Seoul branch, she (not/have) _____ malaria today.
5. If Columbus (not/discover) _____ America, we (not/have) _____ the tobacco problem now.
6. If Teutonic Knights (win) _____ the battle of Tannenberg, we (speak) _____ probably _____ German in Poland today.

7. If my parents (give) _____ me a computer as my birthday present last year instead of that stupid teddy bear, I (play) _____ some fascinating game now.

262. Wybierz właściwą wypowiedź.

1. Aidan hated his sister's boyfriend so much that he refused to attend their wedding ceremony. His sister got so offended that now she will not see him. This summer she and her husband are going to buy a house in Provence.
   a) 'If Aidan had been present at our wedding, I would have invited him to stay with us in Provence.'
   b) 'If Aidan had been present at my wedding, I would invite him to stay with us in Provence.'
2. Annie says she loves her boyfriend Tristan, but when she went out with her friends recently, she told them he was stupid and stank. This happened for the first time, but still her friends began to doubt her affection for Tristan.
   a) 'If Anne loves Tristan, she wouldn't have said such nasty things about him behind his back.'
   b) 'If Anne loved Tristan, she wouldn't have said such nasty things about him behind his back.'
3. Marie is said to be a very good cook, but Yolande very much doubts it.
   a) 'If Marie really cooks as well as she is said to, she would have got a job in a restaurant.'
   b) 'If Marie really cooked as well as she is said to, she would have got a job in a restaurant.'
4. In 1994 Amelia received a scholarship to Rome. At that time Giulio was a postgraduate student at the University of Rome. They have been married for ten years now, have three bambini and are very happy together.
   a) 'If I hadn't gone to Rome in 1994, I wouldn't have met my husband.'
   b) 'If I hadn't gone to Rome in 1994, I wouldn't meet my husband.'
5. Josephine broke her ankle climbing Ben Nevis two summers ago. A Scottish girl who helped her is now her best friend. They are sitting together and recalling the wet and misty day they met.
   a) 'Imagine, Eilidh, if I hadn't broken my ankle, I wouldn't know you!'
   b) 'Imagine, Eilidh, if I didn't break my ankle, I wouldn't have known you!'

263. ☺☺☺ Ułóż wypowiedzi, korzystając z podanych wyrazów.

Wzór: Leslie was severely bitten by wasps when he was three, and now he is very much afraid of wasps. (**be scared, step, nest, wasp**)
'If I hadn't stepped on a wasp nest when I was three, I wouldn't be so scared of wasps now.'

1. Margaret's summer house burned to the ground because she had left a candle burning and went back to town. Today Margaret says: (**candle, leave, stand, house**)
   '_____,

2. Paul wanted to be an artist, but his father persuaded him to study law. Today his father tells him: (**persuade, poor, die, hunger, artist**)
   '_____,

3. Alan's passport is no longer valid. Consequently, he couldn't accompany his wife to Singapore. (**on time, fail, apply, be, passport, Singapore**)
   '_____,

4. Kevin lost a lot of money because his partner cheated him. He is very bitter about it. (**trust, be, richer, less, much**)

'_____ ,

5. Marianne married Steve because her sweetheart, Jock, had been too shy to propose to her. Now she is very unhappy in her marriage. (**be, courage, propose, have, happier**)

'_____ ,

I WISH/IF ONLY

264. ☺☺ Dopasuj wypowiedzi do sytuacji.

1. Bernard regrets he sold his house, because it was much nicer than his present one.
2. Bella is sorry that her friend Mia is moving to New Zealand.
3. Wilma is rather fat and her clothes don't fit her.
4. Arnie is ill and misses his best friend.
5. Harold's whistling irritates Una very much.
6. Delia couldn't go to a party on Sunday because she was too busy.
7. Ina will not get any leave this summer.

a) I wish Bob would come to visit me.
b) I wish you would stop whistling!
c) I wish I hadn't sold my old house.
d) I wish I could get even a day's leave this summer.
e) I wish I could have gone to the party.
f) I wish you weren't moving to New Zealand.
g) I wish I was thinner.

265. ☺☺ Wstaw podany czasownik w odpowiedniej formie.

1. My feet are wet through! I wish I (take) _____ wellingtons instead of sneakers.
2. The gentleman in the next room is snoring so loudly that I cannot sleep. I wish he (stop) _____.
3. This course is really boring. If only we (can/have) _____ a different teacher!
4. Our holiday was ruined. I wish somebody (inform) _____ us the sea is so dirty at Rimini!
5. Don't drop it! I wish you (be) _____ more careful with things.
6. I hate being a secretary. I wish I (not/work) _____ at the office.
7. I can't get the key out of the keyhole now. I wish I (not/try) _____ to open it with a wrong key.
8. My friend died suddenly, so I did not get the chance to say goodbye to her. If only I (can/tell) _____ her how much she had meant to me.

266. ☺☺☺ Uzupełnij wypowiedzi.

Wzór:
Mandy quarrelled with her best friend Eve and told her she was a stupid cow. Now Eve won't talk to her.
Mandy wishes now <u>she hadn't quarrelled with Eve</u>. 'I wish <u>I hadn't told her she was a stupid cow</u>. If only <u>Eve would talk to me again</u>!'

1. Lenny's mother forbade him to play roleplaying games. Lenny thinks this is only because his mother doesn't know what RPG really are, and doesn't care to find out.
   Lenny wishes his mother _____ what RPG really are. 'If only Mum _____! We would have had a great game last night.'
2. Cindy is allergic to milk and can't eat ice cream. Her friends tell her it is delicious. She is angry that they do it, because it only makes her feel more sorry for herself.
   'If only you _____ telling me how delicious ice cream is! I wish I _____, but I can't and you know it!'
3. Philip backed the car out of the garage carelessly and scratched its side badly. Now he has to tell his father about it, and is not feeling very brave.
   Philip wishes _____ damaged the car. 'If only I _____ more careful when I was backing the car out of the garage.'
4. Alex's best shirt has split at the seam and he has no idea how to mend it. He thinks his Gran may know.
   'If I knew how to do it _____ myself, but I don't. I wish Gran _____ it!'
5. Naomi used to enjoy skiing, but she had had a skiing accident and spent a month in hospital. Now she is afraid to start skiing again.
   'If only _____!
   I was in so much pain. I wish _____
   again, but I am too scared. I don't think I will ever put my skis on again.'

KLUCZ

243. *Zero conditional* używamy, mówiąc o tym, co zdarza się zawsze, jeśli zostaną spełnione dane warunki.
  1. c **2.** f **3.** e **4.** d **5.** a **6.** b

244. *Zero conditional* używamy także, mówiąc o prawdach ogólnych lub faktach naukowych.
  1. melts **2.** rusts, rots **3.** grow **4.** evaporates **5.** fall **6.** stings **7.** die **8.** is

245. 1. If you drop blueberries on your shirt, they stain it./If you drop blueberries on your shirt, it gets stained.
  2. If you leave meat in the sun, it rots./Meat rots if you leave it in the sun.
  3. If you step on a viper, it bites./A viper bites if you step on it.
  4. If you watch TV for too long, your eyes grow tired./Your eyes grow tired if you watch TV for too long.
  5. If you leave your laundry hanging in the rain, it gets wet./Your laundry gets wet if you leave it hanging in the rain.
  6. If you wash woollen clothes in hot water, they shrink./Woollen clothes shrink if you wash them in hot water.
  Pamiętaj: jeśli wypowiedź zaczyna się od zdania warunkowego, zdanie wynikowe poprzedza przecinek.

246. *First conditional* różni się od *'zero' conditional* tym, że dotyczy sytuacji sporadycznych, a nie wydarzeń powtarzających się ani prawd ogólnych.
  1. b **2.** g **3.** e **4.** d **5.** f **6.** a **7.** c

247. Jeśli zdanie zaczyna się od zdania warunkowego, występuje w nim przecinek. Jeśli jednak zdanie wynikowe jest pierwsze, nie oddzielamy go przecinkiem od zdania warunkowego.

1. keep, will get **2.** is not, will buy **3.** may, have finished **4.** is going, will not call **5.** must, has been crying **6.** keeps, will have **7.** comes, am leaving **8.** happens, look **9.** can, pay **10.** wins, will have achieved **11.** are planning, do **12.** ought to, wins **13.** has been raining, will be/is going to be **14.** may, can **15.** are, must

248. **1.** Unless it rains soon, the harvest is going to be very poor. (*Unless* wyraża warunek, który uniemożliwia zaistnienie rezultatu zawartego w zdaniu wynikowym.)

2. In case of a thunderstorm, close all the windows. (Konstrukcji *in case of* + rzeczownik używamy głównie do wyrażania ostrzeżeń.)

3. Supposing the car breaks down? (*Supposing/Suppose* wyraża przypuszczenia dotyczące zaistnienia danego warunku.)

4. Suppose the valley gets flooded? (*Supposing/Suppose* wyraża przypuszczenia dotyczące zaistnienia danego warunku.)

5. Provided that you never bring the neighbour's puppy home, you may play with it. (Za pomocą wyrażenia *providing/provided* (*that*) + zakaz można wyrazić pozwolenie uwarunkowane spełnieniem danego warunku.)

6. Providing (that) he stops complaining, he is quite a nice person. (Zdanie z *providing/provided* (*that*) wyraża warunek, który musi zostać spełniony, by zaistniał dany fakt.)

7. Even though there can't be any mushrooms yet, I will anyway go for a walk in the forest. (*Even though/Even if* wyraża zaistnienie danego rezultatu niezależnie od okoliczności.)

8. Even if you don't want to, you will drink this medicine. (*Even if/Even though* wyraża zaistnienie danego rezultatu niezależnie od okoliczności.)

249. **1.** c **2.** f **3.** d **4.** e **5.** g **6.** a **7.** b

250. *Second conditional* używamy, mówiąc o naszych marzeniach.

1. If I had a computer, I could surf the Internet at home.

2. If I wasn't working on Sundays, I could go out with my boyfriend.

3. If I weren't so short-sighted, I could practise archery.

4. If I was/were well-organised, I would have some free time.

5. If I lived in a bigger flat, I could throw big parties.

6. If I had less strict parents, I wouldn't have to be home by 10 pm.

251. **1.** Were it so simple, everyone would be able to write a novel.

2. Should you change your mind, do let me know.

3. Were I to tell him the truth, how should I start?

4. Should the President decide to attend the conference, security would have to be tightened.

5. Were the system to collapse, a social revolution would be inevitable.

Pamiętaj, że zdania warunkowe z inwersją brzmią bardziej oficjalnie niż te same zdania bez inwersji.

252. **1.** b **2.** a **3.** b **4.** b **5.** a **6.** b **7.** a

253. **1.** met, would recognise **2.** rains, will be **3.** are, take **4.** had to, would be **5.** are, will be

254. **1.** If I had more free time, I would go to a hairdresser's.

2. And when it is a hit, I will receive many interesting proposals of new roles.

3. When we close this deal, our company will make twice as much money as last year.

4. If I somehow manage to pass the tests this term, I will study much harder next term.

5. I will be/am going to be a nurse when I grow up.

255. Trzeciego okresu warunkowego (*third conditional*) używamy, mówiąc o sytuacjach, które mogłyby zaistnieć w przeszłości, gdyby został spełniony określony warunek. Ponieważ jednak nie jest to możliwe, bo przeszłości nie da się zmienić, są to zdania całkowicie hipotetyczne.

1. had practised, would have gone

2. had been, would have told

3. hadn't married, wouldn't have left

4. hadn't agreed, wouldn't have employed

5. would have learnt, hadn't been afraid

256. Za pomocą zdań z trzecim okresem warunkowym wyrażamy żal, że coś się stało w przeszłości (zdania 1, 3, 5). Używając *Conditional 3*, możemy także skrytykować czyjeś postępowanie (zdania 2, 4, 6).
  1. e – hadn't gossiped, wouldn't have told
  2. a – hadn't been cribbing, wouldn't have thrown
  3. d – had been writing, wouldn't have got
  4. b – had not criticised, wouldn't have split up
  5. f – hadn't lost it, could have visited
  6. c – had sent, would have had

257. 1. Had Tess been wiser, Larry would not have left her.
  2. Had I known there would be so many mosquitoes in that villa, I would have taken a repellent.
  3. Had the general been more cautious, the decisive battle would not have been lost.
  4. Had they listened to our arguments, they would have realised what mistake they made.
  5. Had Leslie not made this ill-timed remark, Professor Walton would have cancelled the exam.
  Pamiętaj, że zdania warunkowe z inwersją brzmią bardziej oficjalnie niż te same zdania bez inwersji. Nie używamy w nich form skróconych (patrz zdanie 1: *wouldn't* → *would not*; zdanie 2: *would've* → *would have*).

258. 1. hadn't bought, wouldn't have had
  2. had told, would have been able
  3. would you say, sent
  4. had known, wouldn't have made
  5. stopped thinking, would go

259. 1. b 2. a 3. b 4. b 5. a 6. a

260. 1. Robert wouldn't have had to ask Jill to lend him some money if he had taken his wallet with him.
  2. If Andrew hadn't helped me with physics, I wouldn't have passed the final test.
  3. Provided you have a rope, you can climb this rock.
  4. If you played fewer computer games, your eyes wouldn't hurt.
  5. Should you visit Edinburgh, you must see the Museum of Scotland.
  6. Unless you eat less fatty foods, you won't feel better.
  7. If Maureen hadn't climbed a tree, the dog would have bitten her.

261. Najpowszechniej używane są zdania łączące trzeci okres warunkowy z drugim; mówią one o obecnych skutkach jakiegoś przeszłego wydarzenia.
  1. had read, wouldn't now know 2. had studied, wouldn't have 3. had devoted, would be 4. had dared, wouldn't have 5. hadn't discovered, wouldn't have 6. had won, would probably speak (po angielsku bitwa pod Grunwaldem nazywa się 'Battle of Tannenberg') 7. had given, would/could be playing

262. Na ogół występują trzy typy mieszanych okresów warunkowych – pierwszy z trzecim, drugi z trzecim oraz trzeci z drugim. Wybór właściwego *mixed conditional* w bardzo znacznym stopniu zależy od kontekstu.
  1. b – w zdaniu **a** występuje trzeci okres warunkowy, co oznacza, że siostra Aidana mówi o sytuacji w przeszłości; ponieważ jednak dom w Prowansji dopiero będzie kupiony, właściwy jest mieszany okres warunkowy (3rd + 2nd *conditional*), odnoszący skutki dawnego postępowania Aidana do teraźniejszości.
  2. a – oba zdania warunkowe dotyczą teraźniejszości, jednakże zdanie **a** (1st + 3rd *conditional*) wyraża mniejsze wątpliwości przyjaciółek; a tego rodzaju zachowanie zdarzyło się Annie po raz pierwszy.
  3. b – zdanie **a** ogólnie podaje w wątpliwość umiejętności kulinarne Marie (1st + 3rd *conditional*). Yolande jest jednak prawie pewna, że Marie nie umie gotować, stąd zdanie (b) (2nd + 3rd *conditional*) lepiej odpowiada stwierdzeniu '*I very much doubt it*'.
  4. a – Amelia opowiada o sytuacji, która w całości dotyczy przeszłości. Właściwy jest więc trzeci okres warunkowy, a nie mieszany okres warunkowy (3rd + 2nd *conditional*) występujący w zdaniu **b**, który sugerowałby, że swego męża Amelia dopiero spotka.
  5. a – Josephine mówi o warunku, którego zaistnienie w przeszłości wpływa na sytuację teraźniejszą. Zdanie **b** nie ma sensu, gdyż dotyczy warunku w teraźniejszości, a Josephine z pewnością nie chce ponownie złamać sobie nogi w kostce!

263. 1. If I hadn't left the candle burning, my summer house would still be standing.
  2. If I hadn't persuaded you to study law, you would be dying/would have died of hunger as a poor artist.
  3. If I hadn't failed to apply for a new passport on time, I would be in Singapore now.
  4. If I had trusted my partner less, I would be much richer now.
  5. If Jock had had the courage to propose to me, I would be happier now.

264. **1.** c – konstrukcja *I wish* + *past perfect* odnosi się do przeszłości i wyraża żal, że coś się wydarzyło.
2. f – konstrukcja *I wish* + *past simple* lub *past continuous* odnosi się do teraźniejszości i wyraża niezadowolenie z istniejącej sytuacji.
3. g – jak wyżej.
4. a – konstrukcja *I wish... would* odnosi się do przyszłości i wyraża pragnienie, aby coś się wydarzyło. Konstrukcji tej używa się wyłącznie z *action verbs*, nigdy ze *state verbs*.
5. b – jak wyżej.
6. e – konstrukcja *I wish... could* + *past perfect* odnosi się do przeszłości i wyraża żal, że coś się nie wydarzyło lub czegoś nie można było zrobić.
7. d – konstrukcja *I wish... could* odnosi się do przyszłości i wyraża żal, że coś jest niemożliwe.

265. **1.** had taken **2.** would stop **3.** could have **4.** had informed **5.** were **6.** didn't work **7.** hadn't tried **8.** could have told

266. Pamiętaj, że *If only* ma mocniejszy wydźwięk niż *I wish*.
Możliwe odpowiedzi:
1. Lenny wishes his mother would know/find out what RPG really are. 'If only Mum hadn't forbidden me to play RPG! We would have had a great game last night.'
2. 'If only you would stop telling me how delicious ice cream is! I wish I could eat it, but I can't and you know it!'
3. Philip wishes he hadn't damaged the car. 'If only I had been more careful when I was backing the car out of the garage.'
4. 'If I knew how to do it, I would mend my best shirt myself, but I don't. I wish Gran would mend it/would do it!'
5. 'If only I hadn't had that accident! I was in so much pain. I wish I could enjoy skiing/could ski again, but I am too scared. I don't think I will ever put my skis on again.'

REPORTED SPEECH

267. ☺☺ Poniższe zdania to fragmenty wywiadu ze znanym piosenkarzem, Benem Smithem. Przekształć je na mowę zależną.

    Wzór: 'Music is both my job and my philosophy.'
                    Ben Smith said that *music was both his job and his philosophy.*

1. 'My history as an artist is long and complex.'
   Ben Smith said that _____.
2. 'I have recently finished working on my autobiography.'
   Ben Smith said that _____.
3. 'I am going to record a new single soon.'
   Ben Smith said that _____.
4. 'My next tour will probably be to Japan, which I find a truly amazing country.'
   Ben Smith said that _____.
5. 'I'm afraid I will be spending more time sightseeing than giving concerts.'
   Ben Smith said that _____.
6. 'I greatly enjoyed my tour around Poland.'
   Ben Smith said that _____.
7. 'I remember that I met many Polish artists then, who took me to many interesting music events.'
   Ben Smith said that _____.
8. 'I've even been thinking of coming to your country again.'
   Ben Smith said that _____.
9. 'I was only surprised to learn that someone else had received your Fryderyk music award.'
   Ben Smith said that _____.
10. 'That means that I'll be working even harder on my publicity in Central Europe.'
   Ben Smith said that _____.

268. ☺☺ Przekształć poniższe fragmenty wywiadu z Benem Smithem na mowę zależną, zakładając, że wywiad miał miejsce w zeszłym roku.

    Wzór: 'Today is one of my few days at home, in New Orleans.'
                    Ben Smith said that *that day was one of his few days at home, in New Orleans.*

1. 'I bought this house two years ago, because I found it so peaceful here.'
   Ben Smith said that _____.
2. 'I have given over two hundred concerts this year.'
   Ben Smith said that _____.
3. 'Only yesterday I received invitations to some 20 countries.'
   Ben Smith said that _____.
4. 'Last night I played in San Jose, where I will be returning later this week.'
   Ben Smith said that _____.
5. 'I am now working on my 'Best of…' album, for which I have my first studio session tomorrow.'
   Ben Smith said that _____.

6. 'My manager will be able to tell you more about it next week.'
Ben Smith said that _____.

7. 'It is now my greatest ambition to make a film about rock music.'
Ben Smith said that _____.

8. 'I started writing the scenario last year and hopefully the film will be in cinemas next winter.'
Ben Smith said that _____.

269. ☺☺☺ Zdecyduj, które z przekształceń poniższych zdań są bardziej poprawne.

1. 'Storks migrate to Africa in autumn.' You say to your mother:
A. Our teacher told us that storks migrated to Africa in autumn
B. Our teacher told us that storks migrate to Africa in autumn.

2. 'The school will invest in new IT equipment.' One year later you say to your friend:
A. Last year the headmaster told us that the school will invest in new IT equipment.
B. Last year the headmaster told us that the school would invest in new IT equipment.

3. 'I will hand in the report by Friday', Mary said. It is Monday of the same week and you say to your friend:
A. Mary promised that she will hand in the report by Friday.
B. Mary promised that she would hand in the report by Friday.

4. 'Seb is in Africa now.' An hour later you say to your friend:
A. Somebody told me that Seb is in Africa now.
B. Somebody told me that Seba was in Africa now.

5. On that very day you see Seb in a local café. You say to him:
A. Seb! Somebody told me that you are in Africa!
B. Seb! Somebody told me that you were in Africa!

6. 'The audience began clapping when I entered the stage.' A journalist reports:
A. The actor said that the audience began clapping when he entered the stage.
B. The actor said that the audience had begun clapping when he had entered the stage.

REPORTED SPEECH: SEQUENCE OF TENSES

270. ☺☺☺ Zamień poniższe przemówienie rektora uczelni na mowę zależną.

'Dear Students! It is my pleasure to invite you to the Open Days at Garford University.
The event takes place from May 2nd to May 12th and I hope that both you and your parents will participate in at least some of the days.
The Open Days are designed for you to visit the university campus and get a first-hand feel for what it is like to study at Garford University.
You will be meeting our staff, who will show you around our facilities: the library, classrooms and student dorms. Other events include a concert of the university choir and an open-air fair of academic books.
In the past few years the Open Days have been a great success and have convinced many people to study at Garford.

Hopefully this year it will be your turn to enjoy Garford. I am looking forward to meeting all of you!'

The University President addressed the students and said _____

_____

The President added that _____

_____

He said that _____

_____

He also said that _____

_____

The President added _____

_____

The President concluded that _____

_____

271. ☺☺☺ Zamień poniższe przemówienie prezesa firmy na mowę zależną.

'Ladies and Gentlemen, thank you for coming to our Annual General Meeting. After very high profits last year, the year 2005 was another record year for the Company.
A dynamic business climate enabled us to improve our results. We raised the prices, but reduced the costs and, above all, succeeded in our strategy of leadership on the IT market. This success, however, has been overshadowed by the news that next year the government will impose sanctions on the company for anti-competitive practices.
At this place I would only like to repeat that our company is giving this issue its full attention and is actively negotiating with the Minister. Our next meeting with the Minister is scheduled for next week and I expect that it will be a breakthrough in our talks.'

The CEO thanked everyone for coming to their AGM and said _____

_____

The CEO said _____

_____

The CEO added _____

_____

The CEO concluded _____

_____

272. ☺☺☺ Zamień poniższą wypowiedź na mowę zależną.

'We imagine it as a very straightforward process: a team of researchers working together in a laboratory submit the results of their research to a journal, while the editor proof-reads the paper and accepts it for publication.
In fact, it only used to be simple. Today the internet is making free access to scientific results a reality.
Last week, the OECD issued a report describing the consequences of this development. The report shows that the profits of publishers will be declining. But it also signals a change in what has until now been the dominant model of scientific work: the model of a restricted, if not concealed, business.
Online publication has enabled a wider access to research not only to the general public, but also to other researchers.
Increasingly, scientific research will be becoming a truly collaborative activity. Scientists will be able to comment on other people's work while it is still in progress.'

(adapted from: *The Economist*, September 24th, 2005)

During last year's conference the scientist claimed _____

_____

The scientist said _____

_____

He added that _____

_____

He pointed out that _____

_____

The scientist concluded that _____

_____

REPORTED SPEECH:
MODALS AND CONDITIONALS

273. ☺☺ Zamień poniższe zdania na mowę zależną.

1. 'I can give you some tips for your essay, but I will not write it for you.'
He said that _____.
2. 'You may use my car whenever you need it.'
He said that _____.
3. 'Mark's poor grades could be a result of his family problems.'
He said that _____.
4. 'I'm sorry that I couldn't come to your birthday party yesterday.'
He said that _____.
5. 'Life in a city must have been much easier in the past.'
He said that _____.
6. 'I must call Mary and ask if there is anything I could do to help her.'
He said that _____.
7. 'You must report to me every morning at 8 am sharp.'
He said that _____.
8. 'We shouldn't just sit around and wait for what happens.'
He said that _____.
9. 'There may be some problems with your visa.'
He said that _____.
10. 'In a job like mine you can't get stressed over little things.'
He said that _____.

274. ☺☺ Wyraź poniższe przypuszczenia w mowie zależnej.

1. 'If my theory proves correct, I will be acclaimed a genius.'
He said that _____.
2. 'If gunpowder had not been invented, human history would have taken a different course.'
He said that _____.

3. 'If the government concentrated more on domestic policy, it would quickly gain public trust.'

He said that _____.

4. 'If we try hard enough, we will succeed.'

He said that _____.

5. 'If you keep on annoying me, you will get yourself into trouble.'

He said that _____.

6. 'If I were you, I would start looking for another job.'

He said that _____.

7. 'If Richard had foreseen the crisis, he could have taken some steps to prevent it.'

He said that _____.

8. 'I will be very surprised if Charles passes his exam.'

He said that _____.

275. ☺☺☺ Zamień poniższe przemówienie na mowę zależną.

'It may be hard to imagine that the nasty disease we know as flu could turn into a superflu that might kill tens of millions of people within two years.

And yet, if superflu strikes, that is what may well happen.

Many scientists believe that another pandemic is inevitable. Their alarms have even caught the attention of politicians, who are meeting in Canada next month to discuss what can be done to prevent an outbreak and what measures must be taken right away.

If the conference members managed to establish a sensible plan, a major pandemic could be prevented.

However, many commentators seem to doubt that, pointing out that if nothing has been done so far, there is no reason to believe that anything will be done now.'

(adapted from: *The Economist,* September 24th, 2005)

The journalist pointed out that _____

_____, he said, _____

_____

He claimed _____

_____

_____

He maintained _____

_____

_____

However, he said _____

_____

_____

REPORTED SPEECH: QUESTIONS AND ORDERS

276. ☺☺ Zamień poniższe fragmenty rozmowy o pracę na mowę zależną.

Wzór: 'How did you find out about our job offer?'
The interviewer asked *how I had found out about their job offer.*

1. 'What school did you go to?'
The interviewer asked _____.
2. 'Have you completed any additional courses?'
The interviewer asked _____.
3. 'What is your current employment?'
The interviewer asked _____.
4. 'May I see your CV?'
The interviewer asked _____.
5. 'What sort of expectations do you have regarding this job?'
The interviewer asked _____.
6. 'Will it be easy for you to enter into a new environment?'
The interviewer asked _____.
7. 'What sort of improvements would you introduce in our IT department?'
The interviewer asked _____.
8. 'Do you enjoy working in a team?'
The interviewer asked _____.
9. 'Are you planning to have children in the nearest future?'
The interviewer asked _____.
10. 'Is there anything that you might want to ask me?'
The interviewer asked _____.

277. ☺☺ Zamień poniższe fragmenty rozmowy o pracę na mowę zależną.

Wzór: 'Please call me by my first name.'
The interviewer told me *to call her by her first name.*

1. 'Tell me about your career so far.'
The interviewer asked me _____.
2. 'Don't try to impress me, just say what you really think.'
The interviewer asked me _____.
3. 'Fill in our questionnaire.'
The interviewer asked me _____.
4. 'Show me your references, please.'
The interviewer asked me _____.
5. 'Wait in the hall till I contact the manager.'
The interviewer asked me _____.
6. 'Don't be nervous.'
The interviewer asked me _____.
7. 'Don't get your hopes up, because there are 80 candidates for this position.'
The interviewer asked me _____.

8. 'Send us an e-mail with your updated address details.'
   The interviewer asked me _____.
9. 'Report to the reception downstairs for your ticket reimbursement.'
   The interviewer asked me _____.
10. 'Don't talk to the other candidates on your way out.'
   The interviewer asked me _____.

278. ☺☺☺ Zamień poniższą wypowiedź na mowę zależną.

'Would you like to know which courses to take in college?
First, answer the following questions.
Do you prefer straightforward, clear-cut answers, or do you enjoy receiving vague
information that you can interpret for yourself?
How do you feel in a large lecture room filled with people?
Are you perhaps more comfortable in a small group?
Think about courses you took in the past. Did you work well under time pressure? Or
would you rather have had more time to complete some of your assignments?
Did you enjoy individual tasks or are you more of a team-worker?
And last but not least, consider one more question. Will you be willing to devote a lot of
time to your studies at the expense of your private life?
Think it through, because your answers to all these questions will indicate your learning
style and attitude to education.
Take them into account when deciding on your courses.'

My school counsellor asked me _____
He advised me _____
He asked me _____
Then, _____
Next, _____
He also asked me _____
Last but not least, he asked me to _____
namely if _____
_____
He told me _____
He advised me _____

REPORTING VERBS

279. ☺☺ Zamień poniższe zdania na mowę zależną, wykorzystując czasowniki podane poniżej.

warn deny reveal confirm agree complain wonder remind announce admit

1. 'Our company is starting a new advertising campaign.'
   The Director _____.
2. 'The waiters are rude.'
   The guest _____.

3. 'The General has been collaborating with the enemy.'
   The army officials _____.
4. 'Can we reverse the effects of environmental pollution?'
   The scientist _____.
5. 'OK, I will help you.'
   My friend _____.
6. 'Don't touch this wire!'
   The technician _____.
7. 'I did not steal the money!'
   The man _____.
8. 'I made a mistake.'
   The employer _____.
9. 'The meeting will begin at 5 as planned.'
   The secretary _____.
10. 'Don't forget to buy your mother a present.'
    My dad _____.

280. ☺☺ Dobierz z ramki po trzy czasowniki o znaczeniu podobnym do podanych poniżej.

highlight demand maintain mention argue command presume ensure recommend underline guarantee point out notice suggest assure propose suppose maintain allege require emphasize

1. advise   _____
2. assume   _____
3. remark   _____
4. promise   _____
5. claim   _____
6. order   _____
7. stress   _____

281. ☺☺☺ Wykorzystaj czasowniki z poprzednich ćwiczeń, aby przekształcić poniższą wypowiedź na mowę zależną.

'The Global Volunteer Program is the largest such undertaking in the world and you can be sure that you have made the right decision, joining our ranks. But was it a fully conscious decision? It is true that participating in the program may be a lot of fun. But don't forget that it also involves a lot of personal responsibility. Not many of you realize that you will be cooperating in some world-wide projects which are of outmost importance to the existence of entire communities. I would say that some of our actions are comparable to the work of doctors or politicians. There is no place for hesitations and withdrawals. Think it through, before you start your work. You will often feel tired, confused and even discouraged. And yet, at the same time I guarantee that you will love it.'

The Program spokesman emphasized _____and he
_____
But _____. He _____
_____ Yet _____.
_____ He _____
_____. Further, he _____
To conclude, he _____

152

_____. He _____. And yet, at the same time

he _____

KLUCZ

267. 1. ...his history as an artist was long and complex. **2.** ...he had recently finished working on his autobio-graphy. **3.** ...he was going to record a new single soon. **4.** ...his next tour would probably be to Japan, which he found a truly amazing country. **5.** ...he was afraid he would be spending more time sightseeing than giving concerts. **6.** ...he had greatly enjoyed his tour around Poland. **7.** ...he remembered that he had met many Polish artists then, who had taken him to many interesting music events. **8.** ...he had even been thinking of coming to our country again. **9.** ...he had only been surprised to learn that someone else had received our Fryderyk music award. **10.** ...that meant that he would be working even harder on his publicity in Central Europe.

268. 1. ...he had bought that house two years before/earlier, because he had found it so peaceful there. **2.** ...he had given over two hundred concerts that year. **3.** ...only the day before he had received invitations to some 20 countries. **4.** ...the night before he had played in San Jose, where he would be returning later that week. **5.** ...he was then working on his 'Best of...' album, for which he had his first studio session the next day/the following day/the day after. **6.** ...his manager would be able to tell me more about it the following week/the week after. **7.** ...it was then his greatest ambition to make a film about rock music. **8.** ...he had started writing the scenario the year before/in the previous year and that hopefully the film would be in cinemas the following winter.

269. 1 B; mowa zależna nie jest konieczna dla prawd ogólnych. **2** B; wypowiedź jest nieaktualna (odnosi się do zeszłego roku). **3** A; mowa zależna nie jest konieczna, gdyż wypowiedź jest wciąż aktualna (odnosi się do najbliższego piątku). **4** A; mowa zależna nie jest konieczna, gdyż wypowiedź jest wciąż aktualna (Seb jest obecnie w Afryce). **5** B; mowa zależna jest konieczna, gdyż wypowiedź była nieprawdziwa i w ten sposób dystansujemy się do niej. **6** A; gdy dwie czynności przeszłe występują równocześnie albo krótko po sobie, nie używa się mowy zależnej.

270. ...that it was his pleasure to invite them to the Open Days of Garford University.
The President said that the event took place from May 2nd to May 12th and he hoped that both the students and their parents would participate in at least some of the days.
The President added that the Open Days were designed for the students to visit the university campus and get a first-hand feel for what it is/was like to study at Garford University.
He said that the students would be meeting the university staff, who would show them around the university facilities: the library, classrooms and student dorms. Other events included a concert of the university choir and an open-air fair of academic books.
He also said that in the past few years the Open Days had been a great success and had convinced many people to study at Garford.
The President concluded that hopefully that year it would be the students' turn to enjoy Garford and that he was looking forward to meeting all of them.

271. ...that after very high profits the year before/in the previous year, the year 2005 had been another record year for the Company.
The CEO said that a dynamic business climate had enabled them to improve their results. They had raised the prices, but reduced the costs and, above all, succeeded in their strategy of leadership on the IT market.
The CEO added that that success, however, had been overshadowed by the news that the following/next year the government would impose sanctions on the company for anti-competitive practices.
The CEO concluded that at that place he would only like to repeat that their company was giving that issue its full attention and was actively negotiating with the Minister. Their next meeting with the Minister was scheduled for the following week and the CEO expected that it would be a breakthrough in their talks.

272. ...that they imagined it as a very straightforward process: that a team of researchers working together in a laboratory submitted the results of their research to a journal, while the editor proof-read the paper and accepted it for publication.
The scientist said that in fact it had only used to be simple. Today the internet was making free access to scientific results a reality.

He added that in the previous week/the week before, the OECD had issued a report describing the consequences of that development. The report showed that the profits of publishers would be declining. But it also signalled a change in what had until then been the dominant model of scientific work: the model of a restricted, if not concealed, business.

He pointed out that online publication had enabled a wider access to research not only to the general public, but also to other researchers.

The scientist concluded that, increasingly, scientific research would be becoming a truly collaborative activity. Scientists would be able to comment on other people's work while it was still in progress.

273. **1.** he could give me some tips for my essay, but he would not write it for me. **2.** I might use his car whenever I needed it. **3.** Mark's poor grades could be a result of his family problems. **4.** he was sorry that he hadn't been able to come to my birthday party the day before. **5.** life in a city must have been much easier in the past. **6.** he had to call Mary and ask if there was anything he could do to help her. **7.** I had to/must report to him every morning at 8 am sharp. **8.** we shouldn't just sit around and wait for what happened. **9.** there might be some problems with my visa. **10.** in a job like his you couldn't get stressed over little things.

274. **1.** if his theory proved correct, he would be acclaimed a genius. **2.** if gunpowder had not been invented, human history would have taken a different course. **3.** if the government concentrated more on domestic policy, it would quickly gain public trust. **4.** if we tried hard enough, we would succeed. **5.** if I kept on annoying him, I would get myself into trouble. **6.** if he was me, he would start looking for another job. **7.** if Richard had foreseen the crisis, he could have taken some steps to prevent it. **8.** he would be very surprised if Charles passed his exam.

275. ...it might be hard to imagine that the nasty disease we knew as flu could turn into a superflu that might kill tens of millions of people within two years.

And yet, he said, if superflu struck, that was what might well happen.

He claimed that many scientists then believed that another pandemic was inevitable. Their alarms had even caught the attention of politicians, who were meeting in Canada the next/following month to discuss what could be done to prevent an outbreak and what measures had to be taken right away. He maintained that if the conference members managed to establish a sensible plan, a major pandemic could be prevented.

However, he said that many commentators seemed to doubt that, pointing out that if nothing had been done until that time, there was no reason to believe that anything would be done then.

276. **1.** what school I had gone to. **2.** if I had completed any additional courses. **3.** what my current employment was. **4.** if she might see my CV. **5.** what sort of expectations I had regarding that job. **6.** if it would be easy for me to enter into a new environment. **7.** what sort of improvements I would introduce in their IT department. **8.** if I enjoyed working in a team. **9.** if I was planning to have children in the nearest future. **10.** if there was anything that I might want to ask her.

277. **1.** ...to tell her about my career so far. **2.** ...not to try to impress her, just to say what I really thought. **3.** ...to fill in their questionnaire. **4.** ...to show her my references. **5.** ...to wait in the hall till she contacted the manager. **6.** ...not to be nervous. **7.** ...not to get my hopes up, because there were 80 candidates for that position. **8.** ...to send them an e-mail with my updated address details. **9.** ...to report to the reception downstairs for my ticket reimbursement. **10.** ...not to talk to the other candidates on my way out.

278. ...if I would you like to know which courses to take in college.

He advised me first to answer the following questions.

He asked me if I preferred straightforward, clear-cut answers, or if I enjoyed receiving vague information that I could interpret for myself.

Then, he asked me how I felt in a large lecture room filled with people and if I was perhaps more comfortable in a small group.

Next, he asked me to think about courses I had taken in the past. He asked me if I had worked well under time pressure or if I would rather have had more time to complete some of my assignments.

He also asked me if I had enjoyed individual tasks or if I was more of a team-worker.

Last but not least, he asked me to consider one more question, namely if I would be willing to devote a lot of time to my studies at the expense of my private life.

He told me to think it through, because my answers to all those questions would indicate my learning style and attitude to education.

He advised me to take them into account when deciding on my courses.

279. **1.** The Director announced that their company was starting a new advertising campaign. **2.** The guest complained that the waiters were rude. **3.** The army officials revealed that the General had been collaborating with the enemy. **4.** The scientist wondered if we could reverse the effects of environmental pollution. **5.** My friend agreed that he would help me/agreed to help me. **6.** The technician warned me not to touch that wire. **7.** The man denied that he had stolen/denied stealing the money. **8.** The employer admitted that he had made a mistake/admitted to making a mistake. **9.** The secretary confirmed that the meeting would begin at 5 as planned. **10.** My dad reminded me not to forget to buy my mother a present.

280. **1.** recommend, suggest, propose **2.** presume, suppose, maintain **3.** mention, point out, notice **4.** guarantee, ensure, assure **5.** argue, maintain, allege **6.** demand, require, command **7.** emphasize, highlight, underline

281. Proponowana wersja:

...that the Global Volunteer Program was the largest such undertaking in the world and he assured us that we had made the right decision, joining their ranks. But he wondered if it had been a fully conscious decision. He agreed that participating in the program might be a lot of fun. Yet he reminded us that it also involved a lot of personal responsibility. He pointed out that not many of us realized that we would be cooperating in some world-wide projects which were of outmost importance to the existence of entire communities. Further, he claimed that some of their actions were comparable to the work of doctors or politicians. He stressed that there was no place for hesitations and withdrawals. To conclude, he told us to think it through before we started our work. He warned us that we would often feel tired, confused and even discouraged. And yet, at the same time he guaranteed that we would love it.

PARTICIPLE CLAUSES

282. ☺☺ Przekształć podane zdania.

Wzór: Julie cleaned her teeth. Then she went to bed.
After cleaning her teeth, Julie went to bed.

1. First we watched a film. Then we played bridge.
Before _____.
2. June took a painkiller. Then she felt her headache was going away.
After _____.
3. I collected the children from school. Then I drove home.
I _____.
4. Martin was painting the door. He was listening to the news on the radio at the same time.
While _____.
5. I added some salt to the soup, and then I tasted it.
Before _____.
6. Andrew drove to the conference. During the journey he managed to plan his speech.
Andrew _____.

283. ☺☺ Przekształć podane zdania.

Wzór: While Jake was driving home, he run over a badger.
Driving home, Jake run over a badger.

1. While she was unfastening her boot, Martha looked up at her husband.
_____
2. Agnes was ready earlier. She started walking ahead of the group.
_____
3. As I was rummaging through old things in the attic, I found a box of 19th-century photos.
_____
4. I was late for lunch. As a result, I had to eat the leftovers.
_____
5. While I was doing my homework, I tried not to think about my girlfriend.
_____
6. When mother was going shopping, she took the garage keys with her.
_____

284. ☺☺☺ Przekształć podane zdania.

Wzór: After Ronald finished his essay, he went for a walk with the dog.
Having finished his essay, Ronald went for a walk with the dog.

1. We finished lunch. Then we started business talks.
_____
2. The car crashed into a roadside tree after it skidded on ice.
_____
3. The Browns returned home. They noticed it had been burgled.
_____
4. We returned home very tired after the long drive. We went to bed immediately.
_____

5. Teddy paid the debt. Then he promised himself never to borrow money again.

6. Wallace finished 'Anna Karenina'. Then he started reading 'War and Peace'.

KLUCZ

282. *Participle -ing clauses* to zdania podrzędne z imiesłowem czynnym. Zdania z *participle -ing clauses* wprowadzamy przysłówkami *after, before* lub *while*. UWAGA! W zdaniach tego typu podmiot *participle clause* musi być tożsamy z podmiotem zdania głównego.
1. Before playing bridge, we watched a film.
2. After taking a painkiller, June felt her headache was going away. (typowy błąd: *After taking a painkiller, June's headache went away. – to June wzięła proszek, a nie ból głowy!)
3. I drove home after collecting the children from school.
4. While painting the door, Martin was listening to the news on the radio./While listening to the news on the radio, Martin was painting the door.
5. Before tasting the soup, I added some salt to it. – nawet czasowniki, które nigdy nie występują w czasach ciągłych (tzw. *state verbs*, patrz ćw. nr 108, 109), posiadają formy z *-ing*, których możemy używać w zdaniach z *participle clause*.
6. Andrew managed to plan his speech while driving to the conference.

283. *Present participle -ing clauses* używamy, mówiąc o czynnościach równoczesnych (pkt. 1, 3, 5, 6) lub o rezultatach jakiejś czynności (pkt. 2, 4).
1. Unfastening her boot, Martha looked up at her husband.
2. Being ready earlier, Agnes started walking ahead of the group.
3. Rummaging through old things in the attic, I found a box of 19th-century photos.
4. Being late for lunch, I had to eat the leftovers.
5. Doing my homework, I tried not to think about my girlfriend.
6. Going shopping, mother took the garage keys with her.

284. *Past participle -ing clauses* używamy, mówiąc o czynnościach następujących bezpośrednio po sobie.
1. Having finished lunch, we started business talks.
2. Having skidded on ice, the car crashed into a roadside tree.
3. Having returned home, the Browns noticed it had been burgled.
4. Having returned home very tired after the long drive, we went to bed immediately.
5. Having paid the debt, Teddy promised himself never to borrow money again.
6. Having finished 'Anna Karenina', Wallace started reading 'War and Peace'.

RELATIVE CLAUSES

DEFINING RELATIVE CLAUSES

285. ☺☺ Uzupełnij poniższe definicje odpowiednimi wyrażeniami z ramki, używając *relative clauses* z *that/which/who*.

> ~~must be very patient~~   requires good writing skills   has revolutionized human communication   feels superior to others   can predict the future by palm reading has conquered the world book market   can be both dangerous and exciting you can always count on   everybody recognizes   earns heaps of money

1. A teacher is a person   *who must be very patient.*
2. A snob is a person   _____
3. A millionaire is a person   _____
4. Journalism is profession   _____
5. Kite-surfing is a hobby   _____
6. The Internet is an invention   _____
7. Michel Jackson is a name   _____
8. 'Harry Potter' is a book series   _____
9. A good friend is somebody   _____
10. A fortune-teller is a person   _____

286. ☺☺ Połącz poniższe zdania zgodnie z podanym początkiem, używając *defining relative clauses* z *that/which/who*.

1. Stilton is a traditional British cheese. The cheese is protected by the European Union laws.
   Stilton _____
2. You are wearing a necklace. Is the necklace made of silver?
   Is the necklace _____
3. A photo hangs above my bed. The photo shows my great-grandparents.
   The photo _____
4. This is a book. I have been telling you about it.
   This is the book _____
5. One of the job candidates has an interesting CV. He came late to the interview.
   The job candidate _____
6. Some children will get their schoolbooks free of charge. The parents of these children cannot afford to buy the schoolbooks.
   The children _____
7. A boy brought the paper this morning. He has just moved into our neighbourhood.
   The boy _____
8. Some of the company cars will be brought to the garage for inspection. The mileage in these cars exceeds 100,000 miles.
   The company cars _____

9. Every student should select a course. The course best suits his/her area of study.
Every student _____

10. We have organized a charity concert in aid of the citizens of our town. The citizens of our town have suffered in the flood.
We have organized _____

287. ☺☺ W niektórych z poniższych zdań można opuścić zaimki *that/which/who*. Przepisz te zdania bez zaimków.

1. This is one of the best films that I have ever seen.
_____

2. Could you please pass me the book that lies on the table?
_____

3. Are there any other films with this actor that you could recommend?
_____

4. I know the man who has just passed us on the street.
_____

5. During her holidays in Spain Doris met some wonderful people who she is still in touch with.
_____

6. This is a problem that troubles many scientists around the world.
_____

7. Our manager is one of those people who you would like to have as little to do with as possible.
_____

8. The office of the president's deputy was given to a minister who has been his trusted adviser for a long time.
_____

NON-DEFINING RELATIVE CLAUSES

288. ☺☺ Uzupełnij poniższe zdania wyrażeniami z ramki oraz zaimkami *who/which*, dodając odpowiednio przecinki.

> ~~is the capital of Tunisia~~   is the most exclusive residence in town   is a famous American composer   bears the title of the Prince of York   is the author of 'The Name of the Rose'   I have known since high-school   is known as the hottest place on Earth   is called the Oscar of the music industry

1. My uncle lives in Tunis, *which is the capital of Tunisia.* _____
2. Hilary _____ is one of my longest-standing friends.
3. The conference was held at the Summer Palace _____
4. Our school is named after Edward A. MacDowell _____
5. Eminem is this year's winner of the Grammy Award _____
6. The University of Bologne is proud to have Umberto Eco _____ among its lecturers.

7. Prince Andrew _____ is Prince Charles' younger brother.
8. The Death Valley _____ lies in California.

289. ☺☺ Uzupełnij poniższe zdania właściwymi zaimkami względnymi, dodając odpowiednio przecinki.

1. At my new job I met Albert Smith _____ I know from my previous company.
2. This year we are spending our holiday in Bournemouth _____ is an exclusive seaside resort in Britain.
3. The guy serving me at the restaurant turned out to be a psychologist by profession _____ worked as a waiter in his free time to gather observations on people's behaviour.
4. The sheriff decided to offer a high reward for the horse _____ had been stolen before.
5. Agnes _____ not many people in our department are able to get on with is highly praised by the management.
6. This bed & breakfast inn _____ owners have been in the industry for two decades now is immensely popular with tourists.
7. I like to have my tea biscuits with custard _____ a delicious vanilla dessert sauce.
8. The students at our school _____ parents are typically senior company executives or diplomats have already lived and gone to school in several countries around the world.

290. ☺☺ Połącz poniższe zdania, używając *relative clauses*.

1. I find it quite practical to have Albert as my neighbour, because I can always ask him for legal advice. (Albert is an attorney).

   _____

2. My husband is tall and has got blonde hair. (His ancestors came from the Netherlands).

   _____

3. I am going to see the new film with Brad Pitt at the weekend. (I have heard good things about the film).

   _____

4. The results of the final exam were obviously very good. (The students had prepared very hard for that exam).

   _____

5. The employee filed in a resignation. (The management had had high hopes with that employee).

   _____

6. This year an anonymous Iraqi woman has been nominated for the prestigious literary Samuel Johnson Prize. (She has published a blog describing the impact of the war in Iraq on the lives of common people).

   _____

7. My little sister has just announced she is moving to Alaska. (My parents are constantly worried about her).

   _____

8. The Holy Grail was an object of desire of many generations. (It was thought to possess magical powers).

   _____

9. The Faroe Islands are a worthwhile destination for a linguist. (Their inhabitants speak Danish and a local dialect called 'Faroese').

   _____

10. While in exile, Adam Mickiewicz continued to exchange love letters with his beloved Maryla. (He was, however, never allowed to marry her).

   _____

CO-ORDINATE CLAUSES

291. ☺☺ Połącz poniższe zdania za pomocą zaimka *which*.

1. The Minister declined his nomination to the European Parliament. This surprised his fellow party members.

2. The band had to cancel its concert in Poland. All fans very much regretted this fact.

3. Richard turned down the job offer. This later proved the biggest mistake in his life.

4. The acrobat announced he was quitting his circus career. His family was glad to hear that.

5. Jack and Jill are spending Christmas in the Caribbean's. I find this truly appalling.

6. The professor did not allow the students to repeat the exam. This was very mean of him.

7. The host asked his guests to take off their shoes and put on some fluffy slippers that he had brought. Most of the guests considered that offensive.

8. My boyfriend loves playing with my dog. I find this very touching.

9. My mom watches soap operas every day, and I consider it a waste of time.

10. The Joneses have different social backgrounds. This seems to influence the relations between their families.

292. ☺☺ Połącz poniższe zdania za pomocą zaimka *as*.

1. The government has no clear plan what to do. This is something that is obvious from its actions.

2. In some cases love is not a joyful experience. This was the case with Romeo and Juliet.

3. George is not very well educated. This can be observed when we begin talking about history or politics.

4. Tragedy can unite strangers. This was seen during some of the recent terrorist attacks.

5. The monument of the king is much older than what the date underneath suggests. This is evident upon careful examination.

6. Our Manager is very quick-tempered. This could be witnessed during the last Board meeting.

7. When the messenger arrived at the castle, he first went to the temple to thank the gods for a safe journey. That was the custom at the time.

_____

8. Great careers may end in a tragic way. This was the case with the great actor James Dean.

_____

293. ☺☺ Skomentuj poniższe zdania w dowolny sposób, korzystając z wyrażeń w ramce i używając *relative clauses*.

| be very lucky   find funny   be unfair   appreciate   regret   be a pity   be ignorant |
| be proud of |

1. Sam found very cheap accommodation in the centre of London,_ *which was very lucky.*_
2. The summer holidays have passed very quickly, _____
3. Shy students tend to be considered less bright, _____
4. Lucy didn't know who Winston Churchill was, _____
5. My daughter is among the best students in her school, _____
6. Our headmaster tripped and dropped all his books, _____
7. My ex-boyfriend helped me when I was moving flats, _____
8. Not many foreigners have heard about Polish mountain resorts, _____

DEFINING VS. NON-DEFINING RELATIVE CLAUSES

294. ☺☺ Zdecyduj, które z poniższych zdań to *defining*, a które *non-defining relative clauses*. Uzupełnij *non-defining clauses* przecinkami.

1. The customer who is sitting at the table in the corner is a famous actor.
2. Flexibility is a feature which is often expected of job candidates.
3. My husband who is a civil service employee has got very rigid working hours.
4. Staff meetings which are hardly ever productive are nevertheless obligatory for all departments.
5. Children whose parents come from two different countries have the potential advantage of becoming bilingual.
6. My cousins whose parents are both dentists are not allowed to eat chocolate.
7. London which is the destination of many career-seekers from around the world has become a truly global city.
8. The company has finally made an offer that is acceptable to both parties.
9. Last week the City Hall held a press conference with Paulo Coelho who is the author of several international bestsellers.
10. Don't forget to send a birthday card to Peter who is turning 33 next Friday.

295. ☺☺ Uzupełnij poniższy dialog odpowiednimi zaimkami oraz przecinkami tam, gdzie to konieczne.

Lucinda: 'Have you already met the family (1) _____ have moved in downstairs, Albert?'
Albert: 'I'm not sure. Is it the one with a tall fat guy (2) _____ drives a red Porsche?'

Lucinda: 'No, of course not! That's the Joneses (3) _____ have lived here longer than we have.'

Albert: 'Really? Then I guess I don't know who the new family are. Who do you mean?'

Lucinda: 'I mean the Italian couple (4) _____ children are always playing right in front of our windows. I believe the husband (5) _____ is by the way extremely nice is called Paulo.'

Albert: 'Is it the Paulo (6) _____ has brought us a basket of fruit and vegetables the other day?'

Lucinda: 'Yes, that's him! He always carries some bottles with pesticides with him (7) _____ means that he must be a gardener.'

Albert: 'I never knew you were so sharp-eyed, Lucinda! I didn't even know (8) _____ the red car belonged to...'

Lucinda: 'Well, that's true; I easily notice things about other people. I even know whose children are playing outside at the moment. They are the Smiths' boys (9) _____ live upstairs.'

Albert: 'And how do you know that?'

Lucinda: 'By looking at their bikes! John and Jack are the only children in the neighbourhood (10) _____ parents are rich enough to afford something as expensive.'

296. ☺☺ Połącz poniższe zdania zgodnie z podanym początkiem, używając odpowiednich *relative clauses*. Wstaw przecinki tam, gdzie to konieczne.

1. Bob is a fireman. Bob saved my cat once. The cat was trapped in a sewage pipe.
   Bob is the fireman _____

2. After the Battle of Hastings William of Normandy was declared William the Conqueror. In the battle William of Normandy defeated the English king Harold II.
   After the Battle of Hastings _____

3. Abraham Lincoln will be remembered as the man who freed the slaves. During his presidency the Secession War took place.
   Abraham Lincoln _____

4. The princess announced that she had secretly become engaged to the gardener. This infuriated her father.
   The princess _____

5. The rebellion is actually quite a fascinating historical period. Little has been written about the rebellion in history books.
   The rebellion _____

6. Not everybody knows that T.S. Eliot was born in America. The writings of T.S Eliot are considered a remarkable achievement of Modernist poetry.
   Not everybody _____

7. A Professor Smith has come today to talk about the advantages of solar energy. It is not the Professor Smith whom you remember from last-year's lecture.
   The Professor Smith _____

8. The employee has signed a Confidentiality Agreement. According to the Agreement he must treat all documents entrusted to him as strictly confidential.
   The employee _____

9. Some of the children had played seek and hide all day long. These children fell asleep right away in the evening.
   The children _____

10. The bride's family arrived an hour late. By that time the poor girl had cried at least twice.
    _____

WHERE, WHEN, WHY, WHAT

297. ☺☺ Uzupełnij poniższe zdania przysłówkami *where, when* i *why*. Wstaw przecinki tam, gdzie to konieczne.

1. Valencia is one of the remarkable Spanish cities (1) _____ the cafes are always full at any time of the night.
2. Patricia is strikingly overconfident. I'm just waiting for the day (2) _____ her behaviour gets her into trouble.
3. Stratford-upon-Avon (3) _____ William Shakespeare was born is situated in the heart of the English Midlands.
4. The reason (4) _____ so many people came to the opening of the gallery was because they were given a free drink.
5. In the 1980s (5) _____ empty-shelved shops were a frequent sight all around the country exotic fruit was a real luxury.
6. Could you please give me the address details of the hotel (6) _____ you spent your last holidays? It looked very charming in the pictures.
7. In their applications the candidates are requested to enumerate the reasons (7) _____ they would like to join our organization.
8. The times (8) _____ a girl would ask her parents' permission to accept a boy's proposal seem to be irrevocably over.
9. The Grand Banquet (9) _____ the winners of this year's film awards will be announced is organized at the Silver Palace.
10. The years at university (10) _____ all of us were full of energy and ideals and believed that we could change the world belong to my most memorable days.

298. ☺☺ Przekształć poniższe zdania, zastępując podkreślone fragmenty wyrażeniami z *what*.

1. <u>The thing that</u> I found most suspicious about our Chinese teacher was that every 10 seconds he had to look things up in the dictionary.
   _____

2. Santa Claus and the Christmas tree are <u>the things that</u> we usually associate with Christmas.
   _____

3. People with emotional disorders often live in their own little world, but <u>the thing that</u> is even worse is that they are unable to express their feelings.
   _____

4. The behaviour of the witness suggests that he may know something about the accident. <u>The thing that</u> is even more important is that he may also know who was involved in it.
   _____

5. Tell me <u>about something that</u> you would like to get for your 18th birthday.
   _____

6. <u>The fact that</u> is worth mentioning is that Ralph was one of the few students who received the prestigious President's Award.
   _____

7. <u>The thing that</u> we need to discuss here are our chances of receiving a government subsidy.
   _____

8. People chatting over their mobile phones are <u>the thing that</u> annoys me most in cinemas.
   _____

299. ☺☺ Połącz poniższe zdania zgodnie z podanym początkiem, używając odpowiednich *relative clauses*. Dodaj przecinki tam, gdzie to konieczne.

1. Southern Poland is one of the most beautiful parts of this country. All my relatives come from that region.
   Southern Poland _____.
2. You used to live in Egypt. Can you tell me about that time?
   Can you tell me _____?
3. Our teacher has a habit of punctuating his classes with silly jokes. This is the thing that annoys most of us.
   Our teacher's habit _____.
4. The accident happened because the emergency brakes of the train did not work.
   The reason _____.
5. The Lagoon Disco is the most popular dance club in town. Many famous actors spend Saturday nights at that disco.
   The Lagoon Disco _____.
6. True love is something that we all secretly dream about.
   True love _____.
7. The upcoming presidential elections is the thing that is on the minds of all people in our country at the moment.
   The upcoming _____.
8. Patrick decided to start his own business. This was something that nobody would have expected.
   Patrick's decision _____.
9. The Renaissance is a literary period. During that period the achievements of the Antiquity were a great inspiration.
   The Renaissance _____.
10. This chapter of the book deals with the problem of ethics in public life. By the way, the photographs in this chapter have been reproduced from the author's webpage.
    This chapter of the book _____.

KLUCZ

285. **2.** who/that feels superior to others. **3.** who/that earns heaps of money. **4.** which/that requires good writing skills. **5.** which/that can be both dangerous and exciting. **6.** that/which has revolutionized human communication. **7.** which/that everybody recognizes. **8.** which/that has conquered the world book market. **9.** who(m)/that you can always count on. – zaimek *who* może w dopełnieniu przyjmować w stylu formalnym formę *whom*. **10.** who/that can predict the future by palm reading.

286. **1.** Stilton is a traditional British cheese which/that is protected by the European Union laws.
   2. Is the necklace which/that you are wearing made of silver?
   3. The photo which/that hangs above my bed shows my great-grandparents.
   4. This is the book which/that I have been telling you about.
   5. The job candidate who/that came late to the interview has an interesting CV.
   6. The children whose parents cannot afford to buy the schoolbooks will get them free of charge.
   7. The boy who/that brought the paper this morning has just moved into our neighbourhood.
   8. The company cars whose mileage exceeds 100,000 miles will be brought to the garage for inspection. – Zaimek dzierżawczy *whose* stosuje się zarówno do osób, jak i przedmiotów.
   9. Every student should select a course which/that best suits his/her area of study.
   10. We have organized a charity concert in aid of the citizens of our town who/that have suffered in the flood.

287. Jeśli zaimek pełni funkcję dopełnienia w *defining relative clause*, to można go opuścić.

1. This is one of the best films I have ever seen. **2.** Nie można opuścić zaimka. **3.** Are there any other films with this actor you could recommend? **4.** Nie można opuścić zaimka. **5.** During her holidays in Spain Doris met some wonderful people she is still in touch with. **6.** Nie można opuścić zaimka. **7.** Our manager is one of those people you would like to have as little to do with as possible. **8.** Nie można opuścić zaimka.

288. 2. Hilary, who(m) I have known since high-school, is one of my longest-standing friends. – Zaimek *who* może przyjmować formę *whom* w dopełnieniu w stylu formalnym.

3. The conference was held at the Summer Palace, which is the most exclusive residence in town.

4. Our school is named after Edward A. MacDowell, who was a famous American composer.

5. Eminem is this year's winner of the Grammy Award, which is called the Oscar of the music industry.

6. The University of Bologne is proud to have Umberto Eco, who is the author of 'The Name of the Rose', among its lecturers.

7. Prince Andrew, who bears the title of the Prince of York, is Prince Charles' younger brother.

8. The Death Valley, which is known as the hottest place on Earth, lies in California.

289. 1. At my new job I met Albert Smith, who(m) I know from my previous company. – Zaimek *who* może przyjmować formę *whom* w dopełnieniu w stylu formalnym.

2. This year we are spending our holiday in Bournemouth, which is an exclusive seaside resort in Britain.

3. The guy serving me at the restaurant turned out to be a psychologist by profession, who worked as a waiter in his free time to gather observations on people's behaviour.

4. The sheriff decided to offer a high reward for the horse, which had been stolen before.

5. Agnes, who not many people in our department are able to get on with/with whom not many people in our department are able to get on, is highly praised by the management.

6. This bed & breakfast inn, whose owners have been in the industry for two decades now, is immensely popular with tourists. – Zaimek dzierżawczy *whose* stosuje się zarówno do osób, jak i przedmiotów.

7. I like to have my tea biscuits with custard, which is a delicious vanilla dessert sauce.

8. The students at our school, whose parents are typically senior company executives or diplomats, have already lived and gone to school in several countries around the world.

290. 1. I find it quite practical to have Albert, who is an attorney, as my neighbour, because I can always ask him for legal advice.

2. My husband, whose ancestors came from the Netherlands, is tall and has got blonde hair.

3. I am going to see the new film with Brad Pitt, which I have heard good things about/about which have heard good things, at the weekend.

4. The results of the final exam, for which the students had prepared very hard, were obviously very good.

5. The employee, with whom the management had had high hopes/who the management had had high hopes with, filed in a resignation.

6. This year an anonymous Iraqi woman, who has published a blog describing the impact of the war in Iraq on the lives of common people, has been nominated for the prestigious literary Samuel Johnson Prize.

7. My little sister, about whom my parents are constantly worried/who my parents are constantly worried about, has just announced she is moving to Alaska.

8. The Holy Grail, which was thought to possess magical powers, was an object of desire of many generations.

9. The Faroe Islands, whose inhabitants speak Danish and a local dialect called 'Faroese', are a worthwhile destination for a linguist.

10. While in exile, Adam Mickiewicz continued to exchange love letters with his beloved Maryla, who(m) he, however, was never allowed to marry.

291. 1. The Minister declined his nomination to the European Parliament, which surprised his fellow party members.

2. The band had to cancel its concert in Poland, which all fans very much regretted.

3. Richard turned down the job offer, which later proved the biggest mistake in his life.

4. The acrobat announced he was quitting his circus career, which his family was glad to hear.

5. Jack and Jill are spending Christmas in the Caribbean's, which I find truly appalling.

6. The professor did not allow the students to repeat the exam, which was very mean of him.

7. The host asked his guests to take off their shoes and put on some fluffy slippers that he had brought, which most of the guests considered offensive.

8. My boyfriend loves playing with my dog, which I find very touching.

9. My mom watches soap operas every day, which I consider a waste of time.

10. The Joneses have different social backgrounds, which seems to influence the relations between their families.

292. 1. The government has no clear plan what to do, as is obvious from its actions.
2. In some cases love is not a joyful experience, as was the case with Romeo and Juliet.
3. George is not very well educated, as can be observed when we begin talking about history or politics.
4. Tragedy can unite strangers, as was seen during some of the recent terrorist attacks.
5. The monument of the king is much older than what the date underneath suggests, as is evident upon careful examination.
6. Our Manager is very quick-tempered, as could be witnessed during the last Board meeting.
7. When the messenger arrived at the castle, he first went to the temple to thank the gods for a safe journey, as was the custom at the time.
8. Great careers may end in a tragic way, as was the case with the great actor James Dean.

293. Proponowane komentarze:
2. The summer holidays have passed very quickly, which I regret/which is a pity.
3. Shy students tend to be considered less bright, which is unfair.
4. Lucy didn't know who Winston Churchill was, which was ignorant of her.
5. My daughter is among the best students in her school, which I am proud of.
6. Our headmaster tripped and dropped all his books, which we found funny.
7. My ex-boyfriend helped me when I was moving flats, which I appreciated.
8. Not many foreigners have heard about Polish mountain resorts, which I regret/which is a pity.

294. 1. *defining relative clause*, bez przecinków **2.** *defining relative clause*, bez przecinków **3.** *non-defining relative clause*: ..., who is a civil service employee, **4.** *non-defining relative clause*: ..., which are hardly ever productive, **5.** *defining relative clause*, bez przecinków **6.** *non-defining relative clause*: ..., whose parents are both dentists, **7.** *non-defining relative clause*: ..., which is the destination of many career-seekers from around the world, **8.** *defining relative clause*, bez przecinków **9.** *non-defining relative clause* ..., who is the author of several international bestsellers. **10.** *non-defining relative clause* ..., who is turning 33 next Friday.

295. 1. ...who/that have moved in downstairs **2.** ...who/that drives a red Porsche **3.** ..., who have lived here longer than we have. **4.** ...whose children are always playing right in front of our windows. **5.** ..., who is by the way extremely nice, ... **6.** ...who/that has brought us a basket of fruit and vegetables the other day?
7. ..., which means that he must be a gardener. **8.** ...who the red car belonged to... **9.** ..., who live upstairs.
10. ... whose parents are rich enough to afford something as expensive.

296. 1. Bob is the fireman who saved my cat once, which was trapped in a sewage pipe.
2. After the Battle of Hastings, in which he defeated the English king Harold II, William of Normandy was declared William the Conqueror.
3. Abraham Lincoln, during whose presidency the Secession War took place, will be remembered as the man who freed the slaves.
4. The princess announced that she had secretly become engaged to the gardener, which infuriated her father.
5. The rebellion, about which little has been written in history books, is actually quite a fascinating historical period.
6. Not everybody knows that T.S. Eliot, whose writings are considered a remarkable achievement of Modernist poetry, was born in America.
7. The Professor Smith who has come today to tell something about the advantages of solar energy is not the Professor Smith whom you remember from last-year's lecture.
8. The employee has signed a Confidentiality Agreement, according to which he must treat all documents entrusted to him as strictly confidential.
9. The children that had played seek and hide all day long fell asleep right away in the evening.
10. The bride's family arrived an hour late, by which time the poor girl had cried at least twice.

297. 1. where **2.** when **3.** ..., where William Shakespeare was born, ... **4.** why **5.** ..., when empty-shelved shops were a frequent sight all around the country, ... **6.** where **7.** why **8.** when **9.** ..., where the winners of this year's film awards will be announced, ... **10.** ..., when all of us were full of energy and ideals and believed that we could change the world, ...

298. 1. What I found most suspicious **2.** are what we usually associate with Christmas. **3.** but what is even worse is that they are unable to express their feelings. **4.** What is even more important is that **5.** Tell me what you would like to get for your 18th birthday. **6.** What is worth mentioning is that **7.** What we need to discuss here are **8.** are what annoys me most in cinemas.

299. 1. Southern Poland, where all my relatives come from, is one of the most beautiful parts of this country.

2. Can you tell me about the time when you used to live in Egypt?

3. Our teacher's habit of punctuating his classes with silly jokes is what annoys most of us.

4. The reason why the accident happened was because the emergency brakes of the train did not work.

5. The Lagoon Disco, where many famous actors spend Saturday nights, is the most popular dance club in town.

6. True love is what we all secretly dream about.

7. The upcoming presidential elections is what is on the minds of all people in our country at the moment.

8. Patrick's decision to start his own business was what nobody would have expected.

9. The Renaissance is a literary period when the achievements of the Antiquity were a great inspiration.

10. This chapter of the book, where, by the way, the photographs have been reproduced from the author's webpage, deals with the problem of ethics in public life.

EMPHASIS

INVERSION

300. ☺☺ Przekształć poniższe zdania zgodnie z podanym początkiem.

1. Our school has rarely admitted children as bright as your daughter.
   Rarely _____

2. We can seldom rely on the good intentions of others.
   Seldom _____

3. The thief did not know that he was being followed by the detective.
   Little _____

4. Such great excitement has scarcely been witnessed at our company.
   Scarcely _____

5. Great achievements seldom earn great appreciation.
   Seldom _____

6. The king did not realize that his reign was about to end.
   Little _____

7. The government's politics has hardly generated any positive comments.
   Hardly _____

8. One can rarely encounter this species in its natural environment.
   Rarely _____

9. The President did not expect that his speech would stir such criticism.
   Little _____

10. I have seldom seen my mother in a better mood.
    Seldom _____

301. ☺☺ Przekształć poniższe zdania zgodnie z podanym początkiem.

1. The chairman had hardly entered the room when he was attacked by his fellow party members.
   Hardly _____

2. The concert had scarcely begun when the lead singer fainted and fell onto the floor.
   Scarcely _____

3. The great advertising campaign had no sooner begun than it had to be suspended due to the lack of funds.
   No sooner _____

4. The battle had hardly begun when the king called for an armistice.
   Hardly _____

5. I had scarcely left the house when my children began celebrating.
   Scarcely _____

6. The election campaign had no sooner ended than the candidates started planning the next one.
   No sooner _____

7. The travellers had scarcely set off when the fog came down.
   Scarcely _____

8. The robber had no sooner broken into the bank than the alarm went off.
   No sooner _____

9. The couple had hardly come back from their honeymoon when the husband was called away on business.
   Hardly _____

10. The difficult situation had scarcely been solved when another problem appeared.
    Scarcely _____

302. ☺☺☺ Przekształć poniższe zdania, tak aby otrzymać efekt emfazy.

1. The experience was so devastating for him that he had to seek the help of a psychologist.
   _____

2. Her smile was so enchanting that men would do anything to have her smile at least once.
   _____

3. The details of this program are so difficult that even senior staff have to refer to the guidelines for help.
   _____

4. The splendour of the ceremony was such that the guests felt truly overwhelmed.
   _____

5. The rehearsal was so straining that even the extra crew were tired.
   _____

6. Sandra's lover left her after she had divorced her husband. The irony of life is such.
   _____

7. Jane Rowling's books are so popular that she can sell several million copies within a month.
   _____

8. The inequalities in the world are such that one begins to doubt any progress in human thinking.
   _____

INVERSION: NEGATIVE AND RESTRICTIVE EXPRESSIONS

303. ☺☺ Uzupełnij poniższe zdania emfatyczne odpowiednim wyrażeniem z ramki.

such   much as   under no circumstances   only after   never before
not even once   little   rarely   hardly   no sooner

1. _____ my husband tried to pretend that nothing had happened, he did not manage to fool me.

2. _____ had the duchess entered the ballroom than she was surrounded by a swarm of admirers.

3. _____ do genius children become famous as adults.

4. _____ did the groom look at the bride during their wedding.

5. _____ had I begun to enjoy the party when my mobile phone rang.
6. _____ did the candidates expect what tough questions they were going to be asked.
7. _____ are you to touch any of these cables.
8. _____ has humanity faced a greater challenge.
9. _____ was the anger of the Emperor that he had all his counsellors executed.
10. _____ you have struggled through all the formalities, you will truly appreciate the fact that you are a member of our organisation.

304. ☺☺☺ Przekształć poniższe zdania, tak aby otrzymać efekt emfazy za pomocą podkreślonych elementów.

1. You may <u>on no account</u> reveal to Robert that you know the truth.
   _____

2. Dead pigeons are <u>under no circumstances</u> to be touched or moved.
   _____

3. We can learn the truth about that accident <u>only by talking to the witnesses</u>.
   _____

4. Better living conditions are to be found <u>nowhere</u>.
   _____

5. The consequences of this tragedy will become visible <u>only after some time has passed</u>.
   _____

6. The spread of the disease can <u>in no way</u> be prevented.
   _____

7. You should <u>on no account</u> panic or act hastily.
   _____

8. The child will be able to find love and protection <u>only in a good foster family</u>.
   _____

9. The evidence can <u>under no circumstances</u> be accessed by the police.
   _____

10. The origins of the wicker chair-making tradition have <u>in no way</u> been established.
    _____

305. ☺☺☺ Przekształć poniższe zdania, tak aby otrzymać efekt emfazy.

1. Mary did not apologise even once for her scandalous behaviour at the Easter party.
   _____

2. It was apparent at no time that the leader of the rebellion was cooperating with the government.
   _____

3. Democracy has never before been faced with a greater threat.
   _____

4. This man will never again intimidate your family.
   _____

5. I did not get to speak English even once during my English course.
   _____

6. It never at any time occurred to us to call our parents and tell them where we were.
   _____

7. A mistake like that has never happened at our company before.
   _____

8. The legendary football team was never again to win the world cup.
   _____

9. The humiliation of the company has at no time been greater.

10. The gambler did not make a good bet even once.

CLEFT SENTENCES

306. ☺☺☺ Przekształć poniższe zdania, przenosząc nacisk na podkreślone fragmenty za pomocą konstrukcji *It is/was... who/that...*

1. The American scientist Thomas Edison invented the light bulb.

2. Young, promising business sharks are the most frequent victims of the supply and demand forces.

3. Ancient Greeks worshipped Zeus; in Rome the same god was known as Jupiter.

4. According to some sources, the Georgians were first to produce wine.

5. My argument with the manager's assistant contributed to my dismissal, I am sure of that!

6. The school council didn't like the new maths teacher. He had discovered some errors in the council's financial reports.

7. My daughter's little lies hurt me most.

8. The president cared only about fame and power and not the fate of his country.

9. Beth needs support now, not our sarcastic comments.

10. The examiners expect creativity and flexibility from the candidates, not pure textbook knowledge.

307. ☺☺☺ Przekształć poniższe zdania, przenosząc nacisk na podkreślone fragmenty za pomocą konstrukcji *It is/was... who/that...*

1. I love Paris. My boyfriend proposed to me while we were staying in Paris.

2. The shops are usually most busy on Sundays, although people should actually spend that day at home with their families.

3. The future of the organization was decided on that very day.

4. <u>Thanks to the support of his many friends</u>, the retired pilot was able to go on with his life.

_____

5. The treaty was terminated <u>because of the members's obstinacy.</u>

_____

6. One can achieve fluency in a foreign language <u>only by speaking it as much as possible.</u>

_____

7. I have been signed out of hospital <u>at my own request.</u>

_____

8. We understood the idea of electromagnetic fields <u>only after our teacher had forced us to prepare a presentation on that topic.</u>

_____

9. Many members of the British royal family got married <u>in St. George's Chapel situated within Windsor Castle.</u>

_____

10. People began to appreciate the achievements of the previous government <u>only after several months had passed from the new elections.</u>

_____

308. ☺☺☺ Przekształć poniższe zdania, przenosząc nacisk na podkreślone fragmenty za pomocą konstrukcji *What... most was...*

Wzór:
Polish mountains are especially famous for the heather that blooms in September.
What Polish mountains are especially famous for is the heather that blooms in September.

1. The fragile structure of the party tent worried me most.

_____

2. The teachers were shocked at the students' indifference towards the victims of the great flood in their town.

_____

3. The company needs above all to concentrate its efforts on improving its image.

_____

4. The book basically tells us that true friendship is an invaluable and yet rare treasure.

_____

5. He had paid far too much for that second-hand car, which made him angry.

_____

6. Pauline is particularly good at asking people the questions that they least expect.

_____

7. We were most puzzled by the good-humouredness with which they went through their divorce.

_____

8. The fact that the enemy was defeated within just two weeks needs to be stressed here.

_____

9. Jack didn't even try to justify his behaviour, which struck me most.

_____

CONCESSIVE CLAUSES: AS/THOUGH

309. ☺☺☺ Przekształć poniższe zdania, używając konstrukcji *as/though it is/was...*

Wzór: His story seemed obscure at first, but it turned out rather clear in the end.
Obscure though/as his story seemed at first, it turned out rather clear in the end.

1. Though it seems difficult, you must try to make new friends at your new school.
   _____

2. Although we were tired after the journey, we were happy to have come home at last.
   _____

3. The shoes of this brand are very expensive, but they are very durable.
   _____

4. English beers are tasty, but they cannot beat the traditional ale.
   _____

5. Though it seems unfair, you should apologise first to your manager.
   _____

6. My mother is quite impulsive, but she hardly ever panics.
   _____

7. Though the lecture was well-structured, it was not very enlightening.
   _____

8. Although Polish people are quarrelsome, they usually unite in the face of danger.
   _____

9. The new book was well-written, but it never managed to get to the top of bestseller lists.
   _____

310. ☺☺☺ Przekształć poniższe zdania, używając konstrukcji *...as/though it may be/may have been...*

Wzór: The news seems shocking, but we mustn't overreact.
Shocking though/as the news may seem, we mustn't overreact.

1. Our chemistry teacher is demanding, but she is always just in her marks.
   _____

2. Japanese cars are expensive, but they are of very good quality.
   _____

3. Although we tried, we couldn't talk our parents into buying us a dog.
   _____

4. The company's offer was good, but it lacked some bonus options which were available elsewhere.
   _____

5. Our school basketball team is good on the local level, but it won't stand much chance in the national finals.
   _____

6. Though it seems impossible, an average humming-bird is the size of a human nail.
   _____

7. Eve was obviously upset, but she shouldn't have slammed the door running out.
   _____

8. Although the runner tried, he didn't qualify for the final run.

9. I try very hard, but I cannot convince Fred to see a family therapist.

311. ☺☺☺ Przekształć poniższe zdania, używając *concessive clauses* i wyrazów podanych w nawiasach.

Wzór:

The choir had practiced a lot, but their concert was not as successful as expected. (MUCH)
Much as the choir had practiced, their concert was not as successful as expected.

1. I like swimming, but I wouldn't like to spend my entire holidays at the seaside. (MUCH)

2. No matter how angry you were with your employee, you shouldn't have raised your voice. (HOWEVER)

3. Although teaching may seem boring to some people, it gives me a lot of satisfaction. (AS)

4. Although the shop-owner tried to be friendly, the customers could sense that he was bored and irritated. (HOWEVER)

5. Although my uncle was rather good-natured, he could not forgive his wife's infidelity. (THOUGH)

6. No matter what means she used, she couldn't convince her boss to raise her salary. (WHATEVER)

7. The exam was difficult, but it was quite predictable. (AS)

8. Many young women adore little children, but few would be ready to have one of their own. (MUCH)

9. No matter how mean my sister may have been to me, she would always take my side in front of our parents. (HOWEVER)

KLUCZ

Konstrukcje przedstawione w tym rozdziale są typowe dla wypowiedzi pisemnych, nie dla mowy potocznej.

300. 1. Rarely has our school admitted children as bright as your daughter.
2. Seldom can we rely on the good intentions of others.
3. Little did the thief know that he was being followed by the detective.
4. Scarcely has such great excitement been witnessed at our company.
5. Seldom do great achievements earn great appreciation.
6. Little did the king realize that his reign was about to end.
7. Hardly has the government's politics generated any positive comments.
8. Rarely can one encounter this species in its natural environment.
9. Little did the President expect that his speech would stir such criticism.
10. Seldom have I seen my mother in a better mood.

301. **1.** Hardly had the chairman entered the room when he was attacked by his fellow party members.

2. Scarcely had the concert begun when the lead singer fainted and fell onto the floor.

3. No sooner had the great advertising campaign begun than it had to be suspended due to the lack of funds.

4. Hardly had the battle begun when the king called for an armistice.

5. Scarcely had I left the house when my children began celebrating.

6. No sooner had the election campaign ended than the candidates started planning the next one.

7. Scarcely had the travellers set off when the fog came down.

8. No sooner had the robber broken into the bank than the alarm went off.

9. Hardly had the couple come back from their honeymoon when the husband was called away on business.

10. Scarcely had the difficult situation been solved when another problem appeared.

302. **1.** So devastating was the experience for him that he had to seek the help of a psychologist.

2. So enchanting was her smile that men would do anything to have her smile at least once.

3. So difficult are the details of this program that even senior staff have to refer to the guidelines for help.

4. Such was the splendour of the ceremony that the guests felt truly overwhelmed.

5. So straining was the rehearsal that even the extra crew were tired.

6. Sandra's lover left her after she had divorced her husband. Such is the irony of life.

7. So popular are Jane Rowling's books that she can sell several million copies within a month.

8. Such are the inequalities in the world that one begins to doubt any progress in human thinking.

303. **1.** Much as **2.** No sooner **3.** Rarely **4.** Not even once **5.** Hardly **6.** Little **7.** Under no circumstances **8.** Never before **9.** Such **10.** Only after

304. **1.** On no account may you reveal to Robert that you know the truth.

2. Under no circumstances are dead pigeons to be touched or moved.

3. Only by talking to the witnesses can we learn the truth about that accident.

4. Nowhere are better living conditions to be found.

5. Only after some time has passed will the consequences of this tragedy become visible.

6. In no way can the spread of the disease be prevented.

7. On no account should you panic or act hastily.

8. Only in a good foster family will the child be able to find love and protection.

9. Under no circumstances can the evidence be accessed by the police.

10. In no way have the origins of the wicker chair-making tradition been established.

305. **1.** Not even once did Mary apologise for her scandalous behaviour at the Easter party.

2. At no time was it apparent that the leader of the rebellion was cooperating with the government.

3. Never before has democracy been faced with a greater threat.

4. Never again will this man intimidate your family.

5. Not even once did I get to speak English during my English course.

6. At no time did it occur to us to call our parents and tell them where we were.

7. Never before has a mistake like that happened at our company.

8. Never again was the legendary football team to win the world cup.

9. At no time has the humiliation of the company been greater.

10. Not even once did the gambler make a good bet.

306. **1.** It was the American scientist Thomas Edison who/that invented the light bulb.

2. It is young, promising business sharks who/that are the most frequent victims of the supply and demand forces.

3. It was ancient Greeks who/that worshipped Zeus; in Rome the same god was known as Jupiter.

4. According to some sources, it was the Georgians who/that were first to produce wine.

5. It was my argument with the manager's assistant that contributed to my dismissal, I am sure of that!

6. It was the new maths teacher who/that had discovered some errors in the council's financial reports.

7. It is my daughter's little lies that hurt me most.

8. It is/it was only fame and power and not the fate of his country that the president cared about.

9. It is support that Beth needs now, not our sarcastic comments.

10. It is creativity and flexibility that the examiners expect from the candidates, not pure textbook knowledge.

307. **1.** It was while we were staying in Paris that my boyfriend proposed to me.

2. It is on Sundays that the shops are usually most busy, although people should actually spend that day at home with their families.

3. It was on that very day that the future of the organization was decided.

4. It was thanks to the support of his many friends that the retired pilot was able to go on with his life.

5. It was because of the members's obstinacy that the treaty was terminated.

6. It is only by speaking it as much as possible that one can achieve fluency in a foreign language.

7. It is at my own request that I have been signed out of hospital.

8. It was only after our teacher had forced us to prepare a presentation on that topic that we understood the idea of electromagnetic fields.

9. It is in St. George's Chapel situated within Windsor Castle that many members of the British royal family got married.

10. It was only after several months had passed from the new elections that people began to appreciate the achievements of the previous government.

308. **1.** What worried me most was the fragile structure of the party tent.

2. What the teachers were shocked at was the students' indifference towards the victims of the great flood in their town.

3. What the company needs above all is to concentrate its efforts on improving its image.

4. What the book basically tells us is that true friendship is an invaluable and yet rare treasure.

5. What made him angry was that he had paid far too much for that second-hand car.

6. What Pauline is particularly good at is asking people the questions that they least expect.

7. What we were most puzzled by was the good-humouredness with which they went through their divorce.

8. What needs to be stressed here is the fact that the enemy was defeated within just two weeks.

9. What struck me most was that Jack didn't even try to justify his behaviour.

309. **1.** Difficult though/as it seems, you must try to make new friends at your new school.

2. Tired though/as we were after the journey, we were happy to have come home at last.

3. Expensive though/as the shoes of this brand are, they are very durable.

4. Tasty though/as English beers are, they cannot beat the traditional ale.

5. Unfair though/as it seems, you should apologise first to your manager.

6. Impulsive though/as my mother is, she hardly ever panics.

7. Well-structured though/as the lecture was, it was not very enlightening.

8. Quarrelsome though/as Polish people are, they usually unite in the face of danger.

9. Well-written though/as the new book was, it never managed to get to the top of bestseller lists.

310. **1.** Demanding though/as our chemistry teacher may be, she is always just in her marks.

2. Expensive though/as Japanese cars may be, they are of very good quality.

3. Try though/as we might, we couldn't talk our parents into buying us a dog.

4. Good though/as the company's offer may have been, it lacked some bonus options which were available elsewhere.

5. Good though/as our school basketball team may be on the local level, it won't stand much chance in the national finals.

6. Impossible though/as it may seem, an average humming-bird is the size of a human nail.

7. Upset though/as Eve may have been, she shouldn't have slammed the door running out.

8. Try though/as the runner might, he didn't qualify for the final run.

9. Hard though/as I may try, I cannot convince Fred to see a family therapist.

311. **1.** Much though/as I like swimming, I wouldn't like to spend my entire holidays at the seaside.

2. However angry you were with your employee, you shouldn't have raised your voice.

3. Boring as teaching may seem to some people, it gives me a lot of satisfaction.

4. However friendly the shop-owner tried to be, the customers could sense that he was bored and irritated.

5. Rather good-natured though my uncle was, he could not forgive his wife's infidelity.

6. Whatever means she used, she couldn't convince her boss to raise her salary.

7. Difficult as the exam was, it was quite predictable.

8. Much as many young women adore little children, few would be ready to have one of their own.

9. However mean my sister may have been to me, she would always take my side in front of our parents.

PREPOSITIONS

PLACE AND TIME

312. ☺ Wybierz właściwy przyimek.

1. I live <u>on/in/at</u> 25 Rose Street <u>by/in/at</u> Birmingham.
2. My mother lives <u>in/on/at</u> Rose Street too, <u>after/by/in</u> the old church.
3. Let's meet <u>in/on/at</u> three o'clock <u>on/at/after</u> the monument <u>under/in/on</u> the park.
4. On second thoughts, half <u>after/past/by</u> three is a better time.
5. I want to be <u>in/at/on</u> home when my mother comes back <u>from/in/past</u> work.
6. The classes will finish <u>on/at/in</u> noon tomorrow, and then we will all go <u>by/past/to</u> the Houses of Parliament <u>for/to/after</u> a guided tour.
7. I am <u>in/–/at</u> work until a quarter <u>after/to/by</u> seven, and then I am going <u>to/at/–</u> home <u>on/in/by</u> bus.

313. W niektórych linijkach jest za dużo przyimków. Skreśl w tekście niepotrzebne przyimki i wypisz je na marginesie. Linijki bezbłędne zaznacz ✓.

0. It happened in the week between Christmas and ~~to~~ New Year.	<u>to</u>
0. It was the coldest week of the winter. Having spent Christmas	<u>✓</u>
1. with my parents, my husband and I were driving in to the	_____
2. mountains to visit my in-laws. About five kilometres away from	_____
3. my in-law's village the car skidded and landed down in a ditch.	_____
4. We were not harmed, but of course we had to walk in to the	_____
5. village. We set out at a brisk walk. It was getting on late, stars	_____
6. were out and it was freezing cold. Of course, I was worried	_____
7. that we would be lost and freeze up to death. Oh, how I wished	_____
8. I was back in the big city! My husband grew in this region,	_____
9. so he was not afraid of at all. But I? I swear I heard wolves	_____
10. howling somewhere up the mountainside!	_____

314. ☺☺ Wstaw przyimek *at*, *on* lub *in*.

1. Mark is a student _____ Edinburgh University. He lives _____ Edinburgh, too, _____ 17 Church Lane. His flat is _____ the second floor.
2. Our train arrived _____ Paris early enough for us to eat supper _____ Le Chat Noir. It is the best restaurant _____ our district.
3. Let's meet _____ The Golden Lion, _____ the room to the right of the bar.
4. Stratford, the town _____ which Shakespeare was born, is _____ the river Avon.
5. I am spending Easter _____ home. I am going to visit my grandparents _____ Easter Monday. And what are you going to do _____ Easter?
6. Do you remember the little wooden church _____ our village? It burnt down _____ the early morning _____ New Year's Day. It was built _____ the 16th century.

178

7. I saw Suzanne again twelve months after we had so much fun _____ her wedding. I could not believe anyone could have changed so much _____ a year's time.

PREPOSITIONS WITH ADJECTIVES

315. ☺ Połącz połówki zdań.

1. Eating sweets is very bad...
2. I have never been very keen...
3. Julie is worried...
4. My sister is very good...
5. Today father was again late...
6. Mothers are seldom angry...
7. I am tired...

a) ...with their children for a long time.
b) ...for supper.
c) ...about the results of the exam.
d) ...of having to tidy your room again.
e) ...for your teeth.
f) ...at all water sports.
g) ...on horror films.

316. ☺☺ Wybierz właściwy przyimek.

1. The children were so excited with/about/for going to the fun park that they were difficult to control.
2. Andrea Nester was found guilty with/of/for armed robbery and sentenced to prison.
3. Jane's mother is anxious about/for/at her daughter's punk friends, but Jane doesn't care.
4. Never get involved with/in/about any project without asking about deadlines first!
5. I am disappointed to/by/with you! I thought you were a little more mature.
6. Vanessa is extremely jealous of/on/with her handsome husband.
7. Anne's parents were really shocked with/by/from the news that she wanted to marry a Brazilian Indian and live in the jungle.
8. I will never get accustomed with/to/at Lester's way of laughing!
9. Nelly was quite pleased by/with/at her exam results – until the last one.
10. I am quite ashamed of/with/by having got scared by an old newspaper rustling in the dark!

317. ☺☺☺ Wstaw odpowiednie przyimki.

1. He has always been interested _____ visual arts.
2. Small children are totally dependent _____ their parents.
3. Every nation is proud _____ its history.
4. Nowadays, young people are focused _____ education.
5. Be careful _____ this vase: it's very old and valuable.
6. The French region of Burgundy is famous_____ its wines.
7. I agreed, unaware _____ the consequences.

8. Nobody was surprised _____ Angie's changing her mind again.
9. Tama is very keen _____ sailing and windsurfing.
10. Are you ready _____ some very bad news?
11. On hearing the news, Joanna turned pale _____ shock.
12. His art is independent _____ all influence.

PREPOSITIONS WITH NOUNS AND NOUN PHRASES

318. ☺☺ Połącz połówki zdań.

1. Could you please sign this document...
2. Is there anything interesting on...
3. Do you have any concrete proof...
4. Would you consider the idea...
5. Do we know any specialist...
6. A surgeon may refuse to operate...
7. I will not accept responsibility...

a) ...of coming to live with me in Japan?
b) ...on a patient who is related to him.
c) ...in black pen?
d) ...in Oriental languages?
e) ...of Arnold's guilt?
f) ...for my colleague's mistakes.
g) ...TV tonight?

319. ☺☺ Wstaw odpowiednie przyimki.

1. Hilda has such a way _____ smiling that you cannot refuse her anything.
2. Alan never clearly explained the reasons _____ his sudden decision to leave the country.
3. All proceeds from the charity concert go to African children _____ need of reading glasses.
4. Nowadays, children seldom enjoy novels _____ Jules Verne.
5. Can you at least try to see the issue _____ my point of view?
6. It took a long time to convince her, but _____ the end Amanda agreed to perform.
7. The film was so moving that all the girls cried _____ the end.
8. _____ the picture we can see some ruins and a group of travellers.
9. Please open your books _____ page 324.
10. _____ my opinion, this arrangement of furniture is just perfect.

320. ☺☺☺ Uzupełnij zdania wyrazami z ramki.

belief	congratulations	difficulty	discussion	example	interest	knowledge
	marriage	struggle	thought			

1. Let me offer my sincerest _____ on the birth of your son.
2. Did you have any _____ in getting a Russian visa?

3. Mr. Morley's _____ with the Tax Office ended in a total defeat.
4. Guy Gavriel Kay's novels are an _____ of impeccable style.
5. Jonas's _____ in people's honesty is touching, but rather naïve.
6. Marguerite's thorough _____ of Persian carpet-weaving techniques made the Turkish guide look at her with surprise.
7. The professors much enjoyed their weekly _____ about philosophy and literature.
8. Martin never displayed any _____ in chemistry at school, and look at him now! He is finishing his doctorate in chemistry!
9. I hate the _____ of spending the entire summer in the city.
10. Janet's _____ to Nathaniel ended after only a single year.

PREPOSITIONS WITH VERBS

321. ☺☺ W niektórych linijkach jest za dużo przyimków. Skreśl w tekście niepotrzebne przyimki i wypisz je na marginesie. Linijki bezbłędne zaznacz ✓.

0. Holding ~~at~~ the old map in his hand, the treasure seeker	at
0. walked along the sandy shore. He counted 107 steps from	✓
1. the mark Captain Calvados left up on a rock, then turned	_____
2. to south and counted another 701 steps. This should be the	_____
3. place! It didn't look any different from all the other places	_____
4. he walked through, but the treasure seeker began to dig in.	_____
5. After an hour, just when he was about to resign down, the	_____
6. spade struck by something. Soon the treasure seeker saw	_____
7. an old, old chest. He was a rich man! Trembling round with	_____
8. anticipation, he opened up the chest... Inside was Captain	_____
9. Calvados's store of best rum, which had dried up long ago!	_____

322. ☺☺ Połącz części wypowiedzi.

1. I mustn't lose this address. I'd better note it down.
2. The palace park is the largest in the country.
3. The lecturer's voice was low and monotonous.
4. Could I have a little sister, Mummy?
5. Death is a very serious matter.
6. Stop! This bridge is rotten through!

a) I want someone to play with.
b) It is dangerous to walk on.
c) It is much too large to walk round.
d) It was very difficult to listen to.
e) Can you give me some paper to write it on?
f) It is not something to laugh at.

323. ☺☺☺ Wstaw odpowiednie przyimki.

1. I'm afraid I can't agree _____ your point of view.
2. I don't approve _____ his decision.
3. Little Josh insisted _____ being allowed to stay up until midnight.
4. She did apply _____ that job and I think it was a right decision.
5. You must prevent your fiancée _____ leaving now.
6. Mr. Longridge suffers _____ arthritis.
7. Why should I care _____ her problems? She never gave a thought _____ mine!
8. He has succeeded _____ completing his doctoral thesis.
9. My sister has just graduated _____ the university.
10. The castle interiors have been unchanged _____ centuries.
11. Are you familiar _____ this equipment?
12. My brother Leslie is six feet nine inches tall. He towers _____ everyone in our family.
13. The team were shocked _____ the news of their friend's death.
14. Mr. Tibbins resigned _____ the position of the Treasurer.
15. Are you really going to move _____ New Zealand?
16. He used to be a journalist but now he lives _____ writing obituaries.
17. All their sons are allergic _____ birch pollen.
18. Some birds never breed _____ captivity.
19. I felt very sorry _____ our neighbour when she broke her hip.
20. The Cardinal was impressed _____ his favourite artist's new sculpture.

324. ☺☺☺ Wpisz odpowiednie przyimki do zwrotów i wyrażeń z czasownikiem *die*.

1. The only son of the old lord died _____ a duel.
2. Many children in Africa die _____ starvation.
3. He who lives by the sword, dies _____ the sword.
4. The young poet died _____ a broken heart.
5. The sounds of the city died _____ and we heard birdsong.
6. A welcoming smile died _____ her face.
7. Stella's husband died peacefully _____ her arms.
8. Phew, it's hot! I'm dying _____ a drink.
9. Listen! The wind has died _____!
10. Sorry I'm late, the car just died _____ me.
11. When did tyrannosaurs die _____?

KLUCZ

312. Zauważ, że przyimki w tym ćwiczeniu dotyczą określeń czasu lub miejsca (z wyjątkiem dwóch przyimków w pkt. 6 i 7).
1. at, in **2.** in, by **3.** at, at, in **4.** past **5.** at, from **6.** at, to, for (powód) **7.** at, to, – , by (środek transportu)

313. 1. in **2.** OK **3.** down **4.** in **5.** on **6.** OK **7.** up **8.** OK **9.** of **10.** OK

314. 1. at (mówiąc o uniwersytecie w danym mieście, używamy *at*), **in, at, on**
2. in (zazwyczaj po czasowniku *arrive* występuje *at*, np. *arrive at Eustin Station*; jednakże mówiąc o miastach i innych dużych obszarach, używamy *in*), **at** (mówiąc o jakimś budynku z myślą o czynności, jaką się tam wykonuje (np. spożycie posiłku) używamy *at*), **in**
3. at (mówiąc o jakimś budynku jako o miejscu spotkania, używamy *at*), **in**
4. in, on (*on* używamy, mówiąc o położeniu jakiegoś miejsca nad brzegiem rzeki)
5. at, on (mówiąc o jednym dniu świąt, używamy *on*), **at** (natomiast mówiąc o całym okresie świątecznym, używamy *at*)

6. in, in (określając czas za pomocą pory dnia, używamy *in*), **on** (mówiąc o określonym dniu w roku, używamy *on*), **in** (mówiąc o dłuższych okresach, używamy *in*)
7. at (mówiąc o wydarzeniach towarzyskich, spotkaniach itp. używamy *at*), **in** (wyrażenie *in ...'s time* opisuje, po jakim czasie coś się wydarzyło; nie używamy go mówiąc, ile trwała dana czynność)

315. 1. e **2.** g **3.** c **4.** f **5.** b **6.** a **7.** d

316. 1. about **2.** of **3.** about **4.** in **5.** with **6.** of **7.** by **8.** to **9.** with **10.** of

317. 1. in **2.** on **3.** of **4.** on **5.** with **6.** for **7.** of **8.** by **9.** on **10.** for **11.** with **12.** of

318. 1. c **2.** g **3.** e **4.** a **5.** d **6.** b **7.** f

319. 1. of **2.** for **3.** in **4.** by **5.** from **6.** in (*in the end* = wreszcie, w końcu, po długim czasie) **7.** at (*at the end* = pod koniec, na końcu) **8.** In **9.** on **10.** In

320. 1. congratulations **2.** difficulty **3.** struggle **4.** example **5.** belief **6.** knowledge **7.** discussion **8.** interest **9.** thought **10.** marriage

321. 1. up **2.** to **3.** OK **4.** in **5.** down **6.** by **7.** round **8.** up **9.** OK

322. Przyimki często stanowią część dopełnień z bezokolicznikiem. Występują wtedy po bezokoliczniku, niekiedy na końcu zdania. Taka konstrukcja jest szczególnie typowa dla mowy potocznej.
1. e **2.** c **3.** d **4.** a **5.** f **6.** b

323. 1. with **2.** of **3.** on **4.** for **5.** from **6.** from **7.** about, to **8.** in **9.** from **10.** for **11.** with **12.** over **13.** by/at **14.** from **15.** to **16.** by **17.** to **18.** in **19.** for **20.** with/by

324. 1. in **2.** of/from **3.** by **4.** of/from **5.** away (o dźwięku = ucichnąć) **6.** on **7.** in **8.** for **9.** down (o wietrze = ucichnąć) **10.** on (= „samochód mi zdechł") **11.** out (= wyginąć)

PHRASAL VERBS

325. ☺ Połącz sytuację z właściwym zdaniem.

1. Gina is feeding the baby, changing its nappies and watching it to be sure it is safe.
2. Eve is touching the button on her bedside lamp and the light disappears.
3. Nell is checking a word in a dictionary to see if she understands it correctly.
4. Violet is looking at a lovely dress in a shop window. She has to have it!
5. Delia is slowly recovering from the shock of her father's death.
6. Sybil is searching for her red scarf all around the house.
7. Marie is turning a knob and the volume of her radio increases.

a) She is falling for it.
b) She is looking for it.
c) She is looking after it.
d) She is getting over it.
e) She is turning it up.
f) She is switching it off.
g) She is looking it up.

326. ☺☺ Wstaw właściwe słówko.

1. The ghost shrieked and howled, but the magician waved his wand and made it go

   _____.
   a) in   b) on   c) away
2. Please sit _____ and wait for the doctor. He will be with you shortly.
   a) up   b) down   c) in
3. The exam will be _____ in fifteen minutes.
   a) under   b) up   c) over
4. He switched the light _____ and started writing.
   a) on   b) round   c) off
5. Our neighbours are in mourning. Their mother has passed _____.
   a) out   b) away   d) over

327. ☺☺ Wstaw do zdań czasowniki frazowe z ramki w odpowiedniej formie gramatycznej.

break down	come to	hold on	get across	keep on
live up to	pick up	set off	split up	tell off

1. Miriam _____ whistling in her annoying way even after I asked her to stop.
2. If my mother's car _____, we would have caught the last train.
3. When the jockey _____, he was told his horse had been killed.
4. Although Florence is famous for its beauty, it failed to _____ my expectations because it was much too crowded with tourists.
5. When we were living in Sichuan, my four-year-old daughter _____ a little of the local dialect, which amused our Chinese friends very much.
6. _____, he expected to be back home in a weeks' time; he returned after a year.

7. I am sorry to learn that Millie and Michael _____! They were such a nice couple.

8. I am sure that sooner or later the boss _____ you _____ for surfing the Internet during work hours.

9. No matter how often I tell Robert to put the toilet seat down, he will not do it! Do you know any way to _____ it _____ to him?

10. Could you please _____ a while, I'll check if Mr Armadale is in his office.

328. ☺☺ Nie zmieniając podanych fragmentów ułóż nowe zdania, tak aby ich znaczenie było podobne do znaczenia zdań wyjściowych.

Wzór: I couldn't understand what he was suggesting.
          I couldn't _____ getting _____.
          I couldn't understand what he was getting at.

1. On the way to France we visited my uncle and aunt.
   On the way _____ called _____.

2. Looking through old photographs in an antique shop, I accidentally found a wedding photo of my grandparents.
   Looking through old photographs in an antique shop, I came _____
   _____.

3. One thing I have to have in the morning is a cup of coffee.
   One thing I can't do _____ a cup of coffee.

4. You have a guilty look on your face. What have you been doing?
   You have a guilty look on your face. What _____ to?

5. Dorothy asked us not to mention the subject of her MA thesis.
   Dorothy asked us not _____ up with the subject _____.

6. I am expecting meeting your brother with pleasure.
   I am looking _____ meeting your brother.

7. I love talking to you, but I really must continue working.
   I love _____ on with my work.

8. Barbara holds in contempt everyone who is less rich than she.
   Barbara looks _____ on everyone who is less rich than she.

9. It is sad when your children grow too old for listening to bedtime stories!
   It is sad when _____ out of listening _____!

10. Minnie was a sociable child, always ready to do the activities everyone else was doing.
    Minnie was a sociable child, _____ in common activities.

11. Charles quit work when he inherited a fortune.
    Charles _____ came _____ a fortune.

12. I will not tolerate such language from my employees!
    I will not stand _____!

13. Real friends are those you can depend on in time of need.
    Real friends _____ count _____.

14. We must arrange to have Internet access at home.
    We _____ about having _____.

15. If you see Jane, tell her I am interested in how she is getting on.
    If _____ I was _____ after _____.

329. ☺☺☺ Dobierz z ramki przyimki, tak aby powstały czasowniki frazowe z czasownikiem *put* o znaczeniu, jakie sugerują słowa w nawiasach. Wstaw te czasowniki do zdań we właściwej formie gramatycznej.

> PUT + off (2x)   up with   through   down to
> away   forward   down   on

1. (**postpone**)
You can't keep _____ your visit to the dentist! Your teeth will finally fall out!
2. (**tolerate**)
How can you _____ your secretary's incompetence? I would have fired her long ago!
3. (**extinguish**)
We have to _____ the fire very carefully before we leave the camp; otherwise the whole forest might burn.
4. (**connect on the phone**)
Sorry, I can't _____ you _____ to the director right now: he is in a meeting.
5. (**ascribe**)
The present crisis can be _____ the errors in governmental policies.
6. (**propose**)
We are _____ a proposal which should be acceptable to all our partners.
7. (**put in storage**)
The spring's coming, we will soon _____ boots and fur coats.
8. (**kill humanely**)
The horse with a broken leg had to be _____.
9. (**grow fat**)
Mary _____ a lot of weight recently; I am sure she is size 20 now!

330. ☺☺☺ Wybierz właściwy czasownik.

1. I can't bake a cake for you because we have _____ flour.
   a) walked out of   b) run out of   c) made up for
2. After my long illness, I find it difficult to _____ my friends at school.
   a) catch up with   b) put up with   c) get out of
3. Having grown rather plump, Helen decided to _____ sweets and cakes.
   a) call for   b) cut down on   c) get over
4. The short-legged puppy was trying hard to _____ his master.
   a) stand up for   b) keep up with   c) get at
5. When I was driving through Bath, I decided to _____ Keith and Sheila.
   a) go over   b) drop out of   c) drop in on
6. Do you all _____ your boss if he is so short-tempered?
   a) get on with   b) get up to   c) do without

A teraz z czasownikami, które wybrałeś, napisz własne zdania. Spróbuj ułożyć takie zdania, w których można opuścić jeden element czasownika. (Uwaga, to dość trudne zadanie!)

331. ☺☺☺ Zastępując podkreślony fragment ułóż nowe zdania, tak aby ich znaczenie było podobne do znaczenia zdań wyjściowych.

Wzór: Have you heard that the meeting has been <u>cancelled</u>?
          (**off**) *Have you heard that the meeting has been called off?*

1. This form has to be <u>completed</u> in black ink.

   (in) _____

2. Mabel finally <u>discovered</u> what happened to her father.

   (out) _____

3. Justine never <u>made</u> a secret she was told <u>known to anybody</u>.

   (away) _____

4. Mr. and Mrs. McBree offered to <u>educate and take care of</u> the orphan girl as their own daughter.

   (up) _____

5. Can you <u>solve</u> this equation for me, please?

   (out) _____

6. You never <u>stop trying</u>, do you?

   (up) _____

7. Professor Lee says that he will <u>consider</u> our offer.

   (over) _____

8. The appearance of the dish <u>made me unwilling to eat it</u>.

   (off) _____

9. From now on, you will <u>follow</u> my instructions to the letter.

   (out) _____

10. After they arrive, we will <u>give</u> the guests <u>a tour of</u> the conference complex.

    (around) _____

11. Even if I were offered your position, I would <u>refuse the offer</u>.

    (down) _____

12. When you study for the exam, pay attention not to <u>omit</u> chapter seven.

    (out) _____

13. Jamie is in the backyard, <u>using</u> his new bike <u>for the first time</u>.

    (out) _____

14. Don't worry, I will <u>collect</u> you at the airport.

    (up) _____

15. If Father asks about what I was doing last night, I am going to <u>invent</u> some clever story.

    (up) _____

KLUCZ

325. **1.** c **2.** f **3.** g **4.** a **5.** d **6.** b **7.** e

326. **1.** c **2.** b **3.** c **4.** a **5.** b

327. **1.** kept on **2.** had not broken down **3.** came to **4.** live up to **5.** picked up **6.** Setting off **7.** have split up **8.** will tell (you) off **9.** get (it) across **10.** hold on

328. Wszystkie czasowniki frazowe użyte w tym ćwiczeniu, zarówno te składające się z dwóch, jak i z trzech części, są niepodzielne: pomiędzy czasownik a zaimek/zaimki nie można wpisać dopełnienia.

   1. On the way to France we called on my uncle and aunt.

   2. Looking through old photographs in an antique shop, I came across a wedding photo of my grandparents.

   3. One thing I can't do without in the morning is a cup of coffee.

   4. You have a guilty look on your face. What have you been/are you up to?

   5. Dorothy asked us not to come up with the subject of her MA thesis.

   6. I am looking forward to meeting your brother.

   7. I love talking to you, but I really must get on with my work.

   8. Barbara looks down on everyone who is less rich than she.

   9. It is sad when your children grow out of listening to bedtime stories!

   10. Minnie was a sociable child, always ready to join in common activities.

   11. Charles quit work when he came into a fortune.

12. I will not stand for such language from my employees!

13. Real friends are those you can count on in time of need.

14. We must see about having Internet access at home.

15. If you see Jane, tell her I was asking after her.

329. 1. putting off **2.** put up with **3.** put off **4.** put (you) through **5.** put down to **6.** putting forward **7.** put away **8.** put down **9.** has put on

330. 1. b **2.** a **3.** b **4.** b **5.** c **6.** a

W przypadku tych czasowników można opuścić <u>drugi</u> zaimek, lecz wyłącznie wtedy, gdy zdanie nie ma dopełnienia, na przykład:

1. (run out of) Sorry, there's no sugar in your tea, because we've <u>run out</u>.

2. (catch up with) You guys start climbing first, and I'll <u>catch up</u>.

3. (cut down on) I used to smoke a packet a day, but I got so ill that I decided to <u>cut down</u>.

4. (keep up with) We must walk more slowly, little Sheila can't <u>keep up</u>.

5. (drop in on) If you are in our town again, do <u>drop in</u>!

6. (get on with) I used to quarrel with my mother a lot, but now we <u>get on</u> much better.

331. Wszystkie czasowniki frazowe użyte w tym ćwiczeniu można podzielić, wpisując dopełnienie pomiędzy czasownik i przyimek (patrz pkt. 7 – *think our offer over*). Dzieje się tak zwłaszcza w wypadku, gdy dopełnienie wyrażone jest za pomocą zaimka (patrz pkt. 11 – *turn it down*); dłuższe dopełnienia znajdą się raczej po całym czasowniku frazowym.

1. This form has to be filled in in black ink. (Nie należy obawiać się, że obecność dwóch *in* obok siebie to błąd: pierwsze z nich jest częścią czasownika frazowego, drugie – okolicznika sposobu.)

2. Mabel finally found out what happened to her father.

3. Justine never gave away a secret she was told.

4. Mr. and Mrs. McBree offered to bring up the orphan girl as their own daughter.

5. Can you work this equation out for me, please?

6. You never give up, do you?

7. Professor Lee says that he will think our offer over.

8. The appearance of the dish put me off it.

9. From now on, you will carry out my instructions to the letter.

10. After they arrive, we will show the guests around the conference complex.

11. Even if I were offered your position, I would turn it down.

12. When you study for the exam, pay attention not to leave out chapter seven.

13. Jamie is in the backyard, trying out his new bike.

14. Don't worry, I will pick you up at the airport.

15. If Father asks about what I was doing last night, I am going to make up some clever story.

CONJUNCTIONS

THOUGH, ALTHOUGH, ALBEIT

332. ☺☺ Przekształć poniższe zdania, używając spójników *though/even though/ although*.

Wzór:

Despite highly critical reviews, many people went to see the film.

Even though/Although the film had highly critical reviews, many people went to see it.

1. Our civilization is technologically advanced, but it hasn't been able to tame the forces of nature.

   _____

2. The shop assistant tried to be nice, but the customer was clearly in a mood for a quarrel.

   _____

3. Hard-working as John is, he often proves disorganized.

   _____

4. Useless as this exercise may seem to you now, it will prove very useful later on.

   _____

5. Our boss may be demanding, but he is also very fair to us.

   _____

6. Despite bad weather, the turnout at the concert was impressive.

   _____

7. The Minister decided to carry out the reforms, despite the objections of his cabinet members.

   _____

8. National prejudices remain, despite our efforts to eliminate them.

   _____

9. The family lived in poverty, but they considered themselves happy.

   _____

10. Famous as the actor may be, he has no right to be so rude.

   _____

333. ☺☺ Połącz połówki poniższych zdań opowiadających o premierze pewnego filmu.

1. Although the film had good reviews
2. Even though there were some famous names in the cast
3. Though the scenery was picturesque
4. Even though the main story was funny
5. Although the costumes were beautiful
6. Though the film had a substantial budget
7. Although the film had been praised for its soundtrack
8. Even though the film aspired to be an international production
9. Although the director had won some film awards before

a) the theme music was horrible.

b) they did not fit that historical period.

c) the main characters were played by unknown actors.

d) this time he won't have much chance to get any.

e) the visual effects were poor.

f) it was a disappointment.

g) the shots were monotonous.

h) it was very predictable.

i) the cast were overwhelmingly American.

334. ☺☺☺ Zdecyduj, w których z poniższych zdań *though* można zastąpić *albeit*.

1. Though it rained hard, the travellers did not stop for the night.

2. Human beings should not give up their dreams of a better world, though unrealistic.

3. I liked the film, though some parts were quite predictable.

4. He managed to finish his assignment on time, though with difficulty.

5. The complaints of the customer, though justified, did not receive much attention from the management.

6. The critics decided the book had a good story, though simplistic.

DESPITE, IN SPITE OF

335. ☺☺ Przekształć poniższe zdania, używając spójników *in spite of/despite*.

Wzór: Although Mark's parents objected, he decided to marry Kate.
          Despite his parents' objections, Mark decided to marry Kate.

1. There were many obstacles on our way, but we managed to execute our plan.

   _____

2. I had good grades, but I didn't get into all the universities I'd applied to.

   _____

3. There are some obvious differences between the two men and yet their friendship has survived all those years.

   _____

4. Even though Gina had the right qualifications, her boss seemed to be unsure as to her competencies.

   _____

5. The doctor had a year-long experience as a children's psychologist and yet Henry's case was a true challenge for him.

   _____

6. There were many advantages of the course, but I decided not to participate.

   _____

7. The students protested vigorously, but the professor calmly distributed the surprise test.

   _____

8. Jack had outstanding references, but he didn't gain his employer's trust.

   _____

336. ☺☺ Wybierz właściwą wersję zdania.

1. All candidates will have equal chances of being selected, irrespective of/in spite of their nationality.
2. In spite/Despite of some difficult moments, we considered the trip as successful.
3. Despite he is/his being the most experienced one among the sailors, he was terrified.
4. Despite/Irrespective of my admiration for this author, I must say that his latest book was rather weak.
5. He drank alcohol at the party, despite/in spite all the promises he had made to his wife.
6. Despite/Though we could hardly see the singer, we were thrilled to be at the concert.
7. Even though/Despite the situation being pretty much hopeless, we still believe in a miracle.
8. Every child has the right to decent education, in spite of/irrespective of his or her parents' financial means.

337. ☺☺ Uzupełnij poniższy tekst podanymi spójnikami. Każdego z nich można użyć jeden raz; jeden jest zbędny.

despite	no matter	in spite	yet	although	albeit	though

Even (1) _____ Patricia tried to act as though nothing had happened, we knew that something was wrong right away. (2) _____ of all the smiles and assurances, her eyes were telling us that she needed our help, and (3) _____ she wouldn't tell us what it was all about. It's funny how little she trusted us, (4) _____ all the years we have spent together at university. So we just tried to be there for her, knowing that our sheer presence was already of some help, (5) _____ little. We knew that we had to wait patiently, (6) _____ how long it took.

BUT, HOWEVER, NEVERTHELESS

338. ☺ Z rozsypanych liter ułóż właściwe spójniki i uzupełnij nimi poniższe zdania.

1. t b u
   During the performance, the king tried to keep a straight face, _____ couldn't help laughing at one point.
2. r e h v w o e
   We were sure that things will go smoothly. _____, the situation turned out to be more complex than we had thought.
3. e e t h e e s n v r l s
   I think children should be given a lot of freedom. _____, they should also be taught respect towards adults.
4. t y e
   All members of the team had very different backgrounds and _____ they managed to get on perfectly.

5. s e s l h e n e t o n

Our government has promised to pursue a very decisive foreign policy. _____, domestic affairs should not be neglected.

6. n o   h e t   n a h d   h t o r e

Such paintings can hardly be called art. _____, many people seem to like them.

339. ☺☺ Przekształć poniższe zdania, używając spójników podanych w nawiasach.

Wzór:

Although the weather was splendid, the hotels and camping places were empty. (HOWEVER)

The weather was splendid. However, the hotels and camping places were empty.

1. Although many things we learn at school are not very useful later in life, there are also some that are worth memorizing. (HOWEVER)

_____

2. Despite there being a lot of confusion among the rescue staff, all guests managed to be evacuated safely. (NEVERTHELESS)

_____

3. Eccentric as Marion may be, I am sure that you will like her. (YET)

_____

4. Even though your essay does not exhaust the topic, I appreciate the extensive bibliography. (HOWEVER)

_____

5. Although there is not much that could speak in my defense, I would like you to give me a chance to explain my behaviour. (NONETHELESS)

_____

6. Beautiful as the Queen may have been, her vanity was rather unjustified. (NEVERTHELESS)

_____

7. Despite many books devoted to that topic, most people know little about it. (YET)

_____

340. ☺☺ Uzupełnij poniższy tekst podanymi spójnikami. Każdego z nich należy użyć tylko raz; jeden jest zbędny.

however   nevertheless   despite   albeit   but   although

Lately, global warming has returned to public debate, (1) _____ the government's efforts to keep it off its political agenda. For two years now, both the Minister of Environment and the Prime Minister had tried to pretend no such phenomenon as global warming existed. Today, (2) _____, various environmental lobbies have reawakened the discussion on ozone layer protection and various measures to minimize the negative effects of industry on the environment. (3) _____ issues such as national defense and foreign policy are important, the lobbyists claim, the world that surrounds us cannot be neglected. Much has been done recently to protect the country's security, (4) _____ little for its internal health. The lobbies are gaining increasing attention from the media, (5) _____ gradually. Their arguments are also eagerly reaffirmed by specialists from the energy sector.

WHEREAS, WHILE, UNLIKE

341. ☺☺☺ Z każdej grupy wykreśl jeden wyraz, który nie pasuje do pozostałych.

1. whereas, while, but, whilst
2. apart from, though, although, albeit,
3. in spite of, irrespective of, despite, regardless of
4. unlike, in contrast to, contrary to, by contrast
5. nonetheless, nevertheless, notwithstanding, however
6. unlike, yet, however, on the other hand

342. ☺☺☺ Przekształć poniższe zdania, używając wyrazów podanych w nawiasach.

1. Some people like to spend their holidays on the beach. Others prefer active forms of spending their leisure time. (WHEREAS)

   _____

2. John studied medicine. His twin brother dropped out of school and became a street artist. (WHILE)

   _____

3. My wife loves going to the cinema. I don't. (UNLIKE)

   _____

4. The boss enjoyed the Christmas party immensely. His staff didn't. (IN CONTRAST)

   _____

5. Making a career is an important goal to many people. They also stress their desire to have a family. (WHILE)

   _____

6. My younger sister is an extremely quiet person. My older sister is loud and full of life. (BY CONTRAST)

   _____

7. Our company offers you both a personal and a health insurance policy. Our competitors offer only one type of cover. (WHEREAS)

   _____

343. ☺☺☺ Uzupełnij poniższe zdania jednym z wyrazów: A, B lub C.

1. _____ the political scene has gained stability, the economy still needs a lot of improvement.
   A. While   B. Despite   C. Albeit
2. The days in Egypt are very warm. The nights, _____, are very chilly.
   A. in contrast   B. by contrast   C. unlike
3. The book is not at all scary. _____, it is extremely funny at parts.
   A. By contrast   B. On the contrary   C. However
4. _____ other students, Jerry starts studying for his exam long before the exam session.
   A. Irrespective of   B. Whereas   C. Unlike
5. In some countries a particular gesture may be friendly, _____ in others it may be highly offending.
   A. however   B. whereas   C. although

6. _____ the professor spoke fast, his lecture was easy to follow.
   A. While   B. Even though   C. Whereas
7. She was a tough teacher, _____ all children loved her.
   A. while   B. nevertheless   C. yet
8. _____ to most other European countries, Britain has left-side traffic.
   A. In contrast   B. By contrast   C. On the contrary

THEREFORE, THUS, HENCE

344. ☺☺☺ Spośród poniższych wyrazów i wyrażeń wybierz 8 o zbliżonym znaczeniu.

however	gradually	nevertheless	therefore	as a result
whereas	notwithstanding	for that reason	hereby	hence
although	eventually	consequently	while	on the contrary
so	in consequence	thus		

345. ☺☺☺ Użyj wyrazów i wyrażeń wybranych w poprzednim ćwiczeniu, aby uzupełnić poniższe zdania:

1. John had been in such a situation before. _____ he handled it perfectly.
2. The king discovered the rebels' plan and _____ their dream of freedom was over.
3. Most families feature a model where both parents work. _____, the ties between their children and them are becoming weaker.
4. Matthew acted very selfishly and _____ lost many of his supporters.
5. It may rain tomorrow, _____ it is advisable to take umbrellas with you.
6. Many of the e-mails we get every day contain harmful elements. It is _____ crucial that you should delete any e-mails from unknown senders.
7. This book is particularly well-written. _____ it is recommended as a self--reference book for students.

346. ☺☺☺ Uzupełnij tekst poniższymi wyrazami. Każdego wyrazu należy użyć tylko raz; jeden jest zbędny.

therefore	thus	however	consequently	despite	as a result	while

The long-awaited concert of the „Crazy Fish" was to have been the event of the year.
(1) _____, it turned out a complete failure. The band played mainly its hits from the 1970s, (2) _____ the majority of the audience were high-school students, too young to remember those songs. They were (3) _____ obviously disappointed.
(4) _____ some better moments, when the crowds would come alive for a while, it took only 35 minutes for the audience to start getting bored. (5) _____, fights erupted in the back rows, drawing the attention of both the media and the rest of the crowd away from the stage. (6) _____, the concert could be called a true non-starter and it will take a lot of effort for the band to restore its reputation in this country.

KLUCZ

332. 1. Although/Even though our civilization is technologically advanced, it hasn't been able to tame the forces of nature.
2. Although/Even though the shop assistant tried to be nice, the customer was clearly in a mood for a quarrel.
3. Although/Even though John is hard-working, he often proves disorganised.
4. Although/Even though this exercise may seem useless to you now, it will prove very useful later on.
5. Although/Even though our boss is demanding, he is also very fair to us.
6. Although/Even though the weather was bad, the turnout at the concert was impressive.
7. The Minister decided to carry out the reforms, although/even though his cabinet members objected.
8. National prejudices remain, even though/although we have tried to eliminate them.
9. Even though/Although the family lived in poverty, they considered themselves happy.
10. Even though/Although the actor is famous, he has no right to be so rude.

333. 1. f **2.** c **3.** g **4.** h **5.** b **6.** e **7.** a **8.** i **9.** d

334. *Albeit* jest dużo bardziej formalnym spójnikiem niż *though/even though*. Stosowany jest zwykle we wtrąceniach osłabiających moc wyrażeń bezpośrednio je poprzedzających. Nie jest stosowany na początku zdań.
Albeit można zastosować w następujących zdaniach:
2. Human beings should not give up their dreams of a better world, albeit unrealistic.
4. He managed to finish his assignment on time, albeit with difficulty.
6. The critics decided the book had a good story, albeit simplistic.

335. 1. In spite of/Despite many obstacles on our way, we managed to execute our plan.
2. In spite of/Despite my good grades, I didn't get into all the universities I'd applied to.
3. In spite of/Despite some obvious differences between the two men, their friendship has survived all those years.
4. In spite of/Despite Gina's right qualifications, her boss seemed to be unsure as to her competencies.
5. In spite of/Despite the doctor's year-long experience as a children's psychologist, Henry's case was a true challenge for him.
6. In spite of/Despite there being many advantages of the course, I decided not to participate.
7. In spite of/Despite the students' vigorous protests, the professor calmly distributed the surprise test.
8. In spite of/Despite his outstanding references, Jack didn't gain his employer's trust.

336. 1. irrespective of **2.** In spite **3.** his being **4.** Despite **5.** despite **6.** Though **7.** Despite **8.** irrespective of

337. 1. though **2.** In spite **3.** yet **4.** despite **5.** albeit **6.** no matter

338. 1. but **2.** However **3.** Nevertheless **4.** yet **5.** Nonetheless **6.** On the other hand

339. 1. Many things we learn at school are not very useful later in life. However, there are also some that are worth memorizing.
2. There was a lot of confusion among the rescue staff. Nevertheless, all guests managed to be evacuated safely.
3. Marion may be eccentric, yet I am sure that you will like her.
4. Your essay does not exhaust the topic. However, I appreciate the extensive bibliography.
5. There is not much that could speak in my defense. Nonetheless, I would like you to give me a chance to explain my behaviour.
6. The Queen was beautiful. Nevertheless, her vanity was rather unjustified.
7. There are many books devoted to that topic, yet people know little about it.

340. 1. despite **2.** however **3.** although **4.** but **5.** albeit

341. Należy wykreślić następujące wyrazy: **1.** whilst **2.** apart from **3.** irrespective of **4.** contrary to **5.** notwithstanding **6.** unlike

342. 1. Some people like to spend their holidays on the beach, whereas others prefer active forms of spending their leisure time.
2. John studied medicine, while his twin brother dropped out of school and became a street artist.

3. Unlike my wife, I don't like going to the cinema./My wife loves going to the cinema, unlike me.

4. In contrast to his staff, the boss enjoyed the Christmas party immensely.

5. While making a career is an important goal to many people, they also stress their desire to have a family.

6. My younger sister is an extremely quiet person; my older sister is by contrast loud and full of life.

7. Our company offers you both a personal and a health insurance policy, whereas our competitors offer only one type of cover.

343. **1.** A **2.** B **3.** B **4.** C **5.** B **6.** B **7.** C **8.** A

344. so, therefore, as a result, for that reason, hence, thus, consequently, in consequence

345. **1.** Thus/Hence **2.** hence/so **3.** As a result/In consequence **4.** consequently **5.** so **6.** therefore **7.** For that reason/Hence/Thus/Consequently

346. **1.** However **2.** while **3.** therefore **4.** Despite **5.** As a result **6.** Thus

EXPRESSING PREFERENCE

347. ☺☺ Zdecyduj, czy podane zdanie jest gramatycznie poprawne (YES), czy nie (NO). Popraw zdania błędne.

1. I prefer beer to wine. (YES/NO)
2. I'd rather go to the National Museum. (YES/NO)
3. I like ice-cream better than chocolate. (YES/NO)
4. I'd prefer not see John tomorrow. (YES/NO)
5. I'd sooner to play bridge than to dance. (YES/NO)
6. I'd prefer to have gone to Greece instead. (YES/NO)
7. I'd prefer a sandwich than a slice of cake. (YES/NO)
8. I prefer to make friends rather than lose them. (YES/NO)

348. ☺☺ Połącz połówki zdań i odpowiedz na pytania o to, co lubisz.

1. When it comes to winter sports, I prefer snowboarding...
2. If I had a choice, I'd rather have a motorbike...
3. In the evening, I would rather read...
4. Of all drinks, I like...
5. Looking back, I'd rather have gone to university...
6. I prefer watching people dance...
7. I like dogs better...

a) ...than watch TV. And you?
b) ...than have started working just after school. And you?
c) ...to skiing. And you?
d) ...than cats. And you?
e) ...than a car. And you?
f) ...hot chocolate best. And you?
g) ...rather than dancing myself. And you?

349. ☺☺☺ Uzupełnij wypowiedzi.

1. Tristan's mother worries a lot about his safety. Recently Tristan said he would like to go to a survival camp. Tristan's mother says to his father:
   'I'd rather _____. God knows what can happen to him there!'
2. Antoinette loves cats and wants to get one. She is much less keen on having children. She often says:
   'Cats are very clean and quiet, babies just the opposite. I'd sooner _____ _____.'
3. Wilma, who lives in New York, has always dreamed of visiting Spain, but her husband decided that for their great tour of Europe they should go to France and Italy. Wilma complains to a colleague:
   'My husband wants to go to France and Italy, but I'd much _____ _____. He won't even hear of it, because he had already been there and hated it.'

4. Kelly is gossiping with her best friend Zena about her boyfriend Ron. Zena knows that Kelly used to be sweet on Will and asks her about her feelings for him. Kelly admits:
'I'd sooner _____, but it was clear that Will was not interested in me.'

5. Andrew does not have a singing voice, but he loves listening to people sing. This is what he says about it:
'However I try, I cannot sing in tune. That's why I prefer _____ _____ myself.'

6. Elijah found himself in serious financial difficulties and had to borrow some money from his uncle. He paid the debt long ago, but the uncle keeps reminding him about that difficult time in front of the whole family. Elijah regrets:
'I'd prefer _____. What a pity none of them were able to lend me any at that time.'

KLUCZ

347. **1.** YES (*I prefer* można używać z rzeczownikami)
2. YES (za pomocą *I would rather* (*I'd rather*) wyrażamy swoje własne życzenia; używa się go z bezokolicznikiem bez *to*, czyli tzw. **bare infinitive**)
3. YES (*I like sth better than sth* to także sposób wyrażania preferencji)
4. NO – I'd prefer not to see John tomorrow. (*I would prefer* (*I'd prefer*) znaczy to samo, co *I'd rather/I'd sooner*, ale używa się go z pełną formą bezokolicznika, czyli z **full infinitive**)
5. NO – I'd sooner play bridge than dance. (*I would sooner* (*I'd sooner*) używa się identycznie jak *I'd rather*, ale konstrukcja ta występuje nieco rzadziej)
6. YES (zarówno *I'd rather/sooner*, jak *I'd prefer* może występować z **perfect infinitive**. Wtedy, podobnie jak konstrukcja *would like to + perfect infinitive*, dotyczy przeszłości i wyraża życzenie, które nie zostało spełnione)
7. NO – I'd rather have a sandwich than a slice of cake./I'd prefer a sandwich. (przy *would prefer* wymieniamy tylko tę opcję, która nam się bardziej podoba; jeśli chcemy wymienić obie, musimy użyć *would rather*)
8. YES (*I prefer* używamy do wyrażania ogólnych preferencji)

348. **1.** c **2.** e **3.** a **4.** f **5.** b **6.** g **7.** d
Przykładowe odpowiedzi:
1. I prefer skating to snowboarding./I like skating best.
2. I'd have neither. I'd prefer having my own horse.
3. I would rather go out than stay at home.
4. I prefer Earl Grey tea to hot chocolate.
5. I agree. Studying is fun.
6. I prefer to dance, especially when the music is good.
7. Oh, I much prefer cats.

349. Przykładowe wypowiedzi:
1. I'd rather Tristan didn't go to a survival camp.
2. I'd sooner get a cat than have a baby.
3. I'd much prefer to visit Spain.
4. I'd sooner have gone out with Will than with Ron,
5. I prefer listening to people singing rather than singing myself./I prefer to listen to people singing than to sing myself.
6. I'd prefer to have borrowed money from friends.

VOCABULARY

COMPOUND ADJECTIVES

350. ☺☺ Dopasuj słowa z lewej kolumny do słów z prawej kolumny, tak aby powstały przymiotniki złożone. Niekiedy możliwa jest więcej niż jedna kombinacja.

1. long	a) mentioned
2. home	b) minded
3. south	c) inch
4. short	d) lasting
5. second	e) heeled
6. nine	f) time
7. high	g) tempered
8. above	h) made
9. full	i) hand
10. evil	j) west

351. ☺☺☺ Uzupełnij zdania, dobierając z ramki odpowiednią część przymiotnika złożonego.

free	hour	kind	like	looking	made	mannered	minded
minute	ordered	painted	planned	ranging	sized	starred	written

1. Wearing garments of man-_____ fibres is less good for you than wearing linen, wool or silk.
2. Professor Dempsey is famous for his incredibly wide-_____ interests.
3. Go out with good-_____ men, if you please, but marry a _____- hearted one.
4. The ill-_____ expedition ended in a shipwreck, in which all its members but one were drowned.
5. Having inherited a fortune, Jonas began to enjoy a care_____ life of a country gentleman.
6. Nannette is such a well-_____ girl: always polite, attentive, and interested in what her elders have to say to her.
7. The incredibly difficult, seven-_____ negotiations ended in a compromise which satisfied no one.
8. What did you expect? This was a badly-_____ advertising campaign for a badly-_____ novel by a narrow-_____ author!
9. My mother, who likes her life to be well-_____, absolutely hates _____-minute changes of plans.
10. The life-_____ portrait of Lady Marsh was badly-_____ and not at all life_____.

352. ☺☺☺ Zastąp podkreśloną część zdania odpowiednim przymiotnikiem złożonym. Dokonaj innych niezbędnych zmian.

Wzór:

Mr. Besson's attachment to my grandmother, <u>which lasted all his life</u>, was very moving.
Mr. Besson's lifelong attachment to my grandmother was very moving.

1. Leonard's sarcastic comments were particularly <u>unsuitable for</u> the sad situation.
2. In the swamps and on marshy ground soldiers had to use vehicles <u>which can move through all types of terrain</u>.
3. A cat <u>which gets enough to eat</u> will never eat a rat it has caught.
4. A girl <u>who is sixteen years old</u> cannot have a clear idea of her future yet.
5. The construction team, <u>which consisted of seven men</u>, finished roofing the house before the first frost.
6. Lying on the beach all day, Geraldine got badly <u>burnt by the sun</u>.
7. Old Uncle Philip was a man <u>who was always amiable</u>.
8. Kraken, <u>which is a legendary monster with many tentacles living in the sea</u>, was reported to have been seen by fishermen off the coast of Norway.
9. The controversial exhibition, <u>of which everyone has talked much</u>, has been closed down by scandalised city officials.
10. Food <u>which has been frozen very quickly</u> can be stored in a freezer for a very long time.

COMPOUND NOUNS

353. ☺ Uzupełnij poniższe zdania odpowiednimi rzeczownikami złożonymi.

Wzór: A person that works in an office is an *office worker.*

1. A person that learns a foreign language is a _____.
2. A person that plays the piano is a _____.
3. A person that has broken a record is a _____.
4. A person that has broken somebody's heart is a _____.
5. A person that often goes to the theatre is a _____.
6. A person that uses the Internet is an _____.
7. A person that loves animals is an _____.
8. A person that has made a lot of money is a _____.
9. An excessively sentimental film is a _____.
10. An experienced soldier or an elderly person is an _____.

354. ☺☺ Ułóż po dwa rzeczowniki złożone zawierające wyrazy podane w nawiasie, tak aby uzupełnić zdania.

Wzór: (work)
          A. Our teacher has given us a lot of *homework* tonight.
          B. I hate doing *housework*, such as vacuum cleaning or washing windows.

1. (side)
   A. Why don't we go windsurfing at the _____ during our holiday?
   B. John Constable's paintings depicted the English _____.

2. (head)

A. Be quiet please, I've got a terrible _____ today.

B. First-grade students were greeted by the school _____.

3. (night)

A. I like going to our local _____ at the weekend.

B. The bride bought a beautiful new _____ for her honey moon.

4. (broad)

A. _____ are large-format newspapers, generally considered as addressed to well-educated and demanding readers.

B. On tonight's _____ we will continue coverage of the Palestinian conflict.

5. (break)

A. Matilda has been very depressed since the _____ with her last boyfriend.

B. Many war veterans suffered from a nervous _____.

355. ☺☺ Uzupełnij poniższe zdania rzeczownikami złożonymi utworzonymi z wyrazów podanych w ramce.

> hit bank report beauty consumer ~~bottles~~ coat directors dress money company desk ~~wine~~ treatment film winter cash wedding protection summer account pocket

Wzór: The waiter collected empty <u>wine bottles</u> from the tables.

1. The bride wanted to try on her _____.

2. If you present this voucher at the _____, you will get a 10-percent discount.

3. Today a lot of men decide to go for a _____, which used to be reserved for women only.

4. For my trip to Russia I need to get a warmer _____.

5. It was a catchy song that quickly became a _____.

6. Many parents decide to open a junior _____ for their children.

7. In that way their children can learn to save their _____, instead of spending it right away on sweets and toys.

8. The manager is working on the _____, which has to be submitted to the tax office.

9. Quentin Tarantino is one of the world's most famous _____.

10. One of the aims of _____ to is ensure reasonable prices for new products launched on the market.

SELECTED IDIOMS AND SOME CONFUSING WORDS

356. ☺☺ Zdecyduj, którego wyrazu należy użyć w poniższych zdaniach, wykreślając błędną wersję.

1. Our children will need a little time to adapt/adopt to their new school.
2. We must adapt/adopt EU directives concerning environmental protection.
3. Our law office specializes in legal council/counsel for small companies.
4. The city council/counsel is planning to renovate the main street in our town.
5. I have baked this cake specially/especially for you!
6. These glasses have been specially/especially designed for professional drivers.
7. Researchers are investigating how air pollution affects/effects our health.
8. The Prime Minister has promised to affect/effect changes in the government policy on education.
9. Any cases of bullying must be reported to the school principle/principal.
10. Today's lecture will cover the basic principles/principals of chemical reactions.
11. The 19th century is often called the Age of the Industrial/Industrious Revolution.
12. The aim of our scholarship is to support industrial/industrious students who would like to start their own business.

357. ☺☺ Zdecyduj, który z wyrazów właściwie uzupełnia podaną definicję: A czy B.

1. If an idea seems interesting and attractive it is…
   A. appealing.   B. appalling.
2. If somebody acts in a reasonable way, he or she is…
   A. sensitive.   B. sensible.
3. If you have got used to a person or thing…
   A. have become attracted to them.   B. have grown attached to them.
4. The employees of a company are the company's…
   A. personal.   B. personnel.
5. A description of how to cook a particular dish is a…
   A. recipe.   B. receipt.
6. If you are looking for a job, you may ask a company if they have any…
   A. vacations.   B. vacancies.
7. The reason why you do something is your…
   A. motif.   B. motive.
8. When you pay off a loan in several parts, you pay it off…
   A. in rates.   B. in instalments.
9. When you run your own business, you are engaged in an…
   A. economic activity.   B. economical activity.
10. When you take care of an injured person before he or she is taken to hospital you perform…
    A. first aid.   B. first help.

358. ☺☺ Popraw poniższe zdania, zastępując podkreślone błędne fragmenty wyrażeniami podanymi w ramce.

anthem elevated trial consistent likeable current factory achieve use gambling

1. This year our company has <u>realized</u> all its goals.

_____

2. This magazine offers a summary of the <u>actual</u> events.

_____

3. We have a special offer for all customers who <u>take advantage of</u> our services.

_____

4. Work at the steel <u>fabric</u> may be dangerous.

_____

5. Our director's speech was delivered in a <u>pathetic</u> tone.

_____

6. Poker and roulette are two popular <u>hazard</u> games.

_____

7. The national <u>hymn</u> is played on all important occasions.

_____

8. Alex has been very <u>consequent</u> in his work, keeping up good performance.

_____

9. The <u>process</u> of the murderer has lasted two years.

_____

10. Agnes is a very <u>sympathetic</u> person and has many friends.

359. ☺☺ Uzupełnij poniższe zdania właściwymi idiomami, wybierając odpowiedź A, B lub C.

1. As we knew all the questions beforehand, that exam was a piece of…
   A. cake.   B. mind.   C. pie.
2. Agnes hasn't been eating properly, look, she's as thin as a…
   A. rake.   B. straw.   C. string.
3. The weather is horrible, it's raining…
   A. fish and chips.   B. cats and dogs.   C. pins and needles.
4. This street is very busy, so as you drive you must …
   A. have an eye for it. B. have eyes in the   C. keep an eye on it.
                            back of your head.
5. After I threatened to cut his pocket money, my son was as quiet as a…
   A. bird.   B. cat.   C. mouse.
6. It's not a very serious story, you should take it with a grain of…
   A. sugar.   B. flour.   C. salt.
7. This whole situation seemed a little … to me, so I quickly backed out.
   A. foxy   B. birdie   C. fishy
8. It's evident they are sisters, they are as like as two …
   A. peas in a pod.   B. birds in a bush.   C. off pat.
9. When you are in a new environment, a friendly conversation will help you to quickly…
   A. break the ice.   B. pave your way.   C. break the bank.
10. This story can't be true, stop…
   A. having a cow!   B. pulling my leg!   C. having a fit!

360. ☺☺ Zastąp podkreślone części zdania idiomami podanymi poniżej.

a) slip of the tongue

b) be all ears
c) over one's head
d) have a big mouth
e) give (someone) a hand
f) a drop in the ocean
g) have something up one's sleeve
h) sleep on something
i) head over heals
j) call it a day

1. I shouldn't have told Annie about that incident. I know I <u>talk too much</u>!

   _____

2. Gina can't give you the answer right away. She must <u>think it all through over the night</u>.

   _____

3. We appreciate your donation, but it's <u>very little</u> compared to the amount we need to collect.

   _____

4. This bag is too heavy for me, could you <u>help me</u>?

   _____

5. Caroline is <u>very much</u> in love with her fiancé.

   _____

6. Having worked hard from 9 to 5, we decided to <u>stop working and go home</u>.

   _____

7. Did I say 'Steven'? Sorry, that was just <u>a mistake</u> – I meant Sean.

   _____

8. Tell me your story now, <u>I'm eager to hear it</u>.

   _____

9. It seems that Fred still <u>has some secret plan</u>.

   _____

10. This chapter is <u>too difficult for me to understand</u>. I'll have to ask someone for explanation.

    _____

361. ☺☺ Uzupełnij idiomy w poniższych zdaniach wyrazami podanymi w ramce.

teapot	moon	ears	fingers	pan	nut	ball	penny	pudding	twinkling

1. Countries introducing the new regulations have a hard _____ to crack.
2. After the success of its charity action last year, the company wants to keep the _____ rolling.
3. Due to the lack of enthusiasm on the part of the students, the plan to organize a school Christmas party fell on deaf _____.
4. I really hope my plan will work out! Keep your _____ crossed!
5. The trailers of the film look promising, but the audience's reaction at the premiere will be the proof of the _____.
6. All those discussions about the effects of the law are just a storm in the _____.
7. When the headmaster entered the schoolyard, all students disappeared in the _____ of an eye.
8. You are very quiet and seem to have drifted away. A _____ for your thoughts.
9. Our town is very small. An interesting concert or exhibition is organized once in the blue _____.
10. It seems that Gary's sudden interest in ancient history is just a flash in the _____.

362. ☺☺☺ Połącz angielskie słowo z jego polskim odpowiednikiem.

1. ingenious	a. powieść
2. eventually	b. goździk
3. actually	c. niebezpieczeństwo
4. antics	d. pomysłowy
5. conductor	e. przepis
6. lecture	f. zemsta
7. fatal	g. cera
8. hazard	h. zioło
9. receipt	i. dyrygent
10. billion	j. wariat
11. genial	k. wreszcie/w końcu
12. novel	l. miliard
13. revenge	m. serdeczny
14. lunatic	n. oszczędny
15. pathetic	o. właściwie
16. complexion	p. żałosny
17. recipe	q. paragon
18. carnation	r. śmiertelny
19. economical	s. wykład
20. herb	t. wygłupy

363. ☺☺☺ Utwórz zaprzeczenia wyrazów z ramki za pomocą przedrostków *a-*, *dis-*, *mis-*, *in-*, *im-*, *il-*, *ir-*, *non-* lub *un-*, a następnie uzupełnij poniższe zdania.

> ___agreeable ___effective ___fictional ___legal ___lucky ___patient ___polite
> ___political ___predictable ___rational ___responsible ___spelt

1. To ask questions about somebody's earnings is considered very _____.
2. It's _____ of people to drink alcohol and then drive a car.
3. Some people believe it is _____ to see a black cat crossing the street right in front of you.
4. In Poland it is _____ to distil strong spirits at home.
5. Why are you so _____? Just wait a few more days – the parcel should arrive soon.
6. Considering the number of variable factors, the distant future of mankind is _____.
7. Jonathan only reads _____ literature: biographies, travel diaries and studies on history.
8. When the weather is _____, the nicest thing is to curl up in an armchair with a good book and a glass of wine.
9. No discussing politics at the table, please! Let us keep our conversations _____.
10. The letter arrived very late because the addressee's surname was _____.
11. Luke's jealousy is totally _____: his wife does not give him any cause for it whatsoever.
12. His attempts to secure the post of ambassador for his younger son proved _____.

A teraz dodaj po trzy dalsze wyrazy z tymi przedrostkami:
a) a-   amoral, _____
b) dis-   disadvantage, _____

c) in-	inactive,	_____
d) im-	imbalance,	_____
e) il-	illegal,	_____
f) ir-	irregular,	_____
g) mis-	misunderstanding,	_____
h) non-	non-smoking,	_____
i) un-	uncertainty,	_____

364. ☺☺☺ Wstaw odpowiednie wyrażenie.

> against a rainy day   in all weathers   rain or shine   right as rain
> sunshine   under the weather   weather the storm

1. I stayed in bed all weekend because I was feeling (**not very well**) _____ and didn't want to come down with flu.
2. Until the day he died, Lemmy was a good and loyal friend to me (**no matter what my situation was**) _____.
3. Don't worry, kiddo, we will make you (**healthy**) _____ again in this hospital.
4. A great improvement in sales is expected soon, so the company seems to have (**got through difficulties**) _____.
5. This child is a little (**source of happiness**) _____ to me, I can assure you.
6. Count on me, I shall stand by you (**in good and bad times**) _____.
7. I'm not going to spend all the money I got for the novel. At least half of it I'll save (**until a time of need**) _____.

365. ☺☺☺ Połącz w pary części poniższych rozmówek. Podkreśl idiomy i wyrażenia związane z pieniędzmi (oraz ich brakiem), bogactwem i drożyzną. Czy znasz polskie odpowiedniki tych wyrażeń?

1. Why don't you want to marry Ronald? He has a heart of gold.
2. Why did you buy so much tinned food?
3. Where can Michael have gone to? I haven't seen him since morning.
4. I bought this dress in a little boutique just below the castle. It cost me an arm and a leg.
5. This coat must have cost you a small fortune!
6. If you only need a short-term loan to tide you over, why don't you ask Nathaniel?
7. Did you see Tammy's wedding dress? It was magnificent! And she bought it for a song!
8. Did you see Igor and Bella's new furniture? They really splashed out on it!
9. That new Alfa Romeo Brera of yours must have cost you a pretty penny!
10. This genuine leather bag will put your husband back some $1000, lady.

a) Yes, I did. I would never have thought they were well-heeled enough to afford it.
b) No, it was actually cheap as dirt. My colleague bought it and very quickly grew too fat for it, so she sold it to me for peanuts.
c) I paid through the nose. I couldn't help it, I fell in love with that car.
d) Yes, I know! Mere £25 in a second-hand shop, would you believe it!
e) Don't worry! He will turn up like a bad penny the moment supper is on the table.
f) True. But he is also poor as a church mouse, that's why.
g) No wonder, all shops in the Old Town are expensive, but this boutique is a real tear off.
h) Just in case. Plenty is no plague.
i) How much?!? No way! It's daylight robbery!

j) I don't think he can lend me anything. He has just bought a car, so he is probably hard up himself.

KLUCZ

350. **1.** d, f **2.** h **3.** j **4.** g **5.** i **6.** c **7.** e **8.** a **9.** f **10.** b
Compound adjectives to przymiotniki złożone z dwóch, a czasem nawet trzech wyrazów, często połączonych kreską (łącznikiem). Wszystkie przymiotniki złożone użyte w tym ćwiczeniu pisze się z łącznikiem.

351. Uwaga: rzeczownik wchodzący w skład przymiotnika złożonego zawsze jest w liczbie pojedynczej (patrz pkt. 7 oraz pkt. 5 i 6 ćw. 352).
1. man-made **2.** wide-ranging **3.** good-looking, kind-hearted **4.** ill-starred **5.** carefree **6.** well-mannered **7.** seven-hour **8.** badly-planned, badly-written, narrow-minded **9.** well-ordered, last-minute **10.** life-size, badly-painted, lifelike

352. **1.** Leonard's sarcastic comments were particularly ill-suited to the sad situation.
2. In the swamps and on marshy ground soldiers had to use all-terrain vehicles.
3. A well-fed cat will never eat a rat it has caught.
4. A sixteen-year-old girl cannot have a clear idea of her future yet.
5. The seven-man construction team finished roofing the house before the first frost.
6. Lying on the beach all day, Geraldine got badly sunburnt.
7. Old Uncle Philip was a good-humoured man.
8. Kraken, a legendary many-tentacled sea-monster, was reported to have been seen by fishermen off the coast of Norway.
9. The much-talked-of controversial exhibition has been closed down by scandalised city officials.
10. Quick-frozen food can be stored in a freezer for a very long time.

353. **1.** language learner **2.** piano player **3.** record-breaker **4.** heartbreaker **5.** theatre-goer **6.** Internet user **7.** an animal lover **8.** money maker **9.** tearjerker **10.** old-timer

354. **1** A seaside B countryside **2** A headache B headmaster/headmistress **3** A nightclub B nightdress/nightgown **4** A broadsheets B broadcast **5** A break-up B breakdown

355. **1.** wedding dress **2.** cash desk **3.** beauty treatment **4.** winter coat **5.** summer hit **6.** bank account **7.** pocket money **8.** company report **9.** film directors **10.** consumer protection

356. **1.** adapt **2.** adopt **3.** counsel **4.** council **5.** especially **6.** specially **7.** affects **8.** effect **9.** principal **10.** principles **11.** Industrial **12.** industrious

357. **1** A **2** B **3** B **4** B **5** A **6** B **7** B **8** B **9** A **10** A

358. **1.** This year our company has <u>achieved</u> all its goals. 'Realize' oznacza uświadomić coś sobie.
2. This magazine offers a summary of the <u>current</u> events. 'Actual' to faktyczny, rzeczywisty.
3. We have a special offer for all customers who <u>use</u> our services. 'Take advantage of' to wykorzystać.
4. Work at the steel <u>factory</u> may be dangerous. 'Fabric' to tkanina.
5. Our director's speech was delivered in an <u>elevated</u> tone. 'Pathetic' to żałosny.
6. Poker and roulette are two popular <u>gambling</u> games. 'Hazard' to ryzyko.
7. The national <u>anthem</u> is played on all important occasions. 'Hymn' to podniosła pieśń, ale nie hymn państwowy.
8. Alex has been very <u>consistent</u> in his work, keeping up good performance. 'Consequent' to wynikający z czegoś.
9. The <u>trial</u> of the murderer has lasted two years. 'Process' to proces, przebieg czegoś, ale nie proces sądowy.
10. Agnes is a very <u>likeable</u> person and has many friends. 'Sympathetic' to współczujący.

359. **1** A **2** A **3** B **4** B **5** C **6** C **7** C **8** A **9** A **10** B

360. **1.** I know I <u>have a big mouth</u>! **2.** She must <u>sleep on it</u>. **3.** We appreciate your donation, but it's <u>a drop in the ocean</u> compared to the amount we need to collect. **4.** This bag is too heavy for me, could you give <u>me a</u>

hand? **5.** Caroline is <u>head over heals</u> in love with her fiancé. **6.** Having worked hard from 9 to 5, we decided to <u>call it a day</u>. **7.** Sorry, that was just <u>a slip of the tongue</u> – I meant Sean. **8.** Tell me your story now, <u>I'm all ears</u>. **9.** It seems that Fred still <u>has something up his sleeve</u>. **10.** This chapter is <u>over my head</u>. I'll have to ask someone for explanation.

361. **1.** nut **2.** ball **3.** ears **4.** fingers **5.** pudding **6.** teapot **7.** twinkling **8.** penny **9.** moon **10.** pan

362. **1.** d **2.** k **3.** o **4.** t **5.** i **6.** s **7.** r **8.** c **9.** q **10.** l **11.** m **12.** a **13.** f **14.** j **15.** p **16.** g **17.** e **18.** b **19.** n **20.** h
Wyrazy, które w języku polskim i angielskim wyglądają lub brzmią podobnie, ale znaczą całkiem co innego, to tak zwani „fałszywi przyjaciele" – *false friends*. Trzeba na nie bardzo uważać!

363. **1.** impolite **2.** irresponsible **3.** unlucky **4.** illegal **5.** impatient **6.** unpredictable **7.** nonfictional **8.** disagreeable **9.** apolitical **10.** misspelt **11.** irrational **12.** ineffective
a) np. asocial, asynchronous
b) np. disloyal, dissimilar
c) np. incompetent, indecisive
d) np. immoral, impossible (przedrostek *im-* występuje przed **b, m, p**)
e) np. illegible, illogical (przedrostek *il-* występuje przed **l**)
f) np. irresponsible, irreversible (przedrostek *ir-* występuje przed **r**)
g) np. misleading, misprint (przedrostek *mis-* nadaje wyrazowi, z którym się łączy, znaczenie „źle", „omyłkowo")
h) np. non-European, nonconformist
i) np. unpredictable, unwise
Pamiętaj, że przedrostki tworzące przeczenia dodaje się zarówno do przymiotników (np. *irregular*), jak i do rzeczowników (np. *injustice*), a nawet form czasownikowych (np. *misjudge, misquoted*).

364. **1.** under the weather **2.** in all weathers **3.** right as rain **4.** weathered the storm **5.** sunshine **6.** rain or shine **7.** against a rainy day

365. **1.** f – to have a heart of gold (mieć złote serce), to be poor as a church mouse (być biednym jak mysz kościelna)
2. h – plenty is no plague (od przybytku głowa nie boli)
3. e – to turn up like a bad penny (pojawić się niechybnie)
4. g – to cost (somebody) an arm and a leg (kosztować oczy z głowy), to be a tear-off (to zdzierstwo)
5. b – to cost a small fortune (kosztować krocie), to be cheap as dirt (być tanim jak barszcz), to sell/buy (something) for peanuts (sprzedać/kupić za grosze)
6. j – to tide (someone) over (o pożyczce: krótkoterminowa, „do pierwszego"), to be hard up (być bez grosza)
7. d – to buy/sell (something) for a song (sprzedać/kupić za grosze)
8. a – to splash out on (something) (zaszaleć, kupując coś), to be well-heeled (mieć kasę)
9. c – to cost a pretty penny (kosztować ładny grosz), to pay through the nose (wykosztować się, zapłacić o wiele za dużo)
10. i – to put (someone) back some... (sprawić, że będzie uboższy o jakieś...), daylight robbery (rozbój w biały dzień)